PROBLEMS IN MODERN GEOGRAPHY

D0710563

Recreational Geography

PROBLEMS IN MODERN GEOGRAPHY

Series Editor   Richard Lawton *Professor of Geography,*
                         University of Liverpool

PUBLISHED

J. Allan Patmore   *Land and Leisure*
David Herbert   *Urban Geography: A Social Perspective*
Kenneth Warren   *Mineral Resources*
John R. Tarrant   *Agricultural Geography*
Kenneth L. Wallwork   *Derelict Land*

IN PREPARATION

PATRICK LAVERY
Editor

Recreational Geography

A HALSTED PRESS BOOK

JOHN WILEY & SONS
New York

© Patrick Lavery 1974

Published in the U.S.A.
by Halsted Press, a
Division of John Wiley & Sons, Inc.,
New York.

Library of Congress Cataloging in Publication Data
Main entry under title:

Recreational geography.

   "A Halsted Press book."
   Includes bibliographical references.
   1.   Recreation areas—Addresses, essays, lectures.
I.   Lavery, Patrick, ed.
GV182.R37   333.7'8   74-15207

ISBN: 0 470–51888–X

Printed in Great Britain

Contents

List of Illustrations

LIST OF PLATES

TEXT ILLUSTRATIONS AND MAPS

Page

List of Tables

Page

List of Contributors

K. Balmer, BA, PhD
Research Officer, Ministry of State for Urban Affairs, Ottawa, Canada

J. Bradley
Planning Officer, Monmouthshire County Council

J. T. Coppock, MA
Professor of Geography, University of Edinburgh

B. S. Duffield, PhD
Department of Geography, University of Edinburgh

J. Gittins, BA, BSc (Econ)
Lecturer in Geography, St Mary's College, Bangor

F. B. Goldsmith, BSc, PhD
Lecturer, Department of Botany and Microbiology, University College, University of London

J. Hall, BA
Lecturer in Geography, Queen Mary College, University of London

P. Lavery, BA, PhD
Lecturer in Geography, Birkbeck College, University of London

2

D. Mercer
Lecturer in Geography, Monash University, Melbourne, Australia

R. J. C. Munton, BSc, PhD
Lecturer in Geography, Department of Geography, University College, University of London

J. Palmer, BA
Planning Officer, Monmouthshire County Council

J. A. Patmore, MA
Professor of Geography, University of Hull

D. Sewell, PhD
Lecturer in Geography, Department of Geography, University of Edinburgh

R. J. Smith, BSc, PhD
Senior Scientific Officer, Water Resources Board

M. Tanner, MA
Lecturer in Geography, University of Birmingham

G. Wall, BA, PhD
Assistant Professor of Geography, University of Kentucky, Lexington, USA

Preface

OVER the past decade many studies have documented the upsurge of interest in the problems of recreational use of city and countryside areas, following a growing awareness of general pressures on recreational resources. Recreation consists of a broad spectrum of leisure time activities generated as a result of many individual decisions and personal preferences, and epitomised in summer traffic jams and crowded beauty spots, swimming pools or golf courses. These recreational movements and their foci reflect the spatial distribution of demand and supply of available resources, with capacity acting as a link between the two.

While many articles and papers have discussed aspects of recreational research, few comprehensive studies have emerged to present the main elements of the recreational experience. The following chapters attempt to present the main aspects of recreation as an economic and social activity, covering both theoretic and applied recreation studies. Although the title of this book is *Recreational Geography* there is no uniquely geographical approach to recreation, and the contributors are drawn from several professions and serve to emphasise the inter-disciplinary nature of recreational research.

This book deals with the problems of recreation demand, the recreationist's decision-making process, and issues arising from

recreational pressures in forest, national park, coastal and inland areas with particular attention given to the planning and management of recreation resources. The role of urban open space, water resources, and the ecological effects of recreational activity are also discussed. These varied themes are set against a background of British, North American and European experience to present a wide-ranging analysis of the complex issues that stem from the use of land for recreational purposes.

PATRICK LAVERY

Dartford, Kent

CHAPTER ONE

The Demand for Recreation

THE swollen queues of traffic on major holiday routeways every summer, the crowded beaches of the popular holiday regions and the explosion in leisure pursuits of all kinds serve to emphasise the burgeoning demand for outdoor recreation. This chapter attempts a discussion of the measures of demand and the current state of knowledge relating to them, drawing on British and North American experience. Finally the relationship between supply and demand and the problems of priority research areas are considered.

THE NATURE OF DEMAND

The *Countryside Recreation Glossary* defines demand as 'The use of existing facilities and the desire to use recreation facilities either now or in the future'.[1] Demand consists of several components: in the Countryside Commission's seminar on

TABLE 1 *Chief leisure activities in England and Wales**

	ALL MALES					ALL FEMALES				
	Summer Weekends	*Summer Weekdays*	*Winter Weekends*	*Winter Weekdays*	*Overall Average*	*Summer Weekends*	*Summer Weekdays*	*Winter Weekends*	*Winter Weekdays*	*Overall Average*
	Per Cent					Per Cent				
Television	8	17	25	42	23	11	18	30	34	23
Reading	2	5	5	9	5	5	9	9	11	9
Crafts and hobbies	3	3	5	5	4	9	17	15	24	17
Decorating and house/vehicle maintenance	6	8	10	7	8	1	1	2	1	1
Gardening	19	22	4	3	12	12	12	1	1	7
Social activities	3	2	5	2	3	11	7	11	5	9
Drinking	3	4	3	2	3	1	1	2	1	1
Cinema and theatre	1	1	2	1	1	1	1	2	1	1
Non-physical games and misc club activities	3	5	5	8	5	3	4	4	6	4
Physical recreation—as a participant	16	10	12	5	11	6	4	5	2	4
Physical recreation—as a spectator	3	1	7	1	3	1	1	1	—	1
Excursions	18	4	5	1	7	19	5	4	1	7
Park visits and walks	8	7	3	2	5	9	8	2	2	5
Anything else	5	7	6	8	7	7	8	7	7	7
Don't know/no answer	2	4	3	4	3	4	4	5	4	4
BASE 100% (total persons)					2,824					3,451

*Source: *Planning for Leisure*, Government Social Survey (1969)

recreation demand (1970) it was defined as 'The number of persons requiring to take part in a recreation activity'.[2] The people who actually take part in outdoor recreation activities make up the *effective demand*.[3] In addition to this there is *deferred demand* (that is, those who could participate but do not either through lack of knowledge, or lack of facilities, or both); and *potential demand* (that is, those who cannot at present participate and require an improvement in their social and economic circumstances to do so). It is necessary to consider the interaction between these dynamic components of demand and to determine their role and spatial impact on the consumption of recreation resources. Measures of current effective demand are not enough. As Knetsch in his seminal paper on recreation demand states: 'The myth persists that somehow we are able to multiply population figures by recreation activity participation rates obtained from population surveys and call it demand.'[4]

The demand for outdoor recreation must be assessed against total leisure time and the changes in popularity of different leisure pursuits. As Table 1 shows, home-based activities occupy most available leisure time, and watching television, gardening (especially in the summer), crafts and hobbies are dominant. Outdoor recreation *per se* claims an important share, and takes up over 20 per cent of overall leisure time, rising to over 40 per cent on summer weekends.

A breakdown of the chief leisure activities by region (Table 2) emphasises the dominance of swimming, with tennis, fishing and team games some way behind. The more regional surveys of Northern[5] and North Western England[6] reinforce this view. With the exception of swimming (and camping in the Northern Region), the range of demand is similar between the regions of Britain. Formal pursuits predominate, and the urban-oriented activities such as swimming, golf, and team games require large inputs of land and capital. The less formal activities such as fishing or hiking are among a broad range of informal recreations, such as driving for pleasure or picnicking, which are less

TABLE 2   Chief leisure activities by region, Great Britain

	Northern (1969)	North West (1972)	Midlands (1965)*	Metropolitan England (1965)*	South and West (1965)*	Wales (1965)*	Scotland (1965)*
			PER CENT	PARTICIPATING			
Swimming	20	15	11	12	18	7	7
Fishing	6	5	7	6	7	3	5
Camping	10	3	4	4	5	1	2
Golf	2	3	3	3	4	1	6
Hiking	4	3	4	6	4	4	3
Riding	1	–	–	1	1	1	1
Cycling	6	–	1	4	4	3	1
Bowls	3	5	2	2	1	1	5
Tennis	7	6	4	6	6	2	5
Team games	4	3	5	4	6	3	3

* Sources: BTA/University of Keele, *Pilot National Recreation Survey*
Northern Region Planning Committee, *Outdoor Leisure Activities in the Northern Region* (1969)
North West Sports Council, *Leisure in the North West* (1972)

well documented though just as important because of their widespread nature and growing popularity. For example excursions and park visits account for 25 per cent of leisure time on summer weekends (12 per cent in winter) compared with 8 per cent watching television (42 per cent in winter).[7] As 44 per cent of Britain's households have regular use of a car and 8 per cent have two or more cars,[8] many of these excursions involve driving for pleasure. This figure is reinforced by the 69 per cent of British holiday-makers who travelled by car in 1970.[9]

A brief analysis of growth in demand for specific activities gives some perspective to this study of the demand situation. Table 3 utilises changing membership figures as an index of growth in demand, although it is accepted that membership of an organisation does not reflect level of active participation. If growth in membership figures is taken as a *minimum* guide to levels of demand, Table 3 serves to show general trends in the period 1950–70. It is not possible to compare the growth rates

between one activity and another because there is no uniform method of standardising these figures. Given these reservations it is clear that most activities experienced a period of very rapid growth in the 1950s, particularly the water-based activities such as yachting and canoeing. The rapid growth in caravan and camping clubs reflects the trend for more mobile, more flexible holidays. Youth hostelling and cycling experienced a period of relative decline. The overall explosive growth in demand slackened off in the period 1960–70 although the rates of growth remained impressive. It is particularly because the impact of this demand is limited both spatially and through time, that the rates of growth and increasing opportunities for outdoor recreation pose many problems in managing land and water resources for leisure activities. The remainder of this chapter considers the components of the demand situation, and the demand/supply relationship in outdoor recreation.

TABLE 3   *Rates of growth in selected outdoor recreation activities in Great Britain as measured by membership figures*

AVERAGE ANNUAL RATE OF GROWTH

Organisation	1950–60 (per cent)	1960–70 (per cent)
Royal Yachting Association	+44	+30
British Canoe Union	+100	+31
Amateur Rowing Association	+16	
National Federation of Anglers	Not known	+3 (1965–70)
Camping Club	+38	+10
Caravan Club	+40	+22
Ramblers Association	+24	+7
Youth Hostels Association	−1·4	+2·2
National Ski Federation	Not known	+49
Cyclists Touring Club	−4·5	−4·2
British Mountaineering Council	+25	
Membership of National Trust	+38	+7

MEASURES OF DEMAND

Attempts to measure present effective demand fall into four broad categories. These are:

1 Some measure of use of formal recreation facilities using attendance records, membership lists, sales figures, and so on.
2 Home interview surveys or postal surveys using questionnaires to identify current and potential participation rates throughout the whole spectrum of recreation activities.
3 On-site visitor surveys in the main resorts/recreation areas, linked with
4 Demand curve analysis comparing trip generation rates with factors such as distance, travel time, travel cost, accessibility, attractiveness and mobility (ie car ownership).

Membership lists, attendance records and the like do not give an accurate guide to the actual numbers involved in particular recreation activities although they do infer the general trends over past decades.[10] In the absence of accurate records of the frequency and time spent on each activity, this type of data cannot compare activities over time. At best the order of magnitude of increases can be noted and from these it can be seen that caravanning and camping have increased fourfold since 1950, with greater rates of increase for water-based recreation activities (Figure 1). Many informal pursuits such as driving for pleasure, picnicking and general sightseeing go unrecorded, although from the increasingly crowded roads on summer weekends they are clearly growing in popularity, as Table 3 shows.

The BTA/Keele,[11] Northern[12] and North Western Region[13] surveys relied on a sample of home interviews, but were restricted by time and monetary constraints. In the BTA/Keele survey old people were under-reported while the twenty-five to forty-four age group was over-represented, and with a total sample of 3,000 respondents many of the thirty activity subsamples were too small to give significant results. The NW Region survey assessed the effect of the availability and proximity of resources on participation levels, but for some activities the results were inconclusive due to low sample numbers. For

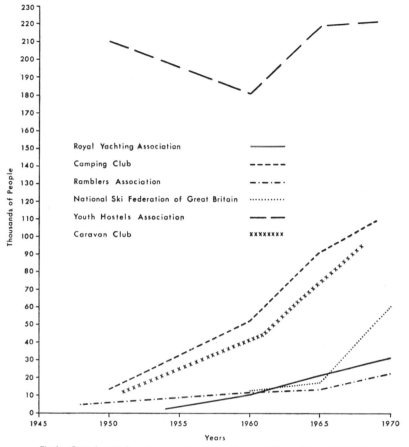

Fig 1   Growth rates for selected outdoor recreation activities in Britain, 1950–70

example sub-samples of respondents playing tennis, bowls, cricket or soccer regularly totalled less than twenty.

In both Britain and North America on-site surveys date back to the 1950s with work by House,[14] Hutchins,[15] Lund[16] and Copeland.[17] Such studies have grown in exponential fashion during the 1960s and almost forty surveys were listed as under way in Britain in 1972.[18] On-site surveys *per se* cannot measure either current or future demand levels, because the participation

levels are observed under prevailing recreation opportunity conditions which are a function of the available supply of recreation resources. This can lead one to assume that people will demand only increasing quantities of what they have, thus perpetuating imbalances in the supply of recreation opportunities.

Moreover for many informal recreation activities no direct charge is made for the recreation resources and therefore the demand for their use as recreation places is a function of first their attractiveness and facilities and, secondly, the relative cost of reaching these places.

Taking demand to be a function of cost, this factor can be expressed in terms of distance or travel time or travel cost; thus the on-site surveys can produce data on trip generation rates from all the towns supplying visitors. This is associated with the idea that demand for a recreation resource can be measured by a curve showing the amount of facilities consumed over a specific range of prices (measured as distance/ travel time or travel cost). Therefore with an increase in costs, demand (ie number of visits) will fall off.

Given that distance is at best a crude measure of the cost function, this approach was adopted by the author for a number of holiday centres in Northern England. For every town providing ten or more visitors, trips per 10,000 resident population

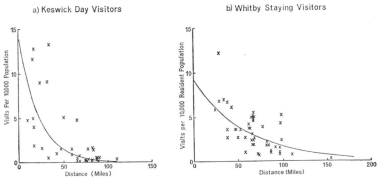

Fig 2a–g   Regression of trip generation rates against distance for selected resorts in Northern England

were plotted against distance of that town from the resort. The regression of trip generation rates against distance varied between resorts, but a test of the correlation coefficients gave significance levels between 5 and 0·1 per cent. As Figure 2 shows, people living within 10 miles of each resort did not appear on the demand curve and their absence is probably due to a

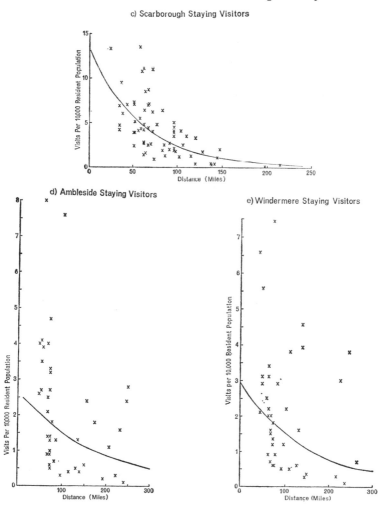

Fig 2

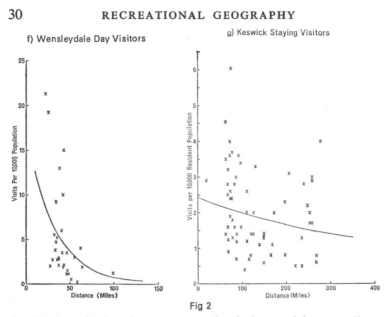

Fig 2

familiarity with local resources and a desire to visit more distant places. Demand was found to be relatively inelastic up to distances of 70 miles from each resort and beyond this point, travel time/travel cost/distance appear to act as background variables.

Both Mansfield[19] and Colenutt[20] have developed trip generation models for day-trip population. Mansfield analysed a cross-section of one year's traffic data from the 1966 Lake District Traffic Survey, using a simplified model of the form:

Y k l = f (Ckl, tkl, Wk, Rkl, Pk)
where Y k l = number of visitors to the i th resort from the k th zone
C k l = money cost of travel from the k th zone
t K l = journey time from the k th zone
W k = level of car-ownership in the k th zone
R k l = overall competitiveness (attractiveness) of the Lake District when compared with alternative recreation facilities available to the population of the k th zone
P k = the population of the k th zone

This model explained 94 per cent of the variation in day trips and 97 per cent of the variation in half-day trips to the Lake

District. Mansfield identified a high price elasticity of demand such that a 10 per cent drop in travel costs (due to road improvements) from every zone would produce a 20 per cent increase in trips from places up to 50 miles, and a 30 per cent increase in trips from zones more than 70 miles from the Lakes. When current and projected road improvement schemes are considered, these findings emphasise the potential growth in demand for recreation in the Lake District.

Colenutt also studied the effect of distance, accessibility and travel time on trip generation rates for day visits to the Forest of Dean.[21] His basic model was:

$$Yi = e^{-X_1}$$

Where Yi = day-trip rate per 100,000 population from origin i
X_1 = distance in road miles from origin town i to approximate centre of Forest of Dean
e = base of natural logarithm.

This equation gave a correlation coefficient of -0.95 for the trip generation function. He then attempted to measure the role of travel time in recreation trip generation using a coefficient of time/coefficient of cost ratio to estimate the value of time for the average motorist. While distance was found to be a crucial factor its effect was non-linear, so that short-distance trippers were not as sensitive to travel time or price changes as longer-distance visitors. The amount of information about recreation opportunities and the amount of time available emerged as the two crucial influences on trip generation rates. However, the use of an area for recreation is also governed by both demand and the available supply of recreation opportunities.

These various empirical attempts to measure demand are based on the premise that price-quantity relationships are crucial to an understanding of the demand situation, even though often in the public sector no direct charge is made for the use of informal recreation resources. Hopefully the construction of a family of demand curves relating to a hierarchy

of recreation facilities/resources can be used to predict the number of recreation trips to and from particular areas. Where such data are available over five or ten year periods it would be possible to estimate the effects of changing mobility and accessibility/journey time/journey costs on levels of current effective demand.

PRESENT EFFECTIVE DEMAND

Given that this represents the number of people who actually take part in outdoor recreation activities, our current state of knowledge of the distribution of available facilities and the incidence and volume of their use at national, regional and local levels is still relatively limited. The theme of demand for outdoor recreation was first substantively developed in 1962 by the Outdoor Recreation Resources Review Commission (ORRRC) in two volumes of a twenty-eight volume study of the United States.[22] Volume 26 deals with *Prospective Demand for Outdoor Recreation* and states that 'The need is not to be able to say what any individual will do but rather to estimate what individual behaviour will add up to when all persons are combined'.[23] Accordingly a multiple regression model was developed using five independent variables—time, population, per capita disposable real income, inter-city car travel, and weekly hours of leisure per employed person. This model produced a good fit when compared with past time-series and explained from 95 to more than 99 per cent of the variations in national park visits. Proctor, in an appendix to the *US National Recreation Survey*, hypothesised that formal outdoor recreation activities fell into four categories: backwoods recreation, boat culture, country club and picnic area recreations, and passive outdoor recreation.[24] He studied the effect of thirty background variables on these four groups of activities, but despite a sophisticated statistical analysis, arrived at rather general conclusions and forecasts. The conclusions of the

ORRRC studies were that the volume of demand for most outdoor recreation activities would treble and in some cases quad-
ruple by the year 2000.[25]

A number of British studies documented an equivalent
upsurge in recreation demand during the 1960s. For example
Burton and Wibberley in *Outdoor Recreation and the British
Countryside* (1965) gave a broad national summary of the
supply of rural land for recreation and produced estimates of
the general levels of demand.[26] In 1965 the British Travel
Association and the University of Keele carried out the field
investigation for a *Pilot National Recreation Survey* which
largely confirmed the ORRRC findings, showing the predomi-
nance of day tripping by car, the growth in available leisure
time and the influence of car-ownership on overall patterns of
recreation.[27] The BTA/Keele study concentrated on informal
recreation, whilst the more recent Government Social Survey
Planning for Leisure revealed more information on sports and
team games.[28] This report found that activities such as visits to
parks, sports, games and excursions to the country or seaside
did not individually take up large proportions of available
leisure periods, but when combined together they made up an
important part of the leisure life of the sample population.
Variations in leisure behaviour were analysed for ten sub-
groups within the sample population, but with a national
sample of 2,682 persons these sub-samples only permit a quali-
tative interpretation. Even so it is clear that demand varies by
time of week and season, at different stages in the life cycle, and
is influenced by car-ownership and socio-economic background.

Recreation surveys for the Northern[29] and North Western
Regions[30] emphasise regional contrasts hitherto masked at the
national level. For example in the survey *Leisure in the North
West* it was found that the inhabitants of Merseyside are more
likely to make outings and to make them more often than the
inhabitants of the Manchester conurbation, demand being

stimulated by the more accessible recreation resources along the Lancashire and Wirral coast.[31] However, the geographical significance of disparities of resources and participation was only identified for these two conurbations; the pattern over the rest of the North West was less clear because of the nature of the sample used.

The Northern Region survey covered thirteen sub-areas consisting of the respective country coastal strips, communication corridors and hinterlands, and considered the extent to which these sub-regions attracted a disproportionate number of participants in general leisure facilities.[32] There was a close correlation between the share of the region's population and the proportion of all activities in each sub-area (R = + 0·98). However when this hypothesis was tested for the Tyneside and Teesside conurbations and their immediate hinterlands some disparities emerged. The Tyneside conurbation had less participants than its population would warrant while the area within 10 miles of Tyneside appeared overloaded. However, while instances of over-use of sub-areas can be identified, no attempt was made in the survey to link these observations with existing provision of facilities or to associate participation levels, location of activity and respondent's place of residence.

Although the Northern Region survey gave a breakdown by thirteen sub-regions the sample was not stratified on this basis, and no interviews were made in the Northumberland and North Riding hinterlands. In some cases interviews were made close to sub-area boundaries with obvious focal points in adjacent sub-regions, and this distorted movement estimates.

DEFERRED DEMAND

Given that this represents demand at present frustrated either by scarcity of facilities or lack of knowledge of the existence of such facilities, the provision of more recreation opportunities and/or better publicity for existing facilities will increase current

effective demand. This was borne out by the Government Social Survey inquiry *Planning for Leisure*, which found that over half the national sample of young people cited inadequate local facilities as the reason for their giving up sports and games.[33]

The GLC survey of the use of open space considered this aspect of demand and found that the size of a park's catchment area is related to its acreage and to some extent its facilities.[34] Table 4 summarises their findings.

TABLE 4   Open space catchments in the GLC area

Type of open space	Function	Size (Acres)	Maximum distance from place of residence
Metropolitan park	Weekend and occasional visits by car/public transport	150	2 miles
District park	Weekend and occasional visits, mainly on foot	50	0·75 miles
Local park	Short visits on foot	5	0·25 miles
Small local park	Limited visits by local residents	Less than 5	Below 0·25 miles

Using these distance and size criteria the GLC identified those areas in Greater London with open space deficiencies (Figure 3). These deficiencies represent two aspects of deferred demand. One is for facilities at local level for people with limited time or mobility, and the second is for facilities at district or metropolitan level catering for families, teenagers, and sportsmen where the demand is heaviest at weekends.

However, to express available facilities in terms of their distances from people's homes results in a statement of level of provision which is based on area and not upon population. This approach measures density of provision by units of area, *not* adequacy of provision by units of population. Although it does provide a measure of accessibility of facilities it is not a satisfactory measure of standards of provision.

In this chapter a deductive approach is made to the problem of

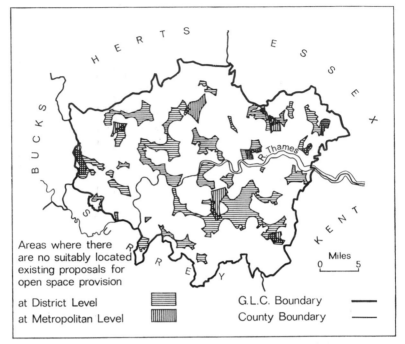

Fig 3   Areas with open space deficiencies in Greater London

identifying the deferred demand sector. An initial distinction is between latent demand associated with recreational activities located inside and outside urban areas (Table 5).

The hypothesis adopted was that those areas at present beyond recreational activity catchments are the localities where deferred demand is most prevalent. Clearly a range of catchments exist simultaneously and deferred demand will differ both in its intensity and variability from one region to another (Figure 4). It is possible to develop a hierarchy of recreation opportunities with progressive specialisation of activities from a local scale upwards, and increasing travel time/accessibility constraints on the present use of these facilities. This approach then needs to be related to population distribution in those areas beyond recreational activity catchments, so that some measure of adequacy of

TABLE 5   Classification of recreational activities by location

ACTIVITIES AWAY FROM HOME

In urban areas	*Outside urban areas*
Most team games	Cycling
Most spectator sports	Hiking
General drinking	Fishing
Miscellaneous club activities	Golf
Cinema and theatre visits	Camping
Swimming	Sailing
Bowls	Riding
Tennis	Hill walking, climbing
Fencing	Natural history
Athletics	Youth hostelling
Skating	Motor sports
Park visits	Winter sports
	Shooting

provision can be obtained. The end product of this approach
would be empirically determined estimates of the extent of deferred demand for a whole range of recreation activities.

A case study was made of recreation provision in the South
West using as a basis the SW Sports Council *Initial Appraisal
of Major Facilities* (1967).[35] Three activities were considered—
golf, fishing, and (indoor) swimming—as these are among the
most popular recreation activities away from home. The
possible catchment area for each activity was plotted (Figure 4)
and the population of the interstitial areas calculated to obtain
a measure of deferred demand. This was done for each activity,
taking the national participation level (by age groups) and
apportioning deferred demand among age-specific groups.[36]
The results are given in Table 6.

The activity participation rates were applied from a national
sample to a county situation and therefore these results only
give the order of magnitude of deferred demand in these three
SW counties. If these figures *are* in the right proportions it is
clear that the existing adequacy of provision varies markedly
from one county to another. Given that the people most likely
to take part in these three activities are drawn largely from the
fifteen to sixty age group, the deferred demand element is most

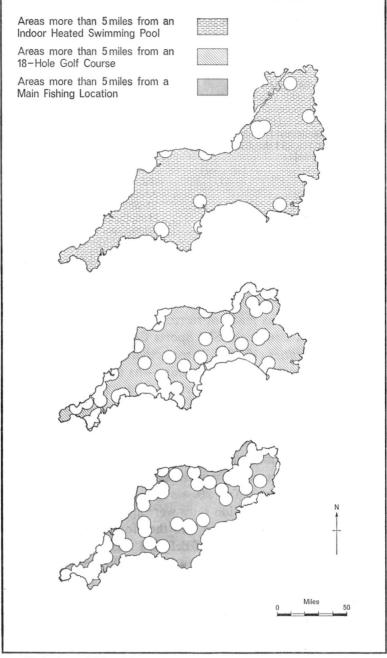

Fig 4 Areas of deferred demand for selected recreational activities in SW England

TABLE 6   Estimated deferred demand for Cornwall, Devon and Somerset*

Cornwall	Fishing	Swimming†	Golf
Deferred demand population	1,469	35,369	1,688
Percentage of county population	0·4%	10%	0·5%
Percentage of 15–45 and 46–60 age groups	0·8%	21%	1·0%

* Figures based on analysis of population of interstitial areas by local administrative areas

† As Cornwall has no indoor heated swimming pools, only those people within easy reach of Plymouth have access to a pool

Devon			
Deferred demand population	19,131	43,519	5,535
Percentage of county population	2·2%	5%	0·6%
Percentage of 15–45 and 46–60 age groups	4%	9%	1%

Somerset			
Deferred demand population	653	45,797	3,326
Percentage of county population	0·1%	7%	0·5%
Percentage of 15–45 and 46–60 age groups	0·18%	12·7%	0·97%

Total deferred demand population	21,253	124,685	10,549
Percentage of 3 counties population	1%	7%	0·6%
Percentage of 15–45 and 46–60 age groups in the 3 counties	2%	12%	1%

Data: *SW Sports Council Initial Appraisal of Major Facilities* (1967) and *Planning for Leisure* (1969). Population data obtained from 1966 sample census, County Reports.

evident for swimming. Virtually all of Cornwall's population and one-tenth of Devon and Somerset (in this age range) live more than 5 miles from an indoor heated swimming pool. All three counties are particularly deficient in such pools. Cornwall has none, Devon four, and Somerset three. Although several holiday resorts have outdoor pools these have only a limited seasonal use. Although deferred demand for golf accounts for only 1 per cent of those likely to play it, the present golf courses are mainly located in or adjacent to coastal resorts, with limited provision inland, particularly in Devon.

These crude estimates of deferred demand are derived from distance-determined catchment areas, and distance may not

adequately measure demand frustrated by scarcity of facilities. Many of the existing golf and fishing facilities may have waiting lists of potential members and during the summer period in this, the most popular holiday region of Britain, the vast influx of visitors will also place heavy demands on the existing facilities. Although the extent of deferred demand for golf and fishing is dwarfed by the scarcity of swimming facilities, all three activities have a potential user population of many thousands, albeit largely scattered through rural areas.

This deferred demand *could* be transferred into current effective demand by greater provision of indoor swimming pools, golf courses and fishing facilities, but all three require considerable expenditure, and golf courses consume large acreages of land. Although the figure for golf is below the Sports Council's recommended standard, part of the present problem stems from maldistribution rather than the absolute shortage of existing facilities for golf.[37] Moreover expenditure in time and money on one type of recreation means that less is available for other activities or resources. In this situation there is a need to know the extent to which recreation activities and their associated resources are substitutes for one another; and the conditioning effect on attendance levels at one area by the existence and characteristics of others. It may be that the degree of substitution between activities or areas is dependent on their inherent attraction and location. Some resources may act as substitutes for one another, others may complement or supplement each other. This whole concept has to be put into manageable terms in relation to particular types of resources or activities.

If this method of measuring deferred demand was refined using regional or sub-regional activity participation rates and applied to a nationwide survey, it should provide a measure of areas of inadequate provision and assist in locating new facilities. In an economic climate where money and resources are scarce, the concept of substitution can be applied to specific

facilities where it is recognised that total deferred demand cannot be met.

POTENTIAL DEMAND

This concept relates to that section of the population who require an improvement in their social and economic circumstances before they can be brought into the effective demand market. This theme is closely tied up with predicting future levels of demand, given changes in population, income, education, free time and the other key variables that influence growth in demand. Potential demand is a crucial concept because we need to identify the future volume and range of recreational activities in order to match predicted levels of demand with the supply of recreation opportunities.

Work by Willmott[38], Rodgers[39] and Young[40] suggests that four basic changes may appear as a result of current trends. These are:

1 Changes in the life cycle of individuals with more and younger marriages.
2 Changes in mobility through diffusion of new transport modes, and a wider diffusion of existing ones.
3 The continued process of urbanisation which may increase participation rates in urban-located activities and decrease non-urban activities.
4 Changes in the form and length of available leisure time.

Rodgers suggests that recreation is determined by—and is an extension of—the life style, and given this assertion a change in life style is required to transform potential demand into future effective demand.[41] This raises the questions, to what extent are life styles changing and what factors influence this change? Willmott develops the thesis that although the average standard of living in Britain in the year 2000 will be substantially higher than it is now, the relative shares of wealth and income of different sections of the population are unlikely to change

fundamentally.[42] In other words, although changes in life cycle, mobility, and leisure time will occur, the social structure of our society is not expected to be radically altered. Any forecast of changes in life styles is inhibited by two contradictory trends—one towards greater cultural homogeneity with a greater diffusion of middle-class tastes and consumption patterns, and the other for many aspects of British social structure to remain unchanged. Despite predictions of increasing affluence and spending power over the next three decades, available evidence suggests that a dichotomy of incomes and associated life styles will remain. There is already a situation where the poorer sections of society are so locked in a vicious circle of economic and social deprivation that they are excluded from many leisure pursuits. Although there is a discretionary element in the potential demand sector, consisting of people without the time to participate, the majority cannot afford most leisure pursuits because of their very low income levels.

FORECASTING DEMAND

The inherent pitfalls in predicting future events have been neatly summed up by M. J. Moroney: 'Economic forecasting like weather forecasting in England is only valid for the next six hours or so.'[43] While this overstates the case it is generally accepted that most estimates of economic and social changes are only valid over a period of five to ten years. This is evident from the transient nature of trends in outdoor recreation demand over the past thirty years.

Most predictive work has analysed recreational patterns in socio-economic terms and multiple regression techniques have been commonly used to project a 'mix' of the key demand variables. For example the ORRRC study report *Prospective Demand for Outdoor Recreation* identified five socio-economic groups within the population and projected trends of causal factors such as age, income and population.[44] Existing parti-

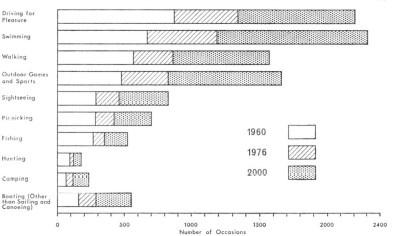

Fig 5   Growth in demand for outdoor recreation in the United States, 1960–2000

cipation rates were applied to future levels of these factors to produce a demand forecast. However, data on participation levels were not available over time and it was assumed that participation rates and socio-economic structure would remain constant. Moreover, opportunity to participate (ie the availability of facilities to persons) was not included as an independent variable. Given these limiting factors the conclusions of this study were that in the United States volume of outdoor recreation activities would at least treble by the year 2000 (Figure 5).

The more recent European Travel Commission *Seminar on Forecasting Tourist Movement* (1971)[45] included a number of papers using a combination of consensus judgement, trend extrapolation, and simple econometric models of the type:

$$T(i + a) = Ti x_1{}^{a1} X_2{}^{a2} X_3 \ldots {}^{an} X_n$$

Where Ti = traffic flow, basic year i
    a = number of years
    X_n = elasticities (ie the sensitivity of the demand for travel to changes in price)
    X_1 = gross national product
    X_2 = gross national product per capita
    X_3 = fare
    X_4 = availability of air services.

Most of the contributions were concerned with international air traffic flows, but econometric models of this type could be adapted to produce general estimates of recreational travel at intra- and inter-regional level. For example a simple predictive model representing the regional recreation system could take the form:

$$Di = Di\, X_1{}^{a1} X_2{}^{a2} X_3{}^{a3} X_4{}^{a4} X_5{}^{a5} X_6 \ldots {}^{an} X_n$$

Where: Di = overall demand for year i
a = year
X_n = elasticities
X_1 = gross regional product
X_2 = gross regional product per capita
X_3 = mean travel costs
X_4 = index of mobility (ie passenger miles per capita)
X_5 = average journey speed
X_6 = average discretionary time per year
X_7 = population (year a).

However, a model of this type is a variation of earlier examples developed by Mansfield and others, and does not offer any conceptual advance on previous work.

The North West Sports Council study used multiple regression analysis to explain participation in particular activities. Two techniques were used.[46] First the regression relationship between eleven activities and sixteen factors was calculated; and direct use of this relationship was made in predicting future demand, by substituting into the equation the values for the activity being studied. Secondly the regression relationship was used to identify which of the sixteen factors were important for individual activities. For example, if the crucial variables influencing fishing were possession of a car licence and men aged fifteen to forty, the proportion of the population with these attributes can be isolated, the basic assumption being that the sub-group participation levels will remain the same up to 1981. In both methods it is necessary to produce a population profile for each year for which predictions are required.

The report suggests that the predictive ability of the equations could be improved by allowing for the fact that the effect of a change in one variable may not be the same at all values of the

other variables. It approaches the problem of quantifying subjective variables by assigning only two possible values, on the
premise that a person has or has not engaged in a specific
activity within the previous twelve months. These are referred
to as 'zero-one variables' and are then used in the same way as
any other numerical variable. As the report points out, this
approach poses considerable problems when interpreting the
results. For example, if participation in turf sports can only
take the values of zero or one, what does an estimated value of
0·25 indicate? The interpretation used is that a person or group
of persons would have a 25 per cent chance of taking part in
turf sports in any twelve-month period. Their conclusion
stresses the need for more detailed demand/supply studies at a
sub-regional level. While their multiple regression technique
needs to be further refined, it may be that an alternative to
regression equations is required. More work is in progress on
the problem of deriving a better equation, with the aid of a
Sports Council grant.

THE DEMAND/SUPPLY RELATIONSHIP
IN OUTDOOR RECREATION

Given the conceptual framework of recreation demand, the
intervening element in the demand-supply equation is capacity.
There are three kinds of capacity: physical, environmental and
ecological.

Physical capacity is the easiest concept to grasp because for
many recreation activities a site imposes physical limits,
although other constraints probably intervene before these are
reached. Thus roads will become jammed and all car park
spaces filled before a beach reaches its physical capacity.

Environmental capacity is the maximum level of recreation
use in terms of numbers and activities that can be accommodated in an area before participants perceive a decline in their
attraction to that locality. This is the most abstract and least

tangible of the capacity concepts, and will vary from one person to another and be influenced by mood, season and weather. Despite its changeable nature this concept has been studied in different recreational environments to produce notional standards of capacity. Dower and McCarthy in their study of Donegal identified a range of resources critical to the development of tourism and recreation, and estimated the capacity of each to take people at any one time.[47] By relating their ideas to further work by Furmidge,[48] Houghton-Evans and Miles[49] it is possible to produce a range of estimates of environmental capacity for different recreation environments. These are outlined in Table 7.

TABLE 7   Suggested space standards for environmental capacity

Type of recreation area	Notional environmental capacity
Major scenic route	20 persons per mile
Minor scenic route	4 persons per mile
Major scenic feature	20 persons per square mile
Major historic site	30 persons per square mile
Woodland area	100 persons per square mile
Picnic area	60 persons per site
Enclosed land	50 persons per square mile
Rough or hill land	5 persons per square mile
Coast or lake shore (basic level)	50 persons per mile
Attractive and accessible coast/beach	400 persons per mile

These are general estimates of environmental standards for countryside areas and the capacity figures might be higher than this in areas close to the major cities or on very accessible stretches of coastline.

Ecological capacity is concerned with the maximum level of recreation use that an area can accommodate before ecological damage or decline occurs. The changes that can take place are influenced by the geology, relief, soils and vegetation cover of the area and the seasonal intensity of its recreational use. A person on horseback has a more noticeable effect than one on foot: so too has the camper. When people come in cars, the wheels of these vehicles can cause more damage than the

visitors. For example, in the New Forest the penetration of cars on to open heathland has destroyed heather and exposed heath and stone.[50] Damage to trees has occurred and access to water and food for wild animals has been restricted; as a result some areas of the forest have lost much biological interest.

The need for adequate and flexible management techniques is implicit in all three concepts of capacity, and these tools can be applied to the resource or its users. Because no direct price mechanism operates in most aspects of the public sector to regulate capacity levels, indirect methods of control can be used such as restrictions on car park signs and traffic flows or more positive measures to substitute resources such as country parks in order to filter off demand from those areas under greatest pressure. Once in a recreation area, the user population can be managed using restraints such as barriers, ditches and limited parking space, with motorless zones in the more fragile habitats. Essentially there is a need to know how many people a recreation facility can take without a change in its physical or ecological character. To date empirical studies are limited and much work remains to be done in translating the whole concept of capacity into usable form.

RECREATION DEMAND: PRIORITY RESEARCH AREAS

The nature of the interaction between supply of and demand for recreation resources needs to be thoroughly examined. Given the concepts of capacity and the underlying assumption that the use of existing recreation resources must eventually reach saturation point, work is needed on the effects of new facilities on participation rates in their surrounding catchment area. Supply of new facilities may transform latent demand into effective demand; changes within the pattern of effective demand may also be created. The degree of substitution should be measured between one kind of facility and another, and

depends on the inherent attraction of different recreation resources in relation to centres of demand. Cesario defines attractiveness as 'drawing power'[51] but this does little to establish what constitutes attractiveness or how it can be measured. It is clearly linked with individual perception of recreation facilities or landscape resources and the motivation of users and their evaluation of resources are two aspects of demand requiring extensive study.

Predictive work requires an understanding of the basic causes of recreational demand and the patterns of movement associated with recreational activities. Synthetic models are being developed such as the gravity model, the opportunity model and the multiple regression model, to define the relationship between trips and measures of attraction, generation and travel resistance. Other factors such as the value of travel time and the impact of intervening opportunities are still fairly obscure. Most work is based on past surveys and the resultant predictions assume that a mix of key variables will remain constant until the forecast target date. Unfortunately recreation consists of ephemeral and constantly changing activities influenced by changes in taste and fashion, and varying circumstances can lead to inaccurate predictions. Much of current research into recreation demand is aimed at describing and interpreting the operation of the whole or parts of the recreation system, and although our understanding of it is as yet very imperfect we do know the main activities which generate the greatest growth and demand for space and we can identify some of the current and potential conflicts with other land-use activities. The conceptual problems associated with research into recreation demand present a challenge to a broad range of disciplines including ecology, economics, biology, geography and planning; and for this reason demand studies may be best tackled on a multi-disciplinary basis. While there is no special geographical approach to recreation studies there is much for the geographer to contribute, as the following chapters show.

Page 49 Caravan camp, Porthcawl

Page 50 (*above*) Informal recreation, St James's Park, London (*below*) Goyt Valley after experiment, visitors enjoying traffic-free lanes

CHAPTER TWO

Perception in Outdoor Recreation

THE values and attributes of any outdoor recreation site, whether a local neighbourhood park or major national wilderness area, are perceived somewhat differently by numerous sub-groups within society. Some of these bodies are highly developed bureaucratic park planning organisations or local government authorities which, through time, have assumed various roles and formalised 'official' attitudes towards the recreation area in question. Other groups are much more loosely structured. Individuals engaging in informal recreation on public land or water often have little in common other than the fact that they enjoy the same activity at the same place under broadly similar environmental conditions. Their attitudes towards the site are rarely made explicit, though in times of stress—as, for example, in the case of a road being routed through a national park or a quarry company announcing plans to extract rock in a prime amenity location—they may band together, sign petitions and

generally object to what is occurring. In practice such criticism comes almost exclusively from well-educated groups who can quickly rally together in a common cause and know precisely how best to communicate their views to a wider public. By the same token such groups traditionally have been composed very largely of hikers, mountaineers, primitive campers, canoeists and naturalists who are very largely concerned with recreational sites at the 'wilderness' end of the environmental continuum. Under stress the precise attitudes of all the various formal and informal groups involved with a particular area are brought to the surface, and it is for this reason that so many investigations made by social scientists have been into isolated resource conflicts involving public recreational land and water resources.

This relative emphasis to date on the environmental attitudes of those individuals and groups involved in fairly clearly defined case studies of extreme stress conditions can be criticised on the grounds that it has tended to direct research attention away from the investigation of perceptions, attitudes and associated decision-making processes of recreationists engaging in numerous more popular activities in less stressful situations. Pleasure driving, boating, swimming, camping and fishing are examples of 'mass' pursuits that are engaged in by millions of participants in the affluent countries of the world, all of whom continually make little-studied decisions to visit particular sites at certain times and by particular routes.

This chapter is concerned with a discussion of some of the main elements of such decision-making processes. This involves such things as attitudes towards, and knowledge of, various recreational sites, and also perception of the home environment, of the distance to the recreational destination and of the journey there. Thus, of the six methodological perspectives for the study of outdoor recreation outlined by Burdge and Field,[1] the focus of the present chapter is very largely on the *social psychological* level—on the way the recreationist perceives the physical and social environment around him, the forces that

appear to shape his view, and the way researchers can attempt to measure and understand his cognitions. Particular attention will be paid to the spatial element in recreational behaviour, though the ideas discussed are drawn from a wide variety of writings mainly in the fields of architecture and landscape architecture, aesthetics, economics, psychology, sociology and engineering, as well as from geography, all of which are concerned with a major interdisciplinary growth-point in the social sciences which can be broadly labelled *environmental psychology*.[2]

The social sciences present two possible lines of approach towards the individual's perception of phenomena such as, for example, beaches, boating lakes, national parks or coastal resorts. The first line of inquiry, to which the greatest attention will be given in this chapter, may be called the *positivistic orientation*. Ground firmly in experimental behaviouristic psychology, it assumes that the elements of the perception process can be isolated and measured objectively. The second approach, which takes its lead from Gestalt psychology and phenomenology, maintains that perceptual processes cannot be measured objectively but that by means of the variety of techniques subsumed under the general heading of *participant observations* the investigator can advance towards a sympathetic 'understanding' of the world as it is experienced by the subject being studied. With the exception of the work of Campbell, Burch and Etzkorn[3] respectively, this latter approach has not yet been used much in recreation research and, for this reason alone, it is given little attention here.

THE RETREAT FROM AGGREGATE STUDIES OF DEMAND

Despite Clawson's early discussion and conceptualisation of the individual recreational experience as a 'package' consisting of five components—the anticipation phase, the journey to the site, the on-site experience, the return journey and the recollection phase[4]—it is only very recently that studies of outdoor

recreation have looked at this most fundamental unit of analysis in demand studies.[5] Most investigations in North America, Western Europe and Australasia up to the present time have been concerned almost exclusively with aggregate studies of demand, focusing on broad patterns of recreational activity at either the national or regional level and on a few relatively easily measured correlates of participation—usually occupation, education, income, age, sex, race and place of residence. However, there are clear signs of a mounting concern over the inadequacies of such macro-scale projects. La Page, for example, has argued strongly that from a number of such surveys in the United States we have only confusing results relating to trends in participation and still have very little idea what people really want in the way of recreation:

> National recreation surveys conducted in 1960 and 1965 indicated that driving for pleasure and walking for pleasure were two of the most popular outdoor activities chosen off a list by approximately 50 per cent of the adult population. The same question asked, in an open-ended fashion, in a 1971 national survey found less than 5 per cent of the population reporting driving and walking for pleasure as outdoor activities! The 1965 survey found that 10 per cent of American adults went camping, while the 1971 survey found that camping was actively engaged in by 21 per cent of American households. This is not growth, it's confusion in terminology![6]

Leigh's detailed investigation of the recreational behaviour patterns of a sample of 157 young adults between the ages of eighteen and twenty-five in an English mining village certainly produced results which were markedly at variance with the picture of frenzied outdoor activity uncovered by a national survey for this age group.[7] Moreover, even if it is conceded that broad-scale national and regional investigations of recreational demand have presented us with a mass of useful information relating to the determinants of participation in selected activities, we are still very much in the dark concerning the preferred environments for these activities. It is one thing to say that X

per cent of a certain socio-economic group went picnicking on so many occasions in a particular year, but on its own this is virtually irrelevant to the recreation planner unless we can provide data relating to the various kinds of environmental settings people choose for this and other pursuits. Thus Van Doren and Lentnek, in their aggregate study of boating in Ohio, concluded: 'It would be helpful to know, for example, the way boaters perceive and evaluate the quality of the aquatic and human recreation environment . . . we need to know why persons choose particular locations for recreation.'[8]

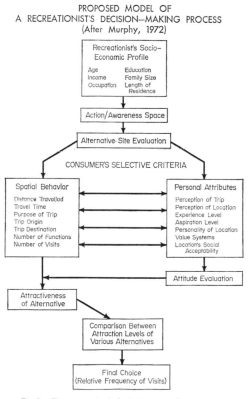

Fig 6   The recreationist's decision-making process

THE RECREATIONIST'S
DECISION-MAKING PROCESS

In simple terms, the process of making a decision involves the following six steps: (i) problem recognition; (ii) goal specification; (iii) procedure selection; (iv) information gathering; (v) evaluation and choice; and (vi) implementation. This process, whether conscious or unconscious, takes place within the context of a particular physical, social and economic environment which constrains the individual in various ways. On *a priori* grounds it would appear that the main 'goal' of recreational behaviour is the maximisation of one's enjoyment or 'satisfaction', but quite obviously, as will be shown below, this can be accomplished in very many different ways depending upon the activity in question and the personality and other characteristics of the individual concerned. A tentative model of the recreationist's decision-making process has been proposed by P. E. Murphy and is illustrated in Figure 6. The author suggested that it consists of three sub-systems: 'the socio-economic profile of the individual, his spatial relationship to the recreation system and his cognitive attributes'.[9] These important determinants of recreational choice will be discussed here through the medium of three basic concepts—*learning*, *image*, and *goal* (or 'need')—which are crucial in helping us to understand both the activity and locational decisions made by recreationists.

LEARNING ENVIRONMENTAL PREFERENCES

Leisure time activity is *learned* behaviour. Children grow up in a particular social and physical environment which strongly moulds their recreational activities and preferences, suggesting what is possible and 'acceptable' and what is not possible. Of course this initial learning phase does not imprint an unmodifiable pattern of leisure activity for the rest of our lives, but there

is growing support for the view that recreational behaviour patterns learnt in childhood are extremely influential in determining the kinds of activities and environmental preferences that we display as adults. The importance of early childhood education for recreation, either by the family or the school, has been clearly underlined by Hendee. In the course of examining three theories of recreational behaviour—the 'familiarity' theory, the 'new experience' and the 'pleasant childhood memory' theory—he concluded that 'activities pleasantly familiar during childhood tend to attract one as an adult . . . and this theoretical framework is, perhaps, one of the most promising'.[10] With reference to migration theory, Rogers has written that 'migration itself should be regarded as one of the more important migration differentials'[11] and the same sentiment can almost certainly be applied to recreational behaviour. A particular type of outdoor activity carried out in a particular setting invariably *itself* acts as an impetus for more recreational activity of the same type; experience breeds more experience. To take two extreme examples, the slum child who has lived all his life in an inner city environment and whose parents have never had access to a car is likely to find this an exciting environment. Michelson lends some support to this view in his account of a group of Boston slum children taken on a holiday to Cape Cod, their first trip out of the city:

> They couldn't imagine, after having been there, why anyone would consider it worth visiting, let alone having as home. It was desolate. There was no 'action'. These boys much preferred the person-centred life style that was part and parcel of the particular arrangement of their 'hot city streets'.[12]

At the other extreme it seems reasonable to suppose that the child of wealthy middle-class parents quickly comes to accept that the car, the boat, the skis and the second home, together with the physical environments associated with these things, are more or less inevitable facts of life, taken-for-granted expectations.

A more important distinction between these two polar groups lies in their different mobility patterns. A high degree of mobility inevitably gives rise to a wide range of environmental experience which in turn acts as a datum against which the quality of various recreational locations can be evaluated. The individual whose 'life space' has encompassed Canada, Australia, much of Western Europe and several parts of Britain is likely to be far more discriminating when it comes to judging the quality of a particular recreational area such as a national park than the person who has left his home city only once in his lifetime. Moreover, the recreational experience gained through a high degree of mobility appears to have an interesting effect on the perception of local neighbourhood recreational facilities. In their comparison of the awareness and use of low-level neighbourhood parks in Vancouver by two groups at opposite ends of the socio-economic scale, Rawley and Peucker, for example, found that with decreasing income people appeared to be more interested in their local parks, to know more about them and to use them more frequently for a greater variety of purposes.[13] For the higher socio-economic group, on the other hand, the foci of much of their leisure time behaviour were private tennis, yacht or country clubs and distant weekend homes, with the result that local parks had a very different 'image', perceived as little more than necessary neighbourhood decoration.

In a more recent article Hendee and his colleagues have incorporated some of the above ideas in a typology of recreational participation designed to suggest how, once set in a pattern, learned activity and environmental preferences probably change through the life cycle (see Figure 7).[14] The authors believe that there exists a continuum from *appreciative-symbolic* activities (such as hiking and mountain climbing), which are strongly favoured by individuals at the 'high' end of the social factor dimension, to *active-expressive* activities preferred by those at the opposite extremity of this scale.

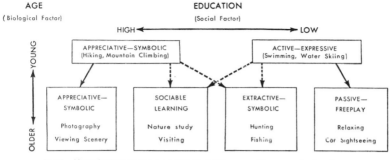

Fig 7 Hypothetical changes in activity preference with age and education

'IMAGE' AND RECREATIONAL MENTAL MAPS

Travel represents an extremely important part of another facet of the whole recreational learning process, for it involves acquiring the information which allows the recreationist to structure a 'mental map' of recreational opportunities, including such things as the perceived distances to the sites (measured in units of subjective time, cost or effort) and their relative quality.[15] Imagine a car-owning migrant who is a complete newcomer to a large city, far from his former residence. Alternatively, consider the example of a person who has arrived by car to spend a vacation in a holiday region that he has never visited before. From talking with friends, from watching television and reading magazines and newspapers the individual in both situations arrives at his destination with some notion of the recreational opportunities available in the region, though these ideas initially are rather vague. His mental map is extremely fuzzy, has huge blanks in it and is likely to bear little relation to reality. He has ideas concerning the location of, and distances to, the few beaches and parks he has heard about and similarly he has some ill-formed views on the facilities available at these sites, their quality, and the kinds of people that go there—in a word, he holds 'images' of the recreational oppor-

tunities available. At first his leisure time behaviour takes on the pattern of a *search*: he explores his new environment and continually modifies his mental map. He discovers new sites, he acquires additional information which results in the re-evaluation of his images of certain routes and locations. In time it is entirely possible that his recreational trip-making may take on something of a stereotyped or habitual character, his action space including only a relatively small number of locations that he has come to know well. However, work by Mercer in Australia[16] and by La Page in the United States[17] suggests that *impulse behaviour* may not be at all uncommon in recreational activity. This involves the individual behaving quite 'irrationally' by taking routeways which he does not know and visiting recreation sites which he has discovered quite by accident.

The interrelated concepts of image, mental map, search, learning, action/awareness space and information have been drawn almost exclusively from the studies of migration at international, national, or intro-urban level.[18] Their direct relevance to recreation research has not yet been fully tested, though they have been employed with some success in a few studies of leisure, the results of which suggest that these concepts are of considerable value in aiding our understanding of individual recreational behaviour at a variety of geographical scales and in locales from the city to the most extensive of wilderness areas.

The relative location of an individual to a set of recreational opportunities certainly seems to have an important influence on his awareness of, and attitudes towards, these opportunities. R. G. Golledge has examined the potential relevance of various learning theories to spatial behaviour and suggests the following three hypotheses.

1 Individuals located closest to a reward (eg recreational opportunity) are most likely to choose that opportunity.

2 Individuals further away from recreational attractions are most likely to exhibit multiple response patterns; and

3 Individuals some distance from recreational opportunities may take longer to form a stereotyped response because of their need to cultivate a larger perceptual horizon.[19]

With the exception of the third hypothesis, which requires longitudinal recreational trip data, these ideas have been tested for trips to outdoor recreation sites in the Melbourne region. Recreational trips to beaches from households in coastal suburbs tend to be strongly oriented towards one, or usually at the most two, proximate beaches; whereas residents in suburbs several miles from the coast exhibit a 'multiple response' pattern which includes a large number of beaches.[20] In general the suburban resident of a large urban complex has only a vague notion of most of the outdoor recreational opportunities available to him. He often has quite a good knowledge of the parks on the edge of the urban area closest to the route from his residence, but has little or no knowledge of similar sites on the other side of the city.[21] Sites close by present a strong 'image', are generally well known, frequently visited and liked, even though, as for example in the case of beaches, they may be quite badly polluted or 'overcrowded'. In her investigation of the users of Toronto beaches, M. L. Barker found that 'there is a tendency among beach users . . . to deny or discount the pollution levels at the place with which they are the most familiar and to express the view that pollution is worse elsewhere'.[22]

Surprisingly, very little research has been carried out on the important question of the information recreationists have at their disposal concerning particular recreational sites, the accuracy of that information, or the way they acquired it. Recent work by Cole in the Grampians region of Western Victoria, Australia, has attempted with some measure of success to apply the principles of a Lynch-type city image study to the large recreational region illustrated in Figure 8a.[23] A variety of

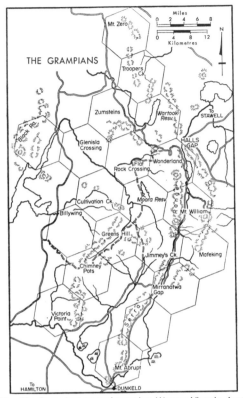

Fig 8a   The Grampians recreation region, Western Victoria, Australia

techniques such as questions relating to the whereabouts of particular locations and photographs illustrating certain sites were used to build up a composite picture of campers' awareness of the region. The results proved extremely interesting (Figure 8b). Large sections of the southern, western and northern Grampians were very rarely visited and little known; they were not a part of the average recreationist's 'awareness space'. But a quite small area in the vicinity of Hall's Gap was used very intensively and was well known. Other parts of the region were judged to be 'not as recreationally desirable' as the Hall's Gap area even though the campers had never visited these other

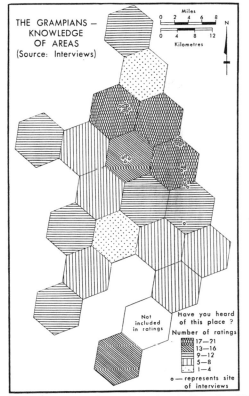

Fig 8b Campers' awareness of recreation region, the Grampians, W Victoria

regions and had only the vaguest idea of what they were like. Using a rather different approach, Murphy attempted to 'manipulate' the spatial behaviour of visitors to Victoria, British Columbia, by feeding a number of control groups different levels of information relating to particular sites.[24] His sample was too small to allow him to formulate a definite conclusion, but the hypothesised relationship between information level and recreational behaviour did appear to be valid: those tourists who had been presented with a large amount of accurate information about a particular location did show a greater tendency to visit that location. The management implications of these

concepts are clear: since the recreational usage made of an area is in large part a function of the information the visitor possesses about the region, this information can be at least partially controlled by recreation management agencies in many different ways[25] to influence choice of recreational area.

Goal

Because travel to and from the outdoor destinations is such an important phase of the recreational experience, the perceived *distance* to the site becomes an important consideration for the recreationist. But this, in turn, is very largely a function of the *goal* of a particular outing. C. K. Campbell has argued that we need to pay far more attention to the aims of various visitor groups rather than assuming, as many researchers do, that these are undifferentiated.[26] Some recreational trips—especially vacation motoring, or the trial and error 'search' behaviour of new residents in a city region—are diffuse in character. In these cases the journey itself is the main activity focus. On such trips, whether they are of a short- or long-term duration, as Wolfe has so ably demonstrated, travel itself may be an inducement for further travel.[27] Other trips are *specific* in character; they are made to a usually predetermined site in order to engage in a particular activity. For the mobile teenage group the time taken to travel to a 'with it' resort would almost certainly be considered well worth the effort, whereas in cognitive terms intervening sites, to all intents and purposes, may be perceived as being farther away or even non-existent. Lentnek *et al* found that different boating populations had varied propensities to travel to the same set of lakes depending upon their individual recreational needs: 'sailors and water skiers tend to have the shortest time-distances, pleasure cruisers somewhat longer, and fishermen and non-specialised boaters the longest of all'.[28]

Further, it is apparent that the goals of any given recreational trip, together with the associated image of the site (if the journey is a specific one), are strongly related to the *role* that the indi-

vidual is playing at the time. A father in a professional occupation and with two children under the age of five may favour
wilderness hiking, which places him firmly within Hendee's
'appreciative-symbolic' category, but on weekend outings in
the summertime he frequently plays the role of 'father', braves
almost intolerable traffic congestion, and takes his young
children to a crowded sandy beach at a popular resort along the
nearest stretch of coast. Such a site and activity choice is a
direct consequence of the recreationist's *role* in a particular
group setting at a particular time. Yet the question might well
be asked: in a photo-choice experiment of recreation site
evaluation—a technique strongly favoured by some researchers
—how would this respondent rate the desirability of a crowded
beach scene?

Conclusion

By its very nature outdoor recreation is discretionary behaviour, involving a relatively unconstrained *choice* of both activities and locations on the part of the recreationist from a vast
array of possibilities. It has been argued here that the investigation of the decision processes associated with these choices
should be a central concern for the researcher in the field of
recreation. Because of the traditionally 'free' nature of outdoor
recreation and the general absence of visitor charges at outdoor
sites this approach, focusing as it does on such behavioural
concepts as user attitudes, information and satisfaction, holds
out promise as a guide to recreation managers in the evaluation
of the relative success of their various planning programmes.[29]
The discussion of ways in which 'perception' studies, broadly
construed, are of relevance in outdoor recreation research has
necessarily been highly selective. Thus, no consideration has
been given to the all-important question of *perceptual capacity*
and *recreational zoning*, both of which are exercising wilderness
area managers, in particular, a great deal at the present time;[30]
research into the grouping of 'environmental personality' types

has been neglected,[31] and the very considerable problems of measurement involved in all such behavioural research have been completely omitted. What appear to be the critical research needs in this area at the present time? First, it is suggested that we need to know far more than we do about the way particular patterns of recreational behaviour and environmental preferences of different groups within society are initially learned and change through the life cycle. This involves two things: the focusing in greater detail on the evolving recreational behaviour patterns of *children*, and a need to collect participation data that would allow us to test ideas suggested by Hendee which were discussed briefly earlier in the chapter.

Secondly, by focusing initially on quite small samples of individuals—ideally, new in-migrants to a country or metropolitan area—to investigate in detail the search and learning processes associated with the development of the recreationist's mental map. Research of this nature would allow us to gain some insight into the way information about recreational sites is diffused, interpreted and acted upon by various groups of recreationalists.

Finally, we require more data on the complex of 'push' and 'pull' factors motivating outdoor recreation behaviour. What are the environmental forces, both social and physical, which act as an impetus for outdoor leisure activity? For example, are dissatisfactions with dwelling-space of the local neighbourhood relevant in this context? Up to the present, aggregate demand models have been far too simplistic on the question of visitor goals—on what it is the tourist is seeking in a particular location at a particular time. In his recent examination of the 'new experience', or compensatory, theory of recreational motivation, Knopp too has argued that 'we cannot assume that any environment is a single, homogeneous entity'.[32] Recreationists in the same park environment may be attracted to it for quite different reasons; for some it may be the 'natural' countryside setting, for others it might be the opportunity for social interaction.

Research into all aspects of recreational 'perception' is in an

Page 67 (*above*) Goyt Valley before experiment (*below*) Goyt Valley after experiment

Page 68 (*above*) Scenic Drive, Blue Ridge Parkway, Appalachians
(*below*) Historical marker, Oregon Trail

KANSAS
HISTORICAL MARKER

ALCOVE SPRINGS & THE OREGON TRAIL

Six miles northwest is Alcove Springs, named in 1846 by appreciative travelers on the Oregon trail who carved the name on the surrounding rocks and trees. One described the Springs as "a beautiful cascade of water . . . altogether one of the most romantic spots I ever saw."

This country was well-known to early-day traders and "mountain men" as well as to later travelers to the Far West. John C. Fremont and his 1842 exploring expedition bivouacked at the Springs, and Marcus Whitman, with a thousand emigrants to Oregon, stopped there in 1843. Utah-bound Mormons and California-bound goldseekers followed, for only a short distance above was Independence Crossing, the famous ford across the Big Blue river. The Donner party, a need of whom later froze or starved in the Sierras, buried its first member, Sarah Keyes, near the Springs in 1846.

The great Tuttle Creek Reservoir at full pool level extends along the Big Blue from Independence Crossing southward nearly to Manhattan.

Erected by Kansas Historical Society and State Highway Commission

early stage of development and has largely been of an isolated and faltering nature, tentatively seeking out concepts from a variety of disciplines and testing them within the recreational context. A major shortcoming of much of this work is that it has been insufficiently grounded in *theory*. However precise and 'objective' our measurements, however elegant our quantitative models, these in themselves are of limited value without a solid theoretical base to build on.

CHAPTER THREE

Routeways and Recreation

... I travel not to go anywhere, but to go.
Robert Louis Stevenson, *Travels with a Donkey*

ROUTEWAYS AND RECREATION PATTERNS

DEEP-ROOTED in the very concept of outdoor recreation is the 'journey to play', the fundamental movement linking residence or workplace to recreation resource. Such movement varies in scale, in duration and in frequency for it must satisfy the wide-ranging variations in demand explored in an earlier chapter. It lacks the studied monotony and regularity of the daily journey to work, but in weekly or seasonal rhythms it can reach even greater intensity and cause even more widespread congestion. Travel takes many forms, from the toddler's tentative trail to a play area a stone's throw from home to the global wanderings of the international jet set. A recreational journey generates its own routes and transport types: the higher reaches

of the Alps have been brought within the range of the ordinary traveller by mountain railways, chair lifts and telepheriques,[1] while cruise liners carry those seeking scenery and sun to the more exotic ports of the world.

The 'journey to play' is far more than a mere adjunct to the recreation experience: it can be, as Stevenson averred, its very focus. For some, the joy lies in the sheer exhilaration of movement. As Fanny Kemble wrote of a pioneer railway journey in 1830, 'You cannot conceive what that sensation of cutting the air was . . . When I closed my eyes this sensation of flying was quite delightful, and strange beyond description.'[2] For others, the journey has its own recreative powers. Not all saw the railway as helpful in this respect: in 1841, A. B. Granville could advise the prospective spa visitor that 'the railroad is out of the question, for the patient would be presently whisked from his home to his destination, ere he knows how that has been done; whereby the object of travelling, as an auxiliary to the mineral water, would be defeated'.[3]

For many, the experience of travel is its own reward, for 'a journey is always an episode, a rounded story in itself'.[4] In this regard, the independence and range conferred by the private car have immeasurably heightened experience. In 1907, Henry James found that the motor car 'contemplatively and touringly used' brought 'a huge extension of life, of experience and consciousness':[5] many find this still, though there are now more than four hundred times as many cars on the roads of Britain. 'Going for a drive' has become the most common form of recreation pursuit in developed temperate lands,[6] though whether this is truly outdoor recreation is more a matter of debate. For most, the car functions simply as an extension to the house, a detachable room with a view. Even in such stirring walking country as the English Lakes, visitors predominantly 'enjoy merely driving about and admiring the scenery'.[7] On two summer weekends in 1966, only 10 per cent of non-holiday car visitors to the Lake District went climbing or fell-walking for a mile or more, and

but 34 per cent admitted to a short walk or stroll less than a mile in length.[8]

The concern of this chapter, however, is not so much the character of recreation journeys as their consequences. The very existence of the 'journey to play', whatever the form of transport, emphasises the fundamental spatial impact of recreation as being largely confined to *lines* of movement linking *nodes* of intensive activity. Few forms of outdoor recreation require the unfettered use of large tracts of countryside: field sports of various kinds are by far the most important in this respect, but these by and large are wholly compatible with agricultural and other uses. For the rest, activities are linear or nodal in expression, restricted to movement along defined routeways linking sites where specific recreation pursuits are carried out. This is as true of water-based as of land-based recreation, though the former is beyond the concern of this chapter.

The crux of recreational planning is therefore the location, design and management of a relatively limited number of sites devoted wholly or partially to recreation, together with a concern for the routes which link them both to each other and to the residences of their users. The interstices within the network have a role in recreation, but it is almost exclusively visual, an area for looking *at* rather than recreating *in*. The limited spatial impact of recreation has not always received the recognition it deserves: in this context, the popular concept of a crowded countryside is of dubious validity, to say the least, even at times of peak recreational pressure. Far more accurate is the planner's view of East Hampshire on an August Sunday afternoon:

> The most apparent feature is the relative unimportance of recreation in terms of actual exclusive land use compared with the acreage of agricultural land and woodland. The recreational uses and activities are scattered in a diffuse pattern on sites surplus to agricultural needs, where pressure has been so great that the agricultural use has been relinquished or where occasionally dual use operates with agriculture or forestry.[9]

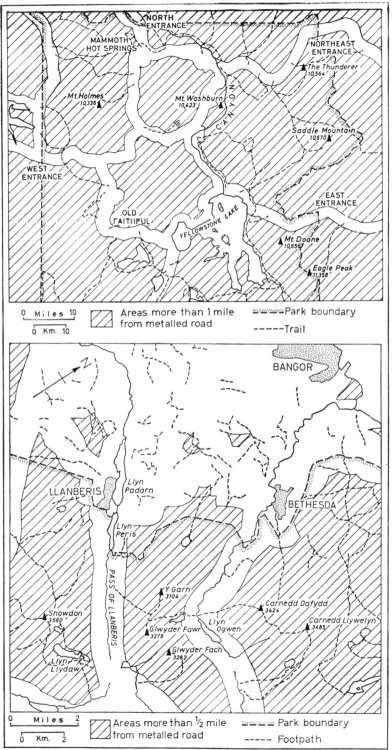

Fig 9   Areas inaccessible to car-borne visitors in parts of Yellowstone National Park, USA, and Snowdonia National Park, Wales

This fundamental pattern can be demonstrated in many ways. The passive, car-borne visitor is obviously confined to the existing road network, which even in densely patterned, cultivated areas affords only limited opportunities for access. Where an area is developed exclusively for the purposes of conservation and recreation, opportunities are likely to be even more restricted (Figure 9). Yellowstone is a classic instance. This pioneer national park is almost half the size of Wales, but few of its visitors stray far from the 300 miles of road and even fewer from its 950 miles of trail. Thus, though traffic densities on the 142-mile long loop road have justified the building of dual carriageways and a flyover junction at Old Faithful, large areas of the park remain undisturbed by an active human presence, glimpsed at most as part of a distant prospect.

TABLE 8   Routeway densities in Wales and in
Yellowstone National Park, USA*

	Total area	Roads	Footpaths and bridleways
	(sq mls)	(miles/sq ml)	(miles/sq ml)
Wales	7,967	1·93	2·24
Yellowstone National Park	3,472	·09	·27

* The data for roads for Wales includes both classified and unclassified roads, but relates to rural roads only.

Even when movement is entirely on foot, the existence of footpaths constrains movement into limited corridors. This is most easily seen in cultivated areas, where the freedom to roam at will is curbed by frequent field boundaries and by the crops themselves, but it remains almost equally true in areas where there is no such restraint on access. On open heather moorland in the Peak District, only 5 per cent of visitors were observed to stray from paths during a 1969 survey of six areas of moor, although the only impediment to free access was the coarse heather itself.[10] Even in the Cairngorms, where there are easy walking conditions on the very short vegetation around 3,500ft,

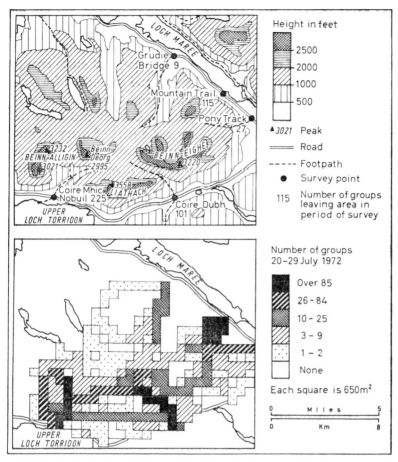

Fig 10   Distribution of walkers in part of the Gairloch Conservation Unit, 20–9 July 1972

only 15 per cent of 2,159 observed summer visitors strayed from the main paths.[11] More recent observations in the Gairlock Conservation Unit confirm these findings (Figure 10). In this relatively lightly used and rugged area, 84·3 per cent of the 477 groups of people interviewed kept to the paths most or all of the time, 15·7 per cent little or hardly at all.[12] Even more striking was the very uneven distribution of recreational activities: all

the areas of heavy use have well-marked footpaths, but not all the footpaths were used to anything like the same degree.

The recognition of this basic pattern of recreational activity eases problems of planning and management, and much energy is rightly expended in catering for demand at nodes of widely varying kinds, as subsequent chapters demonstrate. Consideration of the corridors is not always as well developed from the recreational point of view, yet they are a part of every recreational experience and in themselves may wholly satisfy some types of demand. The remainder of this chapter is therefore devoted to routeways as such, to their importance in terms of accessibility to recreation sites, to their character as a resource in themselves and to their role as an instrument of management.

ROUTEWAYS AND ACCESSIBILITY

Not all journeys or parts of a journey yield the same satisfaction. When the objective is a clearly defined node, the journey may be viewed simply as an impediment to its attainment, people finding travel 'unattractive but a necessary part of getting where they wish to go'.[13] Many, trapped almost immobile in the fumes of a Sunday evening traffic jam, would share Marion Clawson's view that 'the greatest opportunity for improvement of the outdoor recreation experience lies in the two travel phases', not least on the journey home when 'often tired, frequently in a hurry, sometimes broke, the family is in a different mood than when it travelled in the opposite direction'.[14]

Distance, indeed, is perhaps the prime determinant of destination, though the relationship is by no means a simple one. It must vary with the perceived 'attractiveness' of the destination, with its place in the recreational hierarchy. Some sites, of regional or even national importance, may pull people hundreds or even thousands of miles—Stonehenge or Mount Rushmore, the Matterhorn or the Grand Canyon—but the visit may be literally a 'once in a lifetime' experience. The nearest seaside or

open moorland may lure people from conurbations six times a year, while the local park is used every day to exercise the dog. More complex, but more relevant in the present context, are the spatial relationships of alternative destinations. Regional variations in patterns of expressed demand clearly reflect the relative accessibility of different kinds of resource, though more work is needed before any but the most general of relationships can be established. In a study of the Merseyside and Manchester conurbations, for example, it was shown that not only were there wide differences in the number and frequency of recreational trips generated, but that destinations sought also varied (Table 9). This was particularly the case when half-day trips were concerned, and when time was a more evident constraint on opportunity. Merseyside lies within easy reach of the sandy beaches of south Lancashire, north Wirral and North Wales, whereas Manchester, more amorphous and sprawling in form, is both farther removed from open country and more than 35 miles from the nearest coast.[15]

TABLE 9   Variations in recreational trip-taking in North West England

	NW England	Merseyside	Manchester
Full-day trips generated per 100 total sample within previous 4 weeks	52	*70	†38
Per cent of sample making full-day trips within previous 4 weeks	28	*32	†24
Mean distance travelled on full-day trips in miles	43·3	*28·7	†45·5
Per cent of full-day trippers visiting coast	52	58	53
Per cent of half-day trippers visiting coast	35	72	11
Per cent of half-day trippers visiting town parks	19	11	37

* Liverpool County Borough only   † Manchester County Borough only

Despite such variations, it is almost axiomatic that where alternative destinations of roughly equivalent merit are available

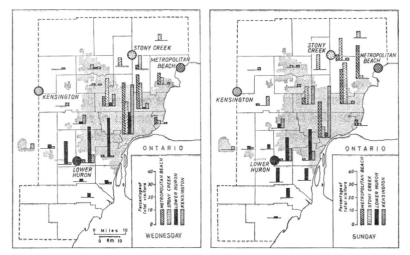

Fig 11   Origin of visitors to four parks of the Huron-Clinton Metropolitan Authority on a typical
Wednesday and Sunday in July 1965

most people on most occasions will choose that closest at hand.
One instance of this is illustrated in Figure 11. The Huron-Clinton Metropolitan Authority was established in 1940 to create
regional recreational facilities for the greater Detroit area: the
resultant parks were conceived entirely as day-use facilities,
all with a peripheral location within forty-five minutes' drive of
the centre of the conurbation. In a survey of four of the parks
made in 1965, 95 per cent of park users were residents of the
Authority's five county district, but each park exerted a particularly strong influence on the areas immediately adjacent,
even though some of these areas were largely non-urban in
character and with a relatively small population.[16] The deprived
inner area of Detroit was a major contributor in every case, but,
not unexpectedly, that contribution was greater on Sundays
and weaker on weekdays, especially in recently created (Stony
Creek) or relatively small (Lower Huron) parks. As in many
other instances, proximity, and accessibility in terms of routeways and of time available, were the key factors.

Accessibility, however, is a relative term. Changes in transport forms and selective improvements in transport routes may both generate an effect, though the direct relationship is not always easy to establish nor are data readily available. In earlier times, the close ties between the developing railway network and the fortunes of individual resorts were classic demonstrations. In the coaching era, Brighton flourished as the nearest point on the Channel coast to London: in 1837, Thomas Creevey could write, '. . . it is *detestable*: the crowd of human beings is not to be endured!'[17] But crowding is a relative term. Although Brighton's population had increased in percentage terms at a greater rate than that of any other English town in the decades 1811–21 and 1821–31, its growth slowed drastically in the 1820s. Fares by coach were relatively high (60p for an outside seat, £1·05 for an inside seat in 1835) and only within the means of comparatively small numbers. The advent of the railway in 1841 brought not only speedier but much cheaper travel, and as the excursionists flowed into the town, so its rate of population growth accelerated anew. In 1837, the number of travellers to Brighton by coach in the whole year was only about 50,000: by 1850, the railway might carry 73,000 in a single week, and on Easter Monday 1862, over 132,000 arrived.[18]

The relative growth of individual resorts was often linked closely to the fortunes of specific railway companies, and visitor hinterlands established in the railway era have had a curious persistence even when the majority of visitors no longer travel by rail. Bournemouth is a case in point. Later to develop, a hundred miles from London and rather more from the industrial West Midlands, the town was unusually dependent on its railway links. It did not possess a railway station until 1870, and the direct route to London through the New Forest was not opened until 1888. In 1874, however, the Somerset & Dorset Railway completed a route over the Mendips between Bournemouth and Bath. There was already a close relationship between the S&D and the Midland Railway (the Midland becoming a joint lessee

of the S&D in 1875), and the Midland hastened to publicise 'through communication between the Midlands and the South Coast by the New Route, without change of carriage or Break of Gauge'.[19] These links were strengthened in ensuing years by through coaches and through trains of which the Pines Express was the most noted. Even today, the links between Bournemouth and the Midlands remain unusually strong, though the S&D was closed in 1966 and by 1968 71·2 per cent of Bournemouth's visitors travelled by car and only 11·7 per cent by rail.[20] In 1968, 17·7 per cent of visitors came from the Greater London area, 22·1 per cent from the Midlands.[21] There are many similar instances: to name but one, Morecambe's close ties with Bradford and the West Riding, unusual for a West Coast resort, owe much to the services provided in earlier years by the Midland Railway, with a link between Airedale and Morecambe being completed as early as 1849.

Contemporary change has come, not only with the advent of the car, but even more with the completion of purpose-built motorways drastically reducing the time consumed in journeys. The potential of such improved accessibility is great,[22] but its importance must not be over-rated, for the friction of distance remains considerable. While it may be true that by 1974 21 million people will live within a three hour journey of the Lake District National Park,[23] it is a pessimistic overstatement to claim that the M6 has done for the Lake District what the railway did for Brighton. A survey of visitors to the Lake District made in 1966, when the M6 was open as far north as Carnforth, showed that between 63·1 per cent and 73·2 per cent of all day and half-day visits on the five days of survey originated within 50 miles of the boundary of the national park: such potential major contributors as Merseyside, Manchester, the West Riding, Teesside and Tyneside all lie beyond this limit (Figure 13). Only between 5·0 and 9·2 per cent had travelled more than 75 miles, the highest total being on Bank Holiday Sunday.[24] The area which even in 1835 Wordsworth felt should be 'deemed a

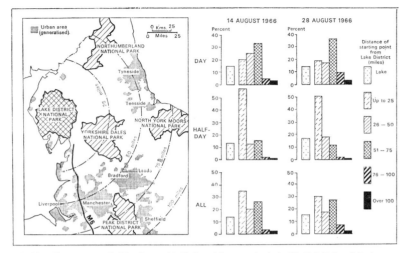

Fig 12   Distance travelled by day and half-day visitors to the Lake District National Park, 14 and 28 August 1966

sort of National property' still functions very much as a regional park, at least as far as non-resident visitors are concerned.

ROUTEWAYS AS RESOURCES

While the location of a site, and the pattern of routeways leading to it, may largely determine the volume and the origins of its visitors, those routeways are themselves a recreation resource of note. For some, the objective of outdoor recreation may not be to reach a particular site, but simply to enjoy the journey for its own sake. Colenutt, in his work on the Forest of Dean, noted that more than 70 per cent of day visitors to the forest from Bristol, Newport, Cardiff and Birmingham did not take the shortest route there on either their outward or their return journeys. Many also sought variety by reducing to a minimum the proportion of their outward route they duplicated on travelling home: the mean percentage of miles duplicated was about 50 per cent for visits from Bristol, Newport, Cardiff

and Birmingham, and as low as 37 per cent when Gloucester was the place of origin.[25]

It may, of course, be argued that this use of the journey as an end in itself is a transient and immature phase of a developing leisure consciousness. In Rodgers' view:

> Perhaps the simple 'going for a drive'—in which arriving at a destination is less the motive than the pleasure of getting there—is an aspect of the 'honeymoon' phase in a society not yet accustomed to seeing the car as a mere beast of burden. Certainly, the longer a family has had a car, the more purposive its use becomes, so that its influence is that of a recreational tool . . . rather than as a recreation in itself.[26]

Some support for this view comes from the USA. While 'driving for pleasure' was the most frequent outdoor recreational pursuit at the beginning of the 1960s,[27] it had been overtaken by 'walking for pleasure' by the middle of the decade.[28] For Britain, however, there is no evidence to suggest any significant slackening of popularity of what was once perceptively termed a 'joy ride'.

This difference between the two countries may well derive from the comparative nature of the resources available. Few tracts of rural America have the intimately meandering and dense network of rural roads which characterises so much of Britain, with the gentle backcloth of an immensely varied, mature agricultural landscape. Though not developed for recreation, and indeed with recreation traffic rarely forming more than a minor share of the total volume, these roads are a profoundly valuable resource. That value lies as much in their ubiquity as in their quality. They are as readily available, and perhaps of even more importance, in the immediate rural hinterland of towns and cities as in the more remote and compellingly beautiful tracts of outstanding scenic quality. Cracknell, indeed, has developed the concept of 'living space', a rural zone surrounding an urban area 'used as an extension of life in the city . . . a vista people can enjoy from their mobile room—their car . . . For every city-dweller it has become,

through the motor car, an integral part of his environment—it is part of the subconscious contract he makes with city living, namely that whenever he wants to, he can get out and enjoy the country.'[29] The capacity of this zone to absorb recreational pressure must be measured to a large degree by the density of its road network and its consequent capacity to absorb recreational traffic.

While rural roads are a near-universal and often undervalued recreation resource, the aristocrats of the system, scenic drives built specially for viewing scenery, are much more rare. In this context, the United States has many lessons to teach. The land in national parks is almost entirely federally owned and devoted to conservation and recreation. The road networks of the parks are designed both to enable the parks to be seen and at the same time to protect them from overuse, by channelling car-borne visitors into limited corridors. Some of the resulting national park roads rightly have an international fame: the Rim Drive at Crater Lake; the Going to the Sun road in Glacier; or the Trail Ridge Road of Rocky Mountain, rising to 12,183ft, to name but a few. In the east is an example even more striking in scale, the 105 mile Skyline Drive of the Shenandoah National Park, linked to the 470 miles of the Blue Ridge Parkway. It is not, however, the mere existence of such roads which is important, but their intrinsic design from a recreation point of view, deliberately opening up vistas, and with adequate lay-bys for the motorist who wants to stop and look.

The British situation is radically different. National parks and other outstanding scenic areas are primarily agricultural land, and their road network must serve the needs of a substantial local population—some 250,000 in national parks alone. There are a few instances of roads developed with recreational users as a foremost concern, scenic drives in the true sense of the term. The Marine Drive around the Great Orme at Llandudno or the private scenic drive near Clovelly are two instances of short toll roads opening up particularly attractive

vistas. The Forestry Commission has also realised some of its potential in this respect. It has developed more than 9,600 miles of private roads in the forests of Great Britain,[30] but these are normally reserved exclusively for vehicles concerned with forest work. Five stretches, however, have been turned into scenic drives, ranging from Dalby and Newtondale Forest Drives in Allerston Forest in North Yorkshire, opened in 1960 and 1969 respectively,[31] to the Cwmcarn Scenic Forest Drive in the Ebbw Forest of South Wales, opened in May 1972 and attracting 17,500 cars in its first season.[32] Other public works have also made a virtue of necessity. The Central Electricity Generating Board, for example, encourages recreational use of the access road to the Rheidol hydro-electric scheme, a 14 mile route from Talybont to Ponterwyd, rising to over 1,000ft.

Routes such as these remain the exception, however, and most car-borne recreation, of necessity, uses existing public roads. All too frequently, frustration replaces satisfaction in the most-used areas. It is not so much the sheer volume of traffic which is the major problem as the lack of adequate opportunity to pause and enjoy the view without causing obstruction and annoyance. This theme impinges closely on management for recreational traffic and will be discussed in more detail in the final section of this chapter.

Away from roads, footpaths are the major routeway resource and the means by which the most intimate personal contact with the rural scene can be achieved. In Britain, their dominantly recreational function is comparatively recent: most now serve primarily a recreational need but this is 'in sharp contrast to the utilitarian purpose which gave rise to many of them'.[33]

Their pattern, as that of our roads, has developed over the centuries in response to local and national needs. Although some footpaths were deliberately planned, many evolved as simple accommodation routes, from farm or cottage to village, and by usage they have acquired the status of legal rights of way. Others developed as drove roads or pack horse routes and often cover long distances.[34]

Page 85 (*above*) Car parking, sea front, Brighton (*below*) car parking, Lake District National Park

Page 86 Urban parks in central London

The resulting legacy is a widespread and frequently dense network (Figure 13), with an estimated 120,000 miles of footpath in England and Wales alone.[35] Densities vary from 0·4 miles per square mile in Devon to 4·4 miles per square mile in Worcestershire, but most counties do not differ substantially from the overall density of 2·05 miles per square mile. Such figures are put in perspective when they are compared with the mileages of rural roads (Table 10): there is a remarkable degree of correspondence between them.

TABLE 10   Rural roads and footpaths in England and Wales

	England	Wales
Mileage of rural roads	94,383	15,306
Mileage of footpaths and bridleways	101,945	17,927
Density of rural roads (miles per square mile)	1·86	1·93
Density of footpaths and bridleways (miles per square mile)	2·03	2·24

Data: Cracknell (1967) and Holroyd (1970)

Footpaths, of course, sustain very varying recreational pressures. At the top end of the scale are those created specifically for recreational use. The North American trails which thread national and state parks and national forests find their British counterpart in the long distance footpaths created by the National Parks and Access to the Countryside Act of 1949. Of the latter, twelve have now been approved, with a combined length of 1,499 miles, though by September 1972 only five had been formally opened.[36] Few people walk the full length of a long distance footpath: their value perhaps lies rather in the stimulus they have given to the wider use of rural footpaths.

More intensive use is often made of shorter-distance routes. Nature trails, first developed in Britain in 1961,[37] have rapidly grown in popularity: a recent inventory lists 341 in the United Kingdom and is by no means complete in its cover.[38] The use of forests for recreation has been encouraged by the creation of forest trails—262 in Great Britain in 1972.[39]

6

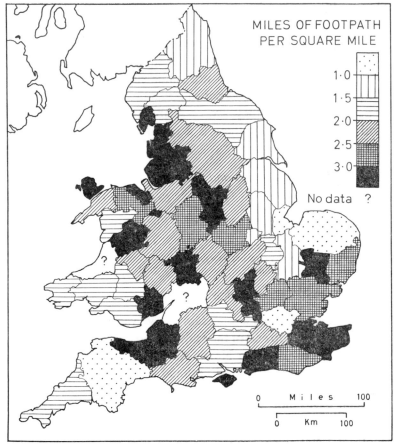

Fig 13   Footpath density in England and Wales

Specialised paths are nevertheless only a tiny fragment of the whole network. The diverse origins of the network mean that that much of it now sees but little use. One illustration of this may be seen in north Lancashire, in a strip of country stretching from the low-lying cultivated land of the eastern Fylde to the open moorland on the higher ground of the Forest of Bowland (Figure 14).[40] The marked variations in density frequently reflect particular historical circumstances. The close network around

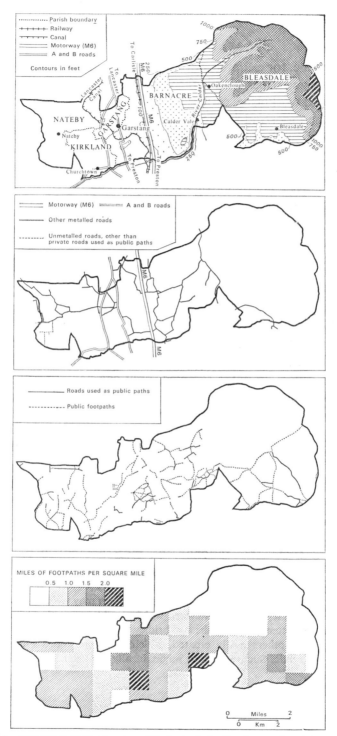

Fig 14   Road and footpath networks and the footpath density of a part of north Lancashire

Calder Vale, for example, developed in response to the building of cotton and paper mills in the valley: a tight mesh of paths link home and workplace, church, school and public house. In contrast, the moorland in the north of Bleasdale parish is totally devoid of public paths; the area is privately owned, and that privacy jealously guarded. Paths as such are far from absent, for many private paths[41] cross the area, their mileage being almost the same as that of public rights of way in the parish as a whole.[42] These private paths are used mainly for access to rough grazing and grouse moor; their obvious attraction for the rambler has led to marked friction.

Throughout the area, path use varies widely. A sample count for an hour on a sunny August Sunday afternoon covered eleven paths scattered through the area. Maximum use (eighty-seven persons) was of a riverside path at Garstang, close to the village and a car park. A path at Bleasdale, well surfaced and signed, and affording attractive views of the fells and the Fylde, had twenty-one users of whom only three lived locally. Of the remaining paths sampled, only one had more than six users and three none at all. The implications of the sample count are substantiated when the physical state of the network is examined (Figure 15). For all practical purposes, the effective network comprises the paths on maps A and B together with a few of the first category on map C. Use itself leads to definition by trampling: there is an inevitable vicious circle in which lack of use leads to a path becoming increasingly hard to trace and therefore increasingly unattractive to the casual user.

Such considerations have led to frequent suggestions that the network should be 'rationalised', most notably in the 1966 White Paper *Leisure in the Countryside* (Cmnd 2928):

> In the Government's view a more radical reform may well be needed, to provide a legislative framework which would permit the development of a system of footpaths and bridleways, some based on existing routes, but others newly created, which would be more suited to modern needs. Such a system might ideally consist of a carefully-

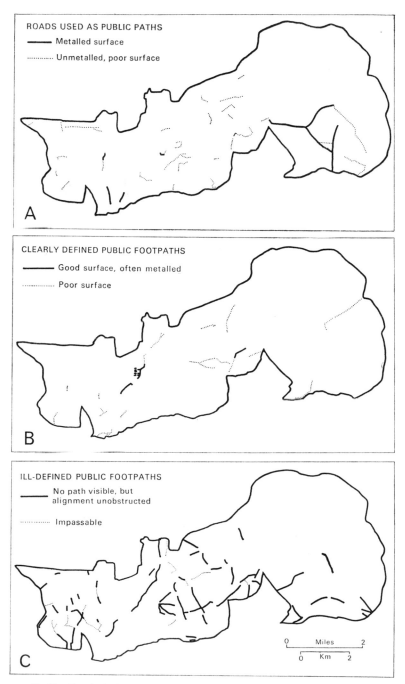

Fig 15   The physical condition of the footpath network of a part of north Lancashire

planned network . . . which, being more regularly used, could be more readily kept fit for use; while the routes which no longer serve any generally useful purpose could be allowed to disappear.

This view met firm rebuttal,[43] not least by the Gosling Committee:

> We approach suggestions of a 'system' and 'a carefully planned network' with great caution because much of the value and charm of footpaths lies in their waywardness.
>   We do not share the view that . . . the present pattern should be re-planned anew. It would be unrealistic to think in this way.[44]

In the event, the Countryside Act of 1968 did no more than reinforce the existing powers of a local authority to seek the closure of paths which are 'unnecessary' or 'not needed for public use' or to divert paths for 'securing efficient use of land or providing a shorter or more commodious path'. In a more positive vein the Act (Section 27) imposed a duty on highway authorities to erect a signpost at every point where a footpath or bridleway leaves a metalled road. Easy recognition is a great incentive to use, and use to the effective maintenance of a right of way.[45]

ROUTEWAYS AND MANAGEMENT

Any study of routeways as recreation resources in themselves must emphasise two fundamental characteristics, their widespread—indeed, near ubiquitous—occurrence and yet the startling variations in the intensity of their use, variations in both space and time. These characteristics, coupled with an inherently linear form, make routeways susceptible to positive management the better to cater for recreational pressures.

Two themes run through the discussion of management in this context, segregation and selection. They are not mutually exclusive themes, but it is convenient to discuss each in turn.

Segregation is management through the horizontal separation of varied demands. 'Heavy traffic, light traffic, cyclists, horse-riders and walkers all have totally different demands and each user sees the countryside in a different way and at a different speed; the convenience and pleasure of each means of travel is less if all types of traffic are on the same road. It would be best to try and separate different types of traffic wherever possible.'[46] Such separation is often enforced by the inherent nature of the routes themselves, by separate networks of motorways, highways and footpaths. The real problems arise when a single routeway sustains heavy volumes of more than one traffic type.

In some areas, the degree of conflict is such that restrictions on particular users are desirable. One experiment of great significance in this direction has been in the Peak Park's Goyt Valley,[47] when, for the first time in Britain, rural roads were closed at weekends to all vehicular traffic except minibuses carrying visitors from car parks at the perimeter of the area. For the duration of the experiment pedestrians had the roads to themselves. In this instance, the scheme was facilitated by particular characteristics of the valley. It contained only three access points, all of them minor roads, and had no resident population requiring exemption. Road closures could therefore be limited in areal extent while the ready availability of alternative through routes meant that traffic diversion caused no hardship of consequence.

Elsewhere in the Peak District, a scheme has been devised for the segregation of different types of traffic on different routes (Figure 16). The importance of the scheme is the very small measure of change it implies:

The plan does not necessitate any radical change in the physical nature of existing routes. Indeed, by sorting traffic it should lessen the need for expensive works or detrimental change. Such a policy is not only visually important, but also functionally important. Its main purpose is to reduce conflict between road users and to make good economical use of an existing pattern.[48]

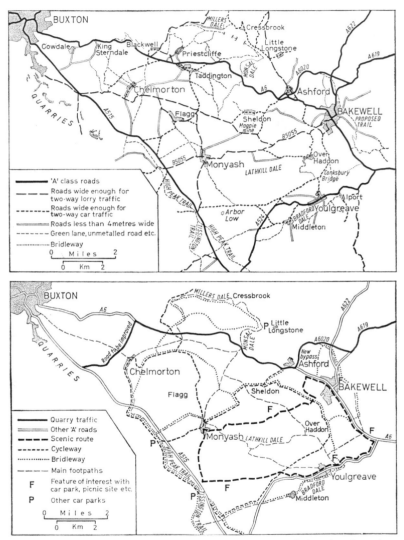

Fig 16 The route network of a part of the Peak District National Park, and a scheme for segregation within it

Segregation in such a context also implies selection, the selection of the most suitable routes for a particular function. Similar schemes have been proposed for other sensitive rural areas, with the aim of restricting different types of traffic to the routes best suited for them and above all for enhancing the quality of the recreational experience for the majority of users.[49]

The crux of the problem is the criterion for selection. Perhaps too often the motorist is seen as the villain of the peace. The road improvements of the 1920s and 1930s in the Lake District brought firm riposte from the Friends of the Lake District:

> It is a perfectly logical case that those who are walking, for their recreation and refreshment, should have the right to a certain space of seclusion. This means closing out motor transport from certain routes and places . . . What is in the legal sense a highway need not admit any inevitable claim to motor traffic. 'Once a highway, always a highway' is an important maxim in defence of liberty, but a very bad maxim if used to suburbanise a mountain area.[50]

Their anger perhaps was justified when an insensitive Ministry of Transport could explain that in making an effective motor road of the grassgrown track over Newlands Hause, 'no works will be executed which will interfere with the road at all as a walking road; indeed it is hoped that the improvements will facilitate its use by pedestrians'. Nevertheless, there must remain obvious grounds for dispute as to whether opening up passes like Newlands and Honister, Wrynose and Hard Knott was of advantage to the ordinary car-borne visitor or not. Even in the Lakes, the persistent walker can still find relative solitude.

Disputes of this character, however, often mask more fundamental issues. Few would question the basic need to impose some restrictions on access, by car or by foot, to protect intrinsic qualities such as wild life or remoteness, but happily the inherent nature of all routeways restricts the direct impact of their traffic to the corridor itself and leaves the interstices but little

affected. The location of the corridors and the type of traffic to which they afford access are rightly of concern, and the criteria for selection important issues of management: even more fundamental must be a continuing care for the whole visual quality of the rural scene, whose observation from the corridors remains an intrinsic recreation experience for the traveller.

CHAPTER FOUR

Car-Owners and Holiday Activities

CAR-OWNERS are privileged people. They possess a personal, independent means of travel which frees them from the confines and vagaries of public transportation. They also tend to be above average in income and educational attainment. Mobility, income and education combine to stimulate an active interest in outdoor recreation so that car-owning households report higher levels of participation than those without cars over almost the whole spectrum of outdoor activities. L. J. Lickorish has summarised the situation as follows:

> If you have a car you are more likely to take a holiday; more likely to spend more time away from home; more likely to become a mobile man or woman, rather than a home spender. You will spend a greater proportion of your income outside the home and outside the complex trade serving the home. You will spend it in the travel trades.[1]

In Britain, slightly more than one-half of all households now

possess a car and more than one-tenth of these own a second car. Comparable figures for the United States are 79 per cent and 34 per cent.[2] The ownership of a car is increasingly becoming the norm rather than the exception in the western world (Table 11).[3]

TABLE 11   Number of private cars (to nearest million)

Country	1960	1965	1967
Austria	0·4	0·8	1·2
Belgium	0·8	1·3	2·1
Canada	4·1	5·3	6·6
Denmark	0·4	0·7	1·1
France	5·5	9·6	12·8
Italy	2·0	5·5	10·2
Netherlands	0·5	1·3	2·5
Norway	0·2	0·5	0·7
Sweden	1·2	1·8	2·3
Switzerland	0·5	0·9	1·4
United Kingdom	5·7	9·2	11·9
United States	61·8	74·9	88·8
West Germany	4·3	9·0	13·5

As the number of car-owning households rises, and as an expanding proportion of car-owners acquire a second vehicle, car-owners will come increasingly to dominate patterns of outdoor recreation as the noise and fumes emitted by the car and its visibility in the landscape mean that car-owners tend to have a greater impact on the environment than those without cars. But while it is justifiable to focus attention upon those with automobiles, a cautionary note is necessary. There will always be families without a car: the elderly, the poor and the infirm often do not have access to an automobile. Moreover, car-owners do leave their vehicles in the garage at times. The increasing attention given to catering for a mobile, car-borne population makes the needs of such minority groups all the more pressing.

A holiday, or a vacation as it is called in North America, is defined as 'at least four nights away from home excluding trips taken primarily for business reasons'. This definition has been

adopted by the British Travel Association, as it was formerly called, as the basis of its many holiday surveys.[4] The major disadvantage of this definition is that it excludes shorter holidays and, in particular, 'long weekends' which have become an increasingly important component of vacation travel.

The estimated number of short holidays taken by residents in Great Britain in the year April 1969 to March 1970 was 47 million and expenditure on these trips was approximately £219 million.[5]

But all available evidence suggests that secondary holidays differ from main holidays in their locations, their lengths, the accommodation utilised, and in their seasonal distributions. A more exhaustive survey of secondary holidays and short stay excursions awaits further research.

CAR-OWNERS AND HOLIDAY DEMAND

Car-owning households generate approximately two-thirds of the effective demand for main holidays in Britain. Almost all car-owners are in the market for vacations, but not all car-owners take a holiday every year. A survey of owners of automobiles in Kingston upon Hull indicated that, while only 7·5 per cent of respondents had not taken a holiday within the five years prior to interview, almost one-third (28·6 per cent) had not been on holiday within the twelve months preceding the investigation.[6] Ties of family and employment restrict recreation opportunities in some households and in others the considerable expense of running a car makes inroads into the family budget. It has been suggested that, for some people, buying a car must serve as a substitute for a holiday and that at lower income levels the spread of automobile ownership tends to have a temporary depressive effect on holiday-making.[7] On the other hand, the Hull study indicated that the first few years of car-ownership are associated with above-average holiday frequencies. The novelty of car-ownership may actually stimulate holiday travel.

The increased use of the automobile has brought about considerable changes in the types of transportation used for holiday travel. Since 1951 the proportion of all holiday-makers travelling to their main holiday destinations in Britain by rail has fallen from almost one-half to less than one-fifth, and in the same period the relative importance of bus and coach transport has also declined markedly. These modes of passenger transport have suffered severely in competition with the car which now carries two-thirds of British holiday-makers to their main holiday destinations (Table 12).[8]

TABLE 12   Method of transport to main holiday destinations in Great Britain, 1951–68 (%)

	1951	1955	1962	1966	1968
Car	27	34	54	64	66
Bus/coach	27	33	18	20	16
Train	47	37	26	16	14
Other	0	0	0	7	5

Almost all British car-owners use their car to reach their holiday destinations in Britain. For instance, 83·9 per cent of a sample of Hull car-owners travelled to their main holiday destination in their own car, 5·8 per cent used another car, and only 10·3 per cent went by some other means of transport.[9] Similarly, almost all American states report that more than 80 per cent and often 90 per cent of their visitors arrive by car. The major exceptions to this generalisation are Alaska, with less than half of its visitors travelling by car, and Hawaii where, as might be expected, all visitors come by plane or boat.[10]

Holiday-makers generate a considerable proportion of the road traffic in popular resort areas. It has been suggested that as much as 40 per cent of the summer traffic in the Lake District National Park is attributable to staying holiday-makers. On Saturdays approximately two-fifths of all traffic leaving the national park was created by holiday-makers returning home, and even on Sundays returning holiday-makers comprised

nearly one-fifth of the total outward flow.[11] One can expect the number of visitors to the Lake District to continue to grow in response to rising levels of car-ownership and improved motorway access but the demand for day trips is more elastic and is likely to rise more rapidly than the demand for holidays and this could markedly affect the day-tripper/holiday-maker ratio.[12]

Regional variations are found in the proportion of holiday-makers who arrive by car. For instance, in 1968 only 62 per cent of visitors spending their main holiday in Yorkshire travelled by car in comparison with 77 per cent in the British Travel Association's South West region.[13] At longer distances, particularly from Britain, where a water barrier must be crossed the car declines slightly in its contribution to the holiday travel pattern as it competes with quicker and less fatiguing air transport: 60 per cent of British holiday-makers who spent their main holiday abroad in 1969 flew to their vacation destinations. Package holidays and charter flights have attracted an important sector of the travel market and charter inclusive tours carried 42·4 per cent of all air passengers leaving Britain in 1966, although charter traffic is of more limited significance for holiday-makers of most other European countries. Nevertheless, the English Channel is not an insuperable barrier to the car driver for foreign travellers to Britain brought approximately 154,400 cars, or one car for every thirty visitors in 1969, and an unknown number hired a car during their vacation.[14]

One of the major advantages of automobile travel is that it appears to be quite cheap. The capital expenditure involved in the purchase of an automobile is likely to be large, but having incurred this outlay the cost of additional increments of travel is comparatively small. This is particularly the case if all seats are occupied. It has been suggested that the private motorist does not attempt to calculate precisely what he pays for his road licence, insurance and maintenance but merely takes into account the cost of petrol and oil. To some extent he is justified

in as much as, having decided to own a car, the capital outlay has been made and at any one time his decision to use the car for travel can be related to the cash cost of the performance of that service.[15]

The car is convenient in that it enables the holiday-maker to convey himself, his family and friends, and his baggage from his home to his holiday destination without the necessity to adhere to the imposed schedule of a time-table. It allows more flexible, variable holidays and also affects the type of accommodation used. The cost of accommodation is likely to be one of the largest items in the holiday budget. The British Travel Association surveys indicated that approximately one-half of all holiday expenses are for accommodation and meals. The average expenditure by British holiday-makers on main holidays in Britain in 1968 was £20·10 per person including fares. The average cost of a holiday in a licensed hotel was £34·40 per person, while the average outlay on a caravan holiday was only £14·10 per person, other types of accommodation falling between these two extremes.[16]

The Hull car-owners survey reflected many broad trends.[17] First over one-third of those interviewed used hotels and boarding houses, and over one-third had self-catering holidays, almost all of these in caravans. The flexibility of holiday location given by the automobile has been associated with an increasing interest in touring holidays as rates of car-ownership have risen. Thus camping (10·2 per cent) was more than double the national figure.[18] The most popular form of main holiday (46·6 per cent) was to stay in one spot[19] and to take trips to other places of interest in the surrounding area. In contrast only 28·4 per cent spent their holiday completely in one resort and a further one-quarter took a touring holiday (Table 13).[20]

These patterns reflect national trends where resorts are increasingly seen as bases from which other places can be visited. Tourists are interested in a wider area and, in consequence, resorts are less able to sell themselves solely by

Page 103 Urban open space, Hackney Marshes

Page 104 (*above*) Snowdonia National Park (*below*) Matkov Kot, Logarska Dolina National Park, Slovenia

TABLE 13   Hull car-owners survey:
accommodation used and type of holiday

Accommodation	Percentage
Hotels and boarding houses	34·4
Caravans	16·0
Camping	10·2
Other self-catering accommodation	17·0
Friends/relations	18·0
Other	4·0

Type of holiday chosen	
Touring holiday	25·0
Stay in one resort but trip in the surrounding area	46·6
Stay spent entirely in one resort	28·4

advertising their own attractions. Car-owners in particular are also concerned with the attributes of the surrounding region. Whereas adjacent resorts once regarded themselves as competitors, it is increasingly being realised that they may be complementary, the one attracting business for the other. Most resorts now regard themselves as part of a wider region of attraction and their brochures publicise the facilities which can be visited from the resort.

Touring has long been a popular way of spending a vacation in North America but Daniel Boorstein has argued that while the automobile has facilitated movement, it has, by encouraging the development of an increasingly standardised leisure landscape, reduced the fascination of travel in that continent: super highways, motels, uniform chain restaurants and the construction of 'tourist traps' are tending to isolate the vacationer from the country through which he passes. He claims:

The automobile itself has been one of the chief insulating agencies. And the insulation has become more effective as we have improved body design from the old open touring car to the new moving 'picture window' through which we can look out from air-conditioned comfort while we hear our familiar radio program. The whizzing cross-country motorist stops at his familiar trademark, refuelling at gas stations of uniform design. His speed makes him reluctant to stop at all. On a

7

train it used to be possible to make a casual acquaintance; the Pullman smoker was a traditionally fertile source of jokes and folklore. Now the train is dying out as a means of long-distance travel. And if we travel by air we are seldom aloft long enough to strike up new acquaintances. But for meeting new people the private automobile is the least promising of all. Even hitchhikers are slowly becoming obsolete as well as illegal.[21]

Touring may now be done in increasing comfort and many tourists now travel with trailers and campers. The total production of recreational vehicles in the United States has grown from 80,300 in 1962 to 728,800 in 1972, and the annual value of recreational vehicle sales is expected to pass $3,000 million by 1972.[22] Catering to the tourist has become a large and profitable business.

In Britain the expansion of touring holidays and the rapid growth of caravans and camping has reduced the profit margins in some sectors of the holiday trade with implications for the structure and morphology of resorts. From an investigation

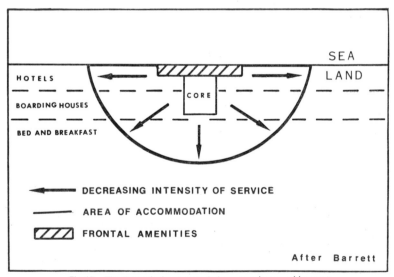

Fig 17   The theoretical accommodation zones in a seaside resort

in 1958 of over eighty coastal holiday resorts in England and Wales, J. A. Barrett drew out generalisations about the building and functional patterns associated with seaside resorts[23] from empirical evidence backed by the resort 'core', consisting of the major shops and business. The intensity of accommodation services decreased as the distance from the core increased (Figure 17). Barrett's thorough, though regrettably unpublished thesis remains the standard reference on the morphology of resorts but it requires updating in the light of the trends which have been outlined. The boarding house has traditionally depended upon visitors who arrived and left on a Saturday and whose stays were best measured in units of a week in length. The rising number of car-borne touring holiday-makers is increasing the demand for shorter over-night stops which magnifies the overheads and decreases the reliability of holiday custom. Visitors staying only one or two nights are less likely to book in advance than those staying for a longer period. In addition, the proliferation of caravans and tents has captured part of the market formerly served by boarding houses and has added a new element to the fringe of seaside resorts. Faced with this competition, and recognising the popularity of self-catering holidays, many boarding house owners have converted their premises to flats. Stability of external form often belies changes in internal function.

IMPACT ON HOLIDAY AREAS

Automobile ownership has reduced the friction of distance and has encouraged a growing proportion of holiday-makers to seek the most desirable vacation areas, with the paradoxical result that recreation activities are becoming both increasingly concentrated and yet more dispersed. The British Travel Association South West holiday region was the most popular destination for British holiday-makers in 1951 when it catered for 14 per cent of British holidays. In 1968 the region attracted 22 per

cent of the British holiday trade and 77 per cent of these visitors arrived by car.[24, 25] At the same time car-owners are penetrating formerly inaccessible places in ever-increasing numbers. This has produced problems and opportunities.[26] The automobile enables car-owners to push more deeply into remote and environmentally often vulnerable areas. Such are the pressures that this can create that the question of cars and car parking in attractive rural areas is regarded as the 'biggest single planning problem connected with countryside leisure'.[27] Improvement of the antiquated roads in rural areas would only encourage more visitors and would remove one of the major attractions of the countryside (see Chapter 3). Such are the pressures of cars upon the countryside that it is being increasingly suggested that cars should be completely excluded from some vulnerable areas of high amenity value by the adoption of traffic-free zones. This, by itself, without alternative provision elsewhere, will not solve the problem but will merely shift its location, for the car-owner will find somewhere where he and his family can play.

In North America, continental Europe and increasingly in Britain, further pressures are being imposed on rural areas, as urban dwellers look for vacation homes.[28, 29, 30] Almost all owners of second homes have previously acquired a car, for easy access is essential if such facilities are to be used to the full. Second homes are used extensively throughout the summer for long weekend stays and longer holidays and in suitable locations they are also used as bases for the enjoyment of winter sports. In Britain the ownership of second homes is currently restricted to a minority of 2 per cent of the population but even a modest rise in demand would greatly increase pressures on rural areas, for summer cottages consume large areas of land.[31] The forest-lakes complexes of Canada and Scandinavia are much more suited to this type of development than Britain, where lake frontage is limited and where most land is already pre-empted.

Many remote rural areas are economically underprivileged, but since rural people own or control the land, which is the basic

resource for most outdoor recreation pursuits, they are in a
position to derive an income from the tourists.[32, 33] The provision of farmhouse accommodation, the letting of camping
and caravan sites, and the sale of fresh fruit and vegetables
might provide supplementary sources of income. However, it
would be wrong to overemphasise these opportunities—it is
only a minority of tourists who stay far from the main lines of
communication.

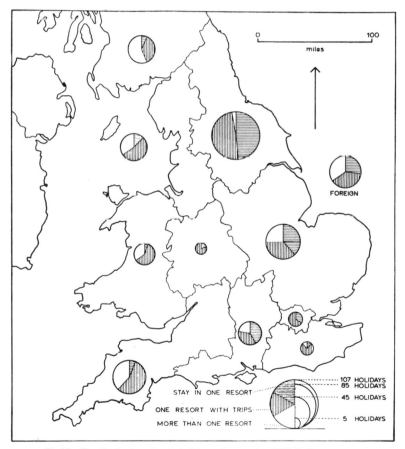

Fig 18   The distribution of main holidays of a sample of 500 Hull car-owners

Mass car-ownership has brought about change in outdoor recreation but there is a strong conservative element even in the recreation habits of car-owners. In 1965, Burton found that the main pattern of holiday movement was to places within the holiday-maker's region of residence or into adjoining regions.[34] This situation has not changed substantially. For instance, the local North East region, the East and the more attractive South West between them catered for half of Hull car-owners' main holidays and two-thirds of all those spent in Britain (Figure 18). More than one-quarter of Hull car-owners spent their last main holiday within fifty miles of their homes.[35] Similarly, despite the international reputation of the Lake District, visitor hinterlands of Keswick, Ambleside and Windermere exhibit a marked regional emphasis (see Chapter 3): in each of the three resorts almost half the staying visitors come from northern England, the main source areas being south-east Lancashire, the North East and the West Riding of Yorkshire.[36]

CONCLUSIONS

Almost all car-owners take holidays but not all of those with an automobile have a holiday every year. The majority of car-owners use their car to reach their holiday destination and many use it to move around while on holiday. Block has described the situation as follows:

> The car-holiday has meant not merely that many holidaymakers travel by a different method but that they have a different kind of holiday . . . Many of them now no longer want to confine their holiday to one place: they either want to keep on the move or to use one place merely as a 'base' for moving about. They demand less service and place a higher value on accessibility and parking facilities . . . When he stays at one place he tends to use it as a base for exploration further afield. Often he will only stay in one place or two, refusing to countenance the Saturday to Saturday booking beloved of old-fashioned hotel-keepers.[37]

However, it would be wrong to overstate the case. The 'car-holiday' as described by Block is still the prerogative of a minority of car-owners. The majority still have their base at only one resort. The most frequently patronised holiday region is still the local one and the main pattern of holiday movement is to places within the car-owner's region of residence or into adjoining regions. The mobility afforded by the car is not so much realised in the distance it enables the vacationer to travel to his holiday destination, as in the opportunities it makes available once that destination has been reached.

CHAPTER FIVE

Urban Open Space and Outdoor Recreation

THOUGH Britain was a pioneer in the public open space movement of the nineteenth century, it is only now realised how little is known about the role of open space and recreational land in the urban environment.

From 1845, large 'Victoria Parks' began to appear on the periphery of towns and cities throughout the country, though most were soon engulfed by the spreading tide of housing. By 1880, emphasis shifted to the more frequent provision of much smaller open spaces, gardens and recreation grounds, often created within the area already built up. Finally, about the turn of the century, the introduction of specially designed children's playgrounds completed the spectrum of facilities we know today.[1]

However, provision was sporadic, the response of private or public philanthropy to evident need rather than the creation of a system conceived as an inherent part of urban expansion. In 1909, the first Town Planning Act[2] listed open space as a major plan-

ning concern: piecemeal, unco-ordinated acquisition and provision of recreational space was to be replaced by a carefully planned, comprehensive approach. Nevertheless, over sixty years later, planners still lack systematic, scientifically-based policies to apply to the complex problems of demand for recreational facilities within the urban fabric. Indeed, the full scale and direction of that demand is only now being measured by more than rule of thumb methods.

Britain is perhaps the most 'urbanised' nation in the world, with approximately 80 per cent of her population living in urban areas. While the process of 'urbanisation', defined as any increase in the proportion of the total population living in urban administrative areas, has slowed down, projected population growth predicts a continued expansion of towns and cities in England and Wales. Although higher real incomes and greater mobility will probably augment the tendency to seek recreation beyond the city, technology is unlikely to produce, in the foreseeable future, a system that will enable the majority of city-dwellers to leave the city for daily and regular weekend recreation. Opportunities must continue to be provided for outdoor recreation within the urban milieu but increasing pressures on urban land resources will necessitate precise, objective arguments for the presence, location and design of such space if recreational land is to withstand competition from residential, commercial and transportation demands. This requirement has been recognised in planning legislation; the new development plan system introduced by the 1969 Planning Act requires carefully structured reasoning to back all structure plan concepts before they appear in the land-use maps of subsequent action area plans.[3] Previously, this initial step was by-passed; the planning of open space was left to the interpretation and personal bias of the individual planner or local authority; and development plans inevitably reflected the existing and the feasible rather than a response to real, identifiable requirements.

Most planners will readily admit that they are ill-equipped to

defend present open space policies and it is no coincidence that recent years have produced a number of excellent leisure-oriented surveys that greatly assist those concerned with the provision of opportunities for outdoor recreation.[4] Three questions are fundamental; planners need to know how much open space is needed, what form it should take, and where it should be located.

For a long time, measures of quantity have been related to the standard of 6 acres of playing fields per 1,000 population first enunciated by the National Playing Fields Association in 1925 and confirmed as recently as 1971.[5] This standard, however, though a valuable rough yardstick, was based on arbitrary assumptions of the numbers likely to need games facilities and of the rates of participation in particular sports.[6] Recent surveys have found that actual levels of participation are much less than those assumed by the NPFA and suggest that the standard for provision of playing pitches could be reduced considerably.[7]

The provision of playing fields, of course, related to only one type of urban open space and the NPFA standard specifically excluded woodlands and commons, ornamental gardens, full-length golf courses and 'open spaces where the playing of organised games by the general public is either discouraged or not permitted'.[8] Successive governments have recommended as a general guide a further acre of ornamental public open space per 1,000 population to add to the 6 acres of playing space.

In recent years, a number of surveys have been carried out that relate to the use of the leisure time, two of these specifically to the use of urban parks. Both indicate that parks are used primarily for passive pursuits. The Greater London Council study used home interview data and indicated the relative popularity of various activities (Table 13).[9]

The Edinburgh study collected interviews on site, giving total figures for autumn, winter and spring (Table 14).[10]

National surveys also emphasise the dominance of informal, passive activities as opposed to organised and active sport, in apparent contradiction to recommended standards which place

TABLE 14a Activities in urban parks (GLC)

Activities	Percentage of all visits
General activities	86*
Watching things and people	19
Activities with children	12
Social activities	10
Organised sport	6
Entertainments	3
Activities with animals	2

*General activities included sitting and walking in parks and playing informally

Note: total of percentages exceeds 100 because some respondents engaged in more than one activity

TABLE 14b Activities in urban parks (Edinburgh)

Activities	Percentage of all visits
Informal, passive pursuits	67
Children's play	14
Casual ball games	15
Organised sport	3

Note: total not equal to 100 per cent due to rounding

emphasis on provision of facilities for active games. The Government Social Survey *Planning for Leisure* indicated that from 60 to 70 per cent of all visits to public open spaces were to take children or simply to go for a walk.[11]

As a reasonably complete picture of recreational habits emerges, even the design of public open space is being questioned.

The real weakness in the contemporary planning of urban open space centres on the question of location. While the importance of correct location is constantly stressed, practical guidelines for establishing what is 'correct' are non-existent. Until recently, most planning policies were based on unsubstantiated assumptions or informed guesses. It was assumed that parks of a certain size or playing pitches of a given standard would attract visitors or players from within a given, arbitrary distance: the distance chosen, however, varied from authority to authority.

While children's playgrounds studies indicate that they have

a very local influence of between one-eighth and one-quarter of a mile, there is far more disagreement on the impact of larger recreational areas. The Greater London Council report suggested that larger areas could be divided into two types: those over 50 acres having a local influence of up to three-quarters of a mile to a mile, and larger parks with a minimum size of 150 acres influencing homes over a 2–5 mile radius. The Edinburgh study supported this theory by dividing parks into those with 'regional', 'city' and 'local' influence. However, a major study by the University of Liverpool for the city's planning department gives a different impression, and suggests that size in itself is an inadequate criterion of attractiveness and range of influence.

The Liverpool study conducted approximately 14,000 interviews at seventy different open spaces. While the general findings agreed with the Greater London Council's conclusion that approximately 75 per cent of all visitors to urban parks come from less than half a mile away, it found little variation with the size of park or the type of facility concerned. Areas with more than 80 per cent of all visitors travelling less than half a mile ranged in size from small children's kick-about areas to parks of well over 100 acres, well-landscaped and with a wide variety of facilities. Areas which did attract a higher proportion of visitors from farther afield had some especially inviting amenity not necessarily related to size, for they ranged from a small, 10 acre wood to a large, particularly appealing park. Only two areas attracted 20 per cent or more of visitors from beyond 3 miles and these were unique in the city, one containing a small children's zoo and the other Liverpool's only riverside promenade. These findings varied little with season and were surprisingly consistent under statistical testing. The acreage of a park is obviously only one index of the facilities provided: the quality of the landscaping is at least as important.

While such survey results are obviously related to specific sites in particular cities, critical questions concerning the level

of provision, type and location of urban open space are gradually being answered by research in England. A great deal more information is still required before planning guidelines can be more than inspired hunches, but more has been accomplished in the last five years than in the previous fifty-five years of urban open space planning.

The utility of such research is beyond doubt; but, while large planning authorities with specialist staff are perhaps capable of deriving objectives and policies suitable to their particular environments, smaller local authorities are poorly equipped to improvise with expertise. This point was illustrated by a study carried out in the summer of 1970 by the University of Liverpool to investigate current open space provision and relevant policies in major urban areas of England and Wales.[12]

Questionnaires were sent to the parks, planning and housing departments of a one-third sample of all urban authorities having populations greater than 50,000.[13] Only 60 per cent of the planning departments studied used a standard concerned with level of open space provision. Surprisingly little variation was observed in the figures adopted: one-fifth followed the NPFA standard and the remainder grouped closely around a mean of 5·6 acres per 1,000 population. Approximately half of the towns and cities relied on a single figure designed to include all types of open space while the other 50 per cent employed a dual standard to define desired acreages of both parks and recreation grounds. A number of cities went further to consider separate standards for children's playgrounds, private sports grounds, educational playing fields and so on, but the small number involved prevented further analysis. Of the authorities using a ratio of parks and other informal areas to recreation grounds and playing fields, all were very close to the mean standard of 1 acre park to 4 acres playing fields, a relatively small deviation from the NPFA standard.

However, while theory seems to favour provision of active recreational space to passive facilities such as parks and

gardens, practice differed dramatically. Having witnessed the acceptance of NPFA recommendations in policy formulation at the local level, and working on the assumption that it is relatively easier to convert public space from one use to another than to acquire new space, one would expect to find that existing open space, while perhaps differing in level from stated objectives, would at least be approximately in the ratio suggested. The inventories collected in the survey gave enough data to determine the existing ratio of active to passive space in twenty-one of the urban authorities and in practice the ratio is reversed: cities devote more land to passive recreation than to active. The average was 1 acre of playing fields and recreation grounds to 2·8 acres of parks, gardens and other informal areas. In addition, questions designed to seek information on new provision showed that for those sites newly opened, under development at the time of the survey, and planned for the next five years, the ratio was 1 : 3 in favour of passive space. These figures clearly indicate that there is little or no dissatisfaction with the existing situation. Although it would be dangerous to assume that participation rates and acreage planned for each activity should correlate exactly, the fact that leisure activity studies have consistently indicated an overwhelming preference for passive recreational pursuits suggests that it is the policy rather than the supply that requires alteration.

On the question of location of facilities, 75 per cent of the local authorities approached indicated dissatisfaction with existing distribution, most commonly identifying inner residential areas and suburban private estates as deficient areas. However, when asked what, if any, guidelines were employed to determine the location of playgrounds, recreation grounds and playing fields, and parks, very few positive responses were forthcoming. (Table 15 summarises the responses.)

Although approximately 50 per cent of the authorities had defined location guidelines for playgrounds, playing fields and parks, most of these were generalised to the point where they

TABLE 15 Urban authorities using location policies

Facility type	No with policy	No without policy	NA
Playground	17 (7)*	19	4
Playing field and recreation ground	13 (3)	22	5
Parks	12 (3)	23	5

* Numbers in parentheses indicate number of authorities using a specific linear distance in the expression of their policy

lost practical value. Statements such as 'one per housing estate' or 'one per neighbourhood' appeared without consideration of the size of the area involved. Playgrounds were most satisfactorily dealt with as it has been generally accepted that playgrounds attract children from up to one-quarter of a mile. However, the six policies for parks and recreation grounds that were expressed in actual distances of facility influence all differed, showing no consistency at all.

The local authority survey was designed to investigate contemporary policy in large cities and towns in England and Wales in the hope that common opinions and policies could be identified that might help to form the basis for more widely accepted guidelines. However, it was found that not only do a large number of urban authorities not utilise planning policies at all in their approach to the complex problems of public open space provision, but that the policies that are used differ considerably from town to town and city to city.

There was, however, a degree of agreement on standards concerned with level of open space provision, focusing on the mean of 5·6 acres per 1,000 population. In addition, there appeared to be common policy agreement on the ratio of active facilities to passive facilities, set at the mean of 4:1 even if the ratio in practice is reversed at approximately 1:2·5. However, the few location policies that exist differ considerably from authority to authority.

Without recognised definitions, comparison of activity and

provision is difficult but the data that could be utilised pointed to a randomness that was difficult to explain. In general, planning policies have been developed at the local level to offset the dearth of nationally recognised guidelines. However, many of these policies are extremely general in nature and often of little practical value. Furthermore, most are based on assumptions rather than detailed empirical work.

While recognising the smaller planning authority's need for advice and guidelines, it must be acknowledged that requirements will vary from community to community. National standards have been supply-based measures, arbitrarily determined, flagrantly misused, and long in need of replacement by more flexible and people-sensitive criteria of open space allocation. Standards are 'quantified statements of supplier goals'[14] which neglect user and community goals as well as the type of quality of the recreation experience supplied. Moreover, the emphasis on self-improvement and middle-class productivity implicit in the supplier's leisure concepts and goals excludes too many alternative forms of provision to serve as the sole basis for community-wide planning of open space. The traditional approach to parks planning based on an arbitrary set of standards is rendered largely irrelevant and ineffective because these standards do not appreciate the differences between the objectives and values of both residents and suppliers, and lack sensitivity to variation in the structure and characteristics of the community. To assume that goals for one city are totally acceptable in another compounds the potential for error.

One also wonders if contemporary approaches fully appreciate the context in which urban parks are being planned. The words contained in the title of this chapter, 'urban open space and outdoor recreation', are frequently used but often misunderstood. 'Urban open space' in its widest sense refers to all areas of the city that are open to the sky and can therefore include parks, private gardens, school grounds, vacant land, parking lots, flat roof-tops, streets, and so on. 'Outdoor recrea-

Page 121 (*above left*) Forestry Commission money box for nature trail booklets — typical 'rural' furniture style (*above right*) toll collection, Dalby Forest Scenic Drive (*below*) Dalby Forest Scenic Drive

Page 122 (*above*) Epping Forest picnic site (*below*) camp ground, Dalby Forest

tion' suggests discretionary time spent out of doors, an activity, however passive, requiring a degree of space and exposure to the elements that cannot be met within four walls. The fact that we are dealing with the interface between these terms is problematic and presents complexities that are only now being identified.

Conceptually, an individual has little difficulty with the word 'urban'; although precise definition is difficult the connotations are many and immediately recognisable. However, looking at the term from a recreationist's point of view, the meaning becomes somewhat obscure. In the developed world, urban man is increasingly mobile and has both the opportunity and the ability to utilise recreational facilities beyond the city boundary. Ex-urban facilities are beginning to offer realistic alternatives to city-based parks for urban-generated leisure activities. This substitutability is not new; the large Victorian parks of the latter half of the nineteenth century, deeply imbedded in the built-up area of contemporary cities, were originally located on the periphery of the developing town or city and could only be reached, by the majority of the population, after quite considerable journeys on foot.

Today, the sites and facilities that satisfy many of the recreational demands of the urban populace are located many miles beyond the city boundary. A recent study of leisure activity patterns in North West England pointed out that only 19 per cent of the half-day recreational trips generated in the region were destined for urban parks, the proportion dropping to only 3 per cent for full-day trips.[15] While the report also stressed the variation from one city to the next related to varying opportunities afforded by location, the relative importance of coastal and countryside destinations is clear. The primary concern of this chapter, and of urban planners, is the provision of those opportunities for participation in outdoor recreation that are located within the built-up area; however, relationships with ex-urban opportunities must always be kept in mind.

8

The word 'outdoor' is also important. A major function of open space in the urban milieu is its ability to cater for games and a variety of other forms of active recreation. A great many of the facilities provided in urban parks, such as pitches for football, hockey and cricket, require relatively extensive areas of land; others, such as tennis, bowls and putting, use land more intensively. Current trends suggest that demands for these recreation facilities might be partially offset by the provision of indoor recreation facilities, sports complexes and community centres. Capital-intensive developments which can include swimming pools, sports halls for five-a-side team sports, squash and handball courts and a wide range of club facilities are undoubtedly capable of satisfying some demands which might otherwise focus on outdoor recreation facilities.

'Recreation', in its broadest sense, includes any activity that man indulges in to 're-create' himself, seeking relief from normal routine. The term commonly connotes a conscious use of leisure time involving a range of activities from watching television to climbing mountains. In this sense, the use of parks and other open spaces within the city is obviously recreation. However, perception of open space, the mere sight of a tree or flower in an otherwise sterile townscape, can offer respite, relief, and satisfaction to the individual that is recreational in every sense of the word. Such amenity function does not necessitate a physical visit to the site; in fact, it may not even require visual contact. The knowledge that space and greenery form a part of one's urban territory may be sufficient to satisfy a wide range of social, emotional, and psychological needs that have often been discussed but can never be adequately quantified. Space designed for visual appreciation only may have different characteristics from space provided for physical use; private gardens, grass verges, the peripheral space around public and semi-public buildings, the landscaped cemetery, all have roles in this wider purpose.

One must also appreciate that activities that may be classified as 'outdoor recreation' occupy a relatively small proportion of one's leisure time. Sillitoe has defined 'leisure time' as the period when a person is not in paid employment, or commuting to such employment, or—for housewives and mothers—when not engaged in domestic duties and caring for the essential needs of the family. Presuming that time spent eating and sleeping is also excluded, he has shown that, for a national sample of 2,824 males living in urban areas, only 35 per cent of one's leisure time is spent outdoors when engaged in gardening, physical recreation, park visits and walks and excursions. For women, a sample of 3,451, the figure is only 23 per cent.[16]

Even the term 'space' has no meaning without due consideration of the more general context of the adjacent urban environment. A space is created by the buildings that surround it. A site planned for outdoor recreation, if responsive to its surroundings, will differ in design in some relation to population density, building type, presence of alternative opportunities, and such socio-economic characteristics of the neighbourhood as age distribution, education level, income and ethnicity. Academics, planners and decision-makers know far too little about the trade-offs inherent in the above discussion. Hypotheses have suggested that demand for public parks within the city can be partially offset by reasonable large private gardens, dual use of educational playing pitches, provision of indoor sports facilities, and access to alternative opportunities on the periphery of the city. The amenity function of space could well be partially satisfied by more imaginative urban design that completely ignores nature and space. Such hypotheses have never been satisfactorily tested.

Clawson has outlined a number of functions which urban open space may perform. Urban space:

provides light and air to buildings;
provides perspectives and vistas of the urban scene;

provides opportunities for recreation in the broadest sense
   of the term;
provides ecological protection; and
serves as city-forming devices or influences.[17]

While this is rather a comprehensive view, it can be seen that
each function bears some relation to either the physical activity
or amenity aspect of outdoor recreation.

Urban design is a conscious attempt to order the built-
environment into a pleasing and efficient whole. Kevin Lynch
has detailed the role of space in creating the identity of the city,
leaving little doubt of the significance of sites and areas planned
primarily for the satisfaction of passive recreation demands.[18]
Similarly, the preservation of natural environments adds to the
quality of urban life in so far as they provide variety and environmental diversity.[19] These environments provide urban
man with opportunity both for contact with nature and for
enhancing his ecological awareness, while facilitating recreational experiences for increasing armies of amateur naturalists
and passive recreationalists.

Open space must be planned recognising its total role in the
urban community. However, it must be stressed that the latent
function of all urban space is to provide the user with a set of
physical, social and psychological satisfactions such as those
derived from active and passive recreation and the appreciation
of one's urban milieu. The challenge of integrating these concerns is a formidable and massive task for planners.

The role of urban open space in shaping man's urban experience has been recognised, as has the disappointment of our park
planning response. Perhaps a community of academics, planners and politicians, recognising the impending crisis of outdoor
recreation[20] and awakened to the problems of urban man, will
be capable of generating more comprehensive, holistic solutions.
Initiatives have been taken, but, at the moment, we are only
planning parks, not open space.

CHAPTER SIX

The Role of National Parks in Outdoor Recreation

INTRODUCTION

THIS chapter examines some of the principles and problems of national parks in England and Wales, and Slovenia, Yugoslavia.

In both countries[1] national parks are neither 'national' nor 'park'. The land is not wholly nationally owned nor are they parks in the commonly accepted sense. Basically they are areas where the cultural landscape is of prime value, showing a subtle blend of man-made and natural features. In terms of 'national excellence' they are 'NATIONAL', even international. Perhaps both countries should take up the suggestion made by A. A. C. Phillips, Assistant Director, Countryside Commission for England and Wales,[2] and rename them 'national landscape

parks'. Such a title would certainly explain in a far better way the aims underlying the designation of such areas.

Recently the National Academy of Sciences of the United States of America put the central question concerning open space:

The provision of adequate facilities and opportunities for outdoor recreation requires an understanding of:
(i)   The needs and desires of potential participants;
(ii) The kinds of environment and their location available to meet these needs;
(iii) The degree, nature and effect of visitor use on these areas;
(iv) The management policies and techniques available.[3]

The role of geographers in this context was clearly put by Lord Shackleton, President of the Royal Geographical Society,[4] when he said '. . . vital decisions affecting the environment are taken all too often on the basis of inadequate facts . . . geographers can help in redressing this by assembling and mapping facts, in comparing relationships and mapping trends'. These have been followed in my studies of two national parks in Wales and Yugoslavia—Snowdonia and Logarska—by measuring two key parameters: recreation environments (the resource base) and visitor pressure. This has been set within the context of multiple land-use management and examined in the light of possible legal, administrative and fiscal reform.

THE STUDY AREAS:
1 SNOWDONIA NATIONAL PARK

The Snowdonia National Park, second largest national park in England and Wales, forms a complex natural, social and economic unit. Designated in 1951 it has an area of 845 square miles in three counties—Merioneth, Caernarvonshire and Denbighshire—but from April 1974 the whole area comes within the new administrative area of Gwynedd. All the land

within the park is privately owned, even that held by national agencies such as the Forestry Commission. Administrative and planning control is vested in the various county councils which function through the respective park planning committees. The Countryside Commission and the Countryside Committee for Wales are purely advisory bodies. The counties come together

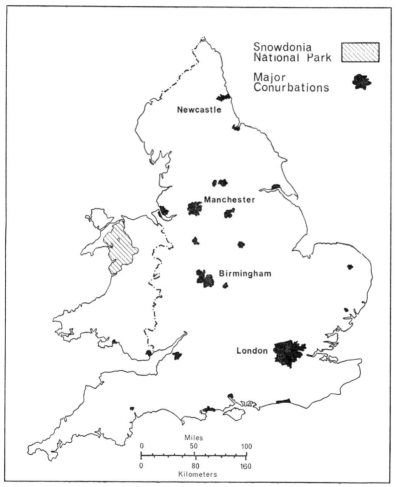

Fig 19   Snowdonia National Park

for joint discussion and the formulation of broad policy in the Snowdonia National Park Joint Advisory Committee. This latter body, even though motivated by the highest principles, has not been a great success, mainly due to legislative, administrative and financial constraints. It is likely, however, in the light of the post-Sandford reforms and changes in local government structure in 1974, that a body with more teeth, staff and funds will be established.

Snowdonia is a major British outdoor recreation area (Figure 19) located within easy reach of the large conurbations of the North West and West Midlands for day visits, and within reach of South East England for weekend visits. It is a popular area for annual holidays with a growing international tourist clientele. The demand for recreational facilities is likely to continue to grow: in spite of country parks located close to urban centres, people will increasingly look to the mountains, rivers, lakes, sea coast and forests of Snowdonia National Park to satisfy many of their recreation demands. Obviously detailed planning for recreational use within the park is needed, together with the provision of more facilities. The application of a positive management policy (including a reorganised administrative and financial structure) and the need to control, and if necessary to reject, potential activities such as mineral exploitation is of paramount importance. In such an area local and national interests must be always carefully balanced. For instance, it is vital to protect the residents' interests, and to preserve their rural-based culture, without which the park could lose its essential character.

2 MATKOV KOT, LOGARSKA DOLINA AND ROBANOV KOT, NATIONAL PARK, SLOVENIA

Although within an area called a 'national park' the three valleys, Matkov, Logarska and Robanov, do not constitute a national park in the United Nations' sense. Nevertheless, the

Robanov Valley is included in the current United Nations' List of National Parks and Equivalent Reserves[5] on account of the outstanding quality of its 'farmland landscape' and the need to conserve this area. The principle feature of the area is the three large glaciated valleys which are part of the Karavanken Mountains. The valleys are well covered with conifer and beech forest, and are surrounded by limestone ridges, which in the

Fig 20   Robanov Valley, Yugoslavia   scale approx 1:2500000

southern section rise to over 2,000m. Access to the area is by a narrow road which follows the Savinja Gorge. There is a rich flora and fauna, particularly birds, deer, chamois and ibex. The Yugoslav/Austrian border runs along the summit ridges but demarcates a political rather than an ecological boundary.

Land-use activities include forestry, which is managed on a carefully planned extraction/replanting programme, livestock rearing of cattle and sheep, recreation, both active and passive,

including hunting which is carefully controlled through hunting associations; and nature conservation.

The area is within travelling distance of such urban centres as Celjie, Maribor and Ljubljana for day visits which are increasing rapidly with growing car-ownership (Figure 20). So far the area has not become part of the international tourist scene on a large scale, though there are likely to be major increases in visitors during the next five years as many secluded areas of Europe are 'discovered'. Currently critical discussions are being held at state level to ascertain the criteria and manner in which this area should be managed.

SOME COMMON POINTS OF REFERENCE— SNOWDONIA/LOGARSKA

However, there are a number of common points of reference between the two study areas which include:

(i)   The nature of the resource base—the 'recreation environment' of mountains, forests, land-use activities and water resources.

(ii)   Visitor profile.

(iii)   Location of the parks in relation to large urban areas.

(iv)   Method of travel to the two areas.

(v)   Length of visit.

(vi)   Main recreational activities undertaken.

(vii)   Visitor pressure/impact.

(viii) Manifestations of visitor pressure.

(xi)   Conflicts between recreation and other land-using activities and between different recreation activities.

(x)   Resource base/visitor pressure interface involving the need for zoning.

(xi)   Local community issues, such as depopulation, ageing communities and the social and economic implications of increasing second home ownership.

(xii) Weaknesses inherent in the existing situation.

LAND-USE ACTIVITIES

Outdoor recreation in upland areas such as Snowdonia and Logarska has been implicitly recognised as a land-using activity for many years. In Britain the Ellison Report, *Forestry, Agriculture and the Multiple Use of Land*,[6] explicitly recognised that recreation use constituted a land-using activity in its own right. Legislation in Slovenia has also recognised this state of affairs.

Today upland areas of Snowdonia and Slovenia are still largely 'wildscape'[7]—'areas which are dominated by nature rather than man'—though relatively little if any of the land in both locations is completely 'natural' today. The landscape in both locations is predominantly semi-natural, but it remains the closest to nature of all landscapes in the respective areas. Current land uses in Snowdonia include extensive sheep and cattle grazing, forestry, quarrying, water collecting, power generation, nature conservation, military training and recreation, while past land uses include slate quarrying and the extraction of metal-liferous ores. In Logarska the main land-using activities are forestry, livestock rearing, nature conservation and recreation, including hunting. Whilst to a degree all land-using activities are competitive we can distinguish three major aspects:

1 *Competitive land-using activities*[8] such as between agriculture, forestry, water conservation, nature conservation, recreation or mining.

2 *Complementary land-using activities.* In the uplands recreational use is complementary to many other uses. For example, hill farming complements extensive pursuits such as hill walking. Although primarily managed at present as timber-producing lands, the forests of Britain can and do cater for extensive and intensive recreation: trees are good places to 'hide' both people and cars. In both Snowdonia and Logarska the role and function of the forest as a base for recreation is likely to

increase dramatically in the next few years. Water conservation and recreation are compatible in many instances, for with modern technology and management it is possible to use reservoirs for sailing and fishing as well as water catchment and storage. Conflicts do arise between different land-using activities and within individual activities, the solving of which is essentially a matter for discussion and compromise within the context of a positive management policy.

3 *Multiple Land Use* should aim at establishing a 'balanced and harmonious use of land and water resources, not on each acre of land or arbitrarily determined management unit, but in the whole pattern of resource use'.[9]

In order to plan the land use of any local area within a national park it is not enough to know the capabilities of the land in that locality. There must also be an evaluation of the whole region or sub-region to which similar planning will apply, and in any integrated plan elements in the natural environment must be combined with factors inherent in the human population. Such integration revolves around the concept of multiple land-use planning.

The uplands of Snowdonia and Slovenia are unique in terms of the variety, range and intensity of recreational use received. Moreover, multiple land-use planning is a necessity in harmonising the variety of uses on a limited area characterised by a harsh physical environment, but including wide variations in amplitude of relief within a small geographical area. Obviously there is a need for conscious planning and decision-making, with some parts of the uplands becoming less important as grazing land and more important as a national playground. Where conflicting interests must be reconciled, the question should be decided from the standpoint of the greatest good of the greatest number of people with due attention being given to maintaining diversity of use. Obviously the management of land and water resources for recreational purposes within the context of the study areas cannot be completely divorced from

their management for other purposes. An integral part of multiple land-use planning is to use each part of the recreation area for the purpose to which it is best suited, with a view to assuring the most effective use of the area as a whole. To attain this objective the extent to which the different uses are compatible or incompatible must be determined. In any large administrative unit such as a national park, most of the uses appropriate to that particular type of area are possible without serious conflict. But in some restricted places within the park—a single farm, nature reserve, forest beat, watershed, 40 acre tract of land or a single acre or lake surface—the number of compatible uses becomes smaller.

Seen thus multiple land-use is a concept of management rather than a system of management, the objective of which is to conserve and wisely use land and water resources so as to produce the greatest benefits for the greatest number of people.

ELEMENTS OF THE
OUTDOOR RECREATION EXPERIENCE

Motivation in outdoor recreation is complex and varied (see Chapter 2). Although there is little work on this it would seem that at least twelve basic elements may be involved (Figure 21). From the standpoint of the resource manager and the visitor the most important of these is probably the effect of increasing numbers of people on the resource base, and the quality of the recreational experience obtained by the individual or group.

Recreation carrying capacity

The recreation carrying capacity of an area can be defined as the level of recreation which an area can sustain without an unacceptable degree of deterioration in the character and quality of the resource or the experience.[10] Although the term 'physical carrying capacity' is usually applied to man-made facilities, it can also be applied to lakes used for sailing and/or

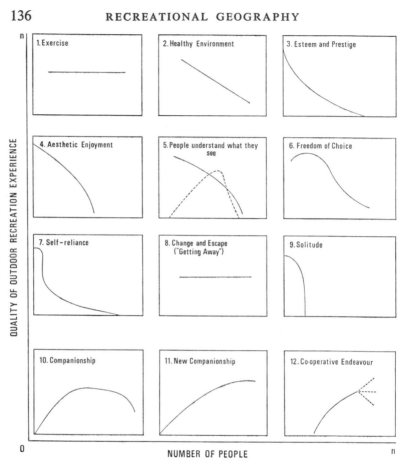

Fig 21   Elements of the outdoor recreation experience[11]

water skiing, to footpaths, and, as in Table 16, to crags used for rock climbing.

Within the national parks examples of areas approaching ecological capacity include in North Snowdonia 'Eryri', the effect of 'gardening' rocks bearing relict arctic/alpine vegetation, or in Logarska the adverse effects of uncontrolled picnic fires on vegetation, both on ground flora and the tree cover.

TABLE 16   The physical carrying capacity of some crags used for rock climbing in Snowdonia

Name of crag	Grades	No of current routes	Approx footage of routes	Carrying* capacity
Cwm Idwal, slabs and walls	E-Ex	56	10,000	80
Milestone Buttress, Tryfan	E-Hvs	28	4,000	32
Dinas Mot, Llanberis Pass	M-Exs	42	13,000	104
Clogwyn ddu Arddu, East Buttress	Vs-Exs	22	5,500	41
Lliwedd	M-Exs	80	24,000	192

* 1 rope of 4 climbers for each 500 vertical ft of rock   E = easy; M = moderate; HVS = hard/very severe; EXS = excessively severe; VS = very severe; EX = extremely severe

Visitor pressure

The current distribution of visitors within Snowdonia and Logarska, although susceptible to seasonal variation, is largely dependent on a range of factors including access, communications and car parking facilities. Time is a key factor in relation to the recreation capacity of, and visitor pressure on, any recreation area. Recreation use tends to be concentrated at least as much in time as space. For example in Snowdonia there is queueing to climb on certain crags while in both study areas traffic congestion at key points at peak periods is excessive. Outdoor recreation areas are often used intensively for only brief periods of time, are moderately used at others and wholly unused for much greater periods.

Patterns of use vary with the weather. Snow brings large numbers of climbers to North Snowdonia and skiers/climbers to Logarska, despite dangerous travelling conditions; while rain during the tourist season results in empty car parks in the park and crowds in nearby urban centres, for example in Snowdonia at Bangor, Caernarvon and resorts along the North Wales coast. Extreme time peaking such as is witnessed during parts of the tourist season and some other occasions during the year almost inevitably means high costs, poor service or both. This extreme time peaking and the resulting areal impact

is one of the major management challenges in the field of outdoor recreation.

The resource base

Many factors combine to make an area attractive to visitors.
Although individual preferences play an important part in
deciding where to go, it is recognised that some factors are of an
objective nature whilst others are highly subjective. A number
of workers such as Blacksell,[12] Duffield and Owen,[13] Lewis[14]
and Linton[15] have attempted to evaluate key elements in this
matrix. In this study of Snowdonia and Logarska, seven elements were selected and amalgamated to form 'recreation
environments', the resource base for recreation. These are
based on a combination of natural and man-made features in a
particular geographical area. The seven elements mapped at a
scale of 1:25,000 were:

1 Scenic resources
   (a) amplitude of relief
   (b) landform landscapes
2 Ecological resources
3 Land-use landscapes
4 Intrinsic resources—ie natural resources for recreation
5 Extrinsic resources—ie man-made resources for recreation
   (a) accommodation facilities
   (b) service facilities
   (c) man-made attractions
6 Roads for recreation
7 Water for recreation.

Nine areas in the Snowdonia National Park were chosen for
study and the 1 km grid square of the Ordnance Survey was used
as a mapping base. In Slovenia a 1 km grid was also used, super-
imposed on a map produced by the Slovene Planning Agency,
Ljubljana. Data were collected by fieldwork and careful desk

Page 139 Blackpool

Page 140 (*above*) Hotel development on the Belgian coast (*below*) sea front development, Hastings

analysis. Information relating to each of the seven elements was collected and the combined rankings used to produce a 'recreation environment map', which attempts to synthesise the scope and availability of those resources which attract and can sustain visitors. The ranking of individual grid squares within the study areas was based on the scale shown in Table 17.

TABLE 17   Recreation environment ranking scale

Total value from the seven element map	Grade
1–12	1
13–20	2
21–26	3
27+	4

1 = Low   4 = High value

Whilst it is certainly possible to criticise the methods used as being far too subjective, from the management aspect it is obvious that once the resources have been listed and mapped a base is available for comprehensive structure planning and development. This is preferable to the piecemeal and often haphazard development which typifies so much of the recreation planning and so-called development in both parks.

People with considerable local knowledge ranked each square for ten activities: rambling, rock climbing, sailing, canoeing, swimming, fishing, field studies, camping, caravanning and picnicking (though Logarska has no water-based activities except fishing). The resulting map (Figure 22) shows the intensity of current recreation pressure and, although subjectively derived, is based on informed impressions which illustrate the range of visitor pressure on Snowdonia and Logarska.

Figure 22 emphasises the role of key areas where natural or man-made resources, or a combination of both, make for high, medium or low recreational use. The nature of recreational impact in areal terms is shown as a series of corridors and nodal points reinforcing the view, often expressed by well-informed observers, that it is nonsense to speak of an overcrowded

9

countryside in blanket terms. They portray what Jean Forbes[16] has called the 'spatial distribution of locational attractiveness'.

True, overcrowding may occur at key locations during the peak season, but even this is not a universal phenomenon. Indeed, it could be argued that under-utilisation is the keynote over most of the two study areas.

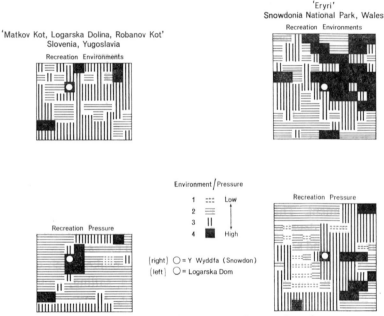

Fig 22   Intensity of recreational use, Snowdonia and Logarska

ANALYSIS AND INTERPRETATION

Tentative conclusions based on resource evaluation, visitor pressure and land-use practice in the Snowdonia National Park and Matkov Kot, Logarska and Robanov Kot National Park indicate that:

1   The potential of these areas expressed in terms of 'recreational environments' is not being fully exploited.

2 Even in areas where visitor pressure is high this is by no means a blanket impact.

3 In areas of high pressure—nodal points—redistribution of visitors could be aided by positive management.

4 Future discussions concerning the problems of landscape conservation and catering for increasing numbers of visitors should also be concentrated on redistributing visitors.

5 There is a very strong case for restricting development in some locations on two grounds:

(a) For the sake of the 'natural landscape', ecology and value of wilderness, some valleys and upland areas should be left remote and inaccessible. We should close some existing roads, save to all-year residents, thereby rendering such areas accessible only to those who travel on foot and to uphold the avowed aim of maintaining diversity.

(b) It is better to try and concentrate economic development in a few well-chosen sites.

6 The conflict of recreation with other land uses has emerged as being less of a problem than it is often made out to be. Findings suggest that forestry plantations (conifers) and reservoirs (Snowdonia) add to, rather than detract from, the recreational potential of an area.

7 The question of agriculture is not so easily solved. However if farming and recreation are to exist side by side, it cannot be at the farmer's expense.

MANAGING NATIONAL PARKS FOR FUTURE RECREATIONAL USE

The key to the future of both parks lies in positive management backed up by legal, administrative and fiscal reform. The role and function of national parks in England, Wales and Slovenia must be clearly stated, with particular attention being

given to general zoning of land-using activities, or with particular attention to outdoor recreation. This policy must be incorporated within an overall structure plan for the park, drawn up by the park's own planning staff led by a person of proven ability, and set within the context of a 'national land-use strategy' and a national recreation strategy.

At individual park level, management should use the techniques already available to optimise the attainment of the stated objectives. These techniques include: resource manipulation, guiding visitors by interpretation, restricting access, segregating conflicting activities and the use of physical and economic measures, interpretative techniques, administrative policies, effective staff deployment and financial aid.

CONCLUSION

In the case of Snowdonia and Logarska the concept of multiple land-use should be developed within the context of an integrated support programme for agriculture, forestry, tourism and social infrastructure. In England and Wales the best approach would be to vest such powers in planning boards for all national parks. Failing this, they should be vested in the newly constituted (post-1974) local authorities. In both instances the body might well be given some of the teeth of the now defunct Rural Development Boards, upon which *all* interests are represented in their own right. In Logarska the answer would probably revolve around management through the local commune, adequately staffed, financed and guided from the state legislature in Ljubljana.

Provided that principles and priorities are right, it should be possible by legal and administrative reform, national funding and positive management to ensure that we hand on to our successors, both residents and visitors alike, high-quality scenic areas such as the Snowdonia National Park, Wales, and the Matkov, Robanov and Logarska National Park, Slovenia.

CHAPTER SEVEN

Forest Recreation

CLEARING the woodlands is a dominant theme in the history and folklore of man's colonisation of Western Europe and North America. Nowadays preserving or even adding to the existing forest area predominates. In managing the man-modified ecosystem in such new forests, trees are seen not only as a resource to be harvested but also as a resort to which urban dwellers can travel for their recreation.

This chapter begins with a description of the broad patterns of forest ownership and use in Britain and the United States and then focuses on the varying patterns of forest use displayed by different groups of users. With so much forest land owned by public agencies, its use can be subjected to political control within a broad range of ecological tolerances.

BRITAIN'S FORESTS

Forests and woodlands cover 4,596,060 acres or about 8 per cent of Great Britain and only 4 per cent of Northern Ireland

(elsewhere in Western Europe the figure averages about 30 per cent). Forests are usually areas planted and managed primarily for *timber production*, which is not the primary purpose in *amenity* woodlands. Table 18 summarises the major categories of forest ownership and timber production. Generally speaking the more accessible, more mature, more productive, often smaller, broad-leaved amenity woodlands of the lowlands are in private ownership and the usually younger, less appealing, less productive, coniferous commercial forests of the uplands are managed by the Forestry Commission.

TABLE 18   Forest land use and ownership statistics,
Great Britain

Forestry Commission (March 1972)		*Private owners (1970–1)*	
	acres		acres
Forest land	2,164,596	1,877,960 productive woodland (b)	1,210,790 acres of commercial forests in 4,000 ownerships
planted 1,850,779	(a)		
to be planted 318,817		741,300 unproductive and scrub land (c)	1,408,470 acres mainly non-commercial in 30,000 ownerships
Other land	835,198	valuable for shelter, shooting and amenity	
(mainly agricultural)			
Total	3,002,265		

a, b and c give a total of about 4,447·8 acres of forest and woodland, about 8 per cent of the land area of Great Britain. In 1965 hardwood species covered 28 per cent of the forest area, and represented 46 per cent of the growing timber.
receipts totalling £7,000,000 1971–2
visitors est 12–15,000,000 *day visits* 1968

Data: Forestry Commission *52nd Annual Report and Accounts 1971–2*; *Forestry Policy* 1972; Countryside in 1970 Third Conference *Reports*

Three-quarters of the Commission's forests have yet to be thinned and so appear like a stockade to the visitor. Afforestation by the Commission in Scotland had covered 948,864 acres with trees by 1972, thereby confounding Dr Johnson's observation that 'A tree in Scotland is as rare as a horse in Venice'. But despite a rapid extension of planting only about 7 per cent

of Britain's timber is home-grown. Forest product imports valued at £740 million in 1971 should be compared with a state grant to the Forestry Commission of £233 million in the whole period 1919–72.[1]

The Forestry Commission's role

During World War I Britain was compelled to use nearly one-third of her scarce resources of growing timber. Mindful of the strategic difficulties, the Acland Report of 1917 proposed a state forestry authority that would afforest about 1,976,800 acres of rough grazing land, mainly with softwood species, in about eighty years. Accordingly, the Forestry Commission was created in 1919 for the purpose of 'promoting the establishment and maintenance in Great Britain of adequate reserves of growing trees'.[2] Production forestry overshadowed planting for amenity and recreational use throughout the early years. But the Commission acquired all the former Crown forests (except Windsor), some of which had been wildlife sanctuaries for royal hunting parties since Norman times. The 'ancient and ornamental' woodlands of the New Forest and the Forest of Dean were traversed by public roads and offered diverse species, glades and clearings for visitors. The Commission considered how it might replicate such features in its newly-planted forests. Argyll was designated as the first *forest park* in 1936, in an attempt to do this: seven others followed.[3] The last, Hardknott, existed until 1959, by which time public annoyance at the visual threat of afforestation in the Dunnerdale area of the Lake District led the Commission to sell their unplanted land to the National Trust.

Figure 23 shows the seven national forest parks and tree-cover of Great Britain in relation to centres of population. Most of the major forests are remote from the zone of about thirty-one miles from urban centres which circumscribes the majority of half-day drives for pleasure and trips to leisure facilities. (Much longer day trips are made to the coast and

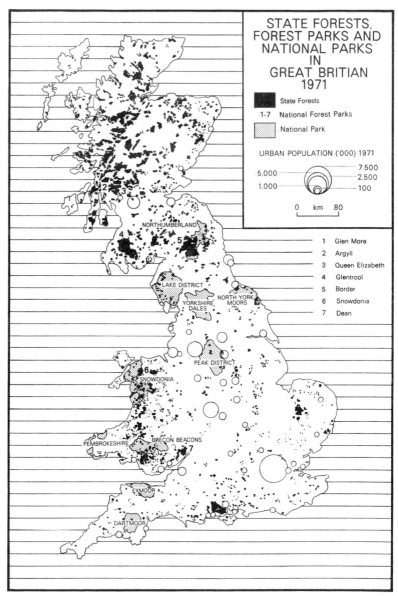

STATE FORESTS,
FOREST PARKS AND
NATIONAL PARKS
IN
GREAT BRITIAN
1971

■ State Forests

1-7 National Forest Parks

▨ National Park

URBAN POPULATION ('000) 1971

5,000 ⋯⋯⋯ 7,500
⋯⋯⋯ 2,500
1,000 ⋯⋯⋯ 100

0   km   80

1   Glen More
2   Argyll
3   Queen Elizabeth
4   Glentrool
5   Border
6   Snowdonia
7   Dean

NORTHUMBERLAND

LAKE DISTRICT

YORKSHIRE
DALES

NORTH YORK
MOORS

PEAK DISTRICT

SNOWDONIA

PEMBROKESHIRE

BRECON BEACONS

EXMOOR

DARTMOOR

Fig 23   Tree-cover, national parks and forest parks and population centres in Great Britain

popular areas like the national parks.) Figure 23 also shows the ten national parks which extend over 3,365,502 of the 37,336,810 acres of England and Wales. The parks are neither nationally owned nor dominated by a parkland function. Existing uses—mainly hill farming and forestry—continue. Afforestation proposals for the parks often annoy conservationists, who cite the parks' functions: the preservation and enhancement of natural beauty, and the promotion of public access and enjoyment. Tree planting should be subjected to land-use planning controls, argues the Countryside Commission, especially where skylines and open moorland might be transgressed.[4]

Changing policy?

Apart from the short statement in the Commission's *Forty-Fourth Annual Report* (1964) that the Forestry Commission should 'give due attention to the aesthetic and protective roles of the forest and . . . encourage open air recreation' there has been less encouragement of forest recreation in Britain than in Western Europe or North America. An upsurge in recreation was anticipated by the Countryside Acts[5] of 1967–8 which enabled the Forestry Commissioners to 'provide, arrange for or assist in the provision of, tourist, recreational or sporting facilities'. In the two years from March 1970 the number of picnic sites in forests rose from 133 to 195, car parks from 122 to 150, and forest trails and walks from 124 to 262. Even so, Professor S. D. Richardson would see this as a timid effort. In a racy lecture which had shown the imaginative recreation provision of the Danish State Forest Service, he argued that in Britain especially 'the forester of the future must become a *resort* rather than a *resource* manager'.[6] His comments attracted a riposte from the Commission's senior officer for Wales: 'foresters and forests can contribute . . . facilities for quiet enjoyment of the air, exercise and the countryside . . . These things can be provided in forests and woodlands with least damage to

the environment if they are scattered, uneconomic and free, rather than concentrated, economic and charged for.'[7]

A similar tone pervades the Commission's first major statement on recreation, made in 1971.[8] Although timber production was still the 'primary objective', it was acknowledged that 'nearly all forests are likely to become places where people will at least want to walk and picnic'. Regional recreation plans would locate suitable sites for car parks, camping and caravanning, field sports, fishing and riding. But 'the regular use of forest roads by motor vehicles for recreational purposes' was to be prohibited.

Restricting car access in forests

Lord Taylor called the Commission's policy to restrict vehicles to peripheral car parks around forests '[protecting] . . . the hiker and picnicker from the pursuit of the motor car',[9] which the Commission justified 'partly for management reasons and partly in the belief that a majority of the public want to see the peace and seclusion of the forests preserved'. But it is estimated that 95 per cent of the public do not visit Commission forests, in most cases because they cannot drive through them. Only a small part of the Commission's 9,097 mile network of forest roads is open to the public. Forest roads may be unused four years out of five, and in any case weekday working would not interfere with weekend visitors. Existing scenic forest drives have proved popular at Dalby and Newtondale, North Yorkshire; Hamsterley, County Durham; Cwmcarn, Monmouthshire; and at Gortin Glen, Lough Navar and Ballycastle, Northern Ireland. Given the right roadside facilities, the car can become a vehicle of great potential *instructiveness*, and not, as the Forestry Commission would seem to see it, a 'monster of great potential destructiveness' (echoing *Traffic in Towns*).[10] 'A "pretty road",' said Nan Fairbrother, 'after all means a road through pretty country, and "pretty country" in turn means chiefly what we see from the road.'[11] Scenic drives enable

the landscape designer to respond to moving vistas instead of just displaying static elements of vegetation and water.[12]

Other public and private woodlands

Many of the most popular open spaces for urban dwellers are the wooded areas in or near to towns. London's royal parks and the Vienna woods would have little appeal without trees! The 5,930 acres of Epping Forest to the north east of London are expressly managed to ensure its 'use and enjoyment [by] the public for all time'. Amenity woodlands are proposed as centre-pieces for the new city of Milton Keynes, the expanding city of Peterborough and, under the title of Hanley Forest Park, to bring a green corridor to the derelict industrial landscape of Stoke-on-Trent.

The public are often actively discouraged from entering many of the small private deciduous woodlands in Britain. Such woods are often used to protect pheasants, which unfortunately seek the areas enjoyed by the public, open valley floors and the edges of lakes and woods. By co-operating to form the Countryside Club, fifty woodland owners in South East England get the equivalent of a good shooting rental by charging families £10·50 a year to enter their 4,942 acres. In the remoter uplands other owners offer their forested land for shooting, deer stalking, wildfowling and fishing by syndicates.

Private owners in Britain (and the Netherlands) derive considerable tax and estate duty concessions from their timber, and such benefits may be tolerated in future only when accompanied by better public access. Section 55 of the Danish Conservation of Nature Act 1969 decreed that 'private woodland . . . of 12 acres and over to which there leads a public road or path . . . shall be open to the public'.

UNITED STATES FORESTS

Initially the United States Forest Service was charged with

'the responsibility for promoting the conservation and best use of the Nation's forest lands'. A significant clarification of purpose was made by the Multiple Use–Sustained Yield Act 1960, in which Congress stated that the national forests 'shall be administered for outdoor recreation, range, timber, watershed and wildlife and fish purposes' and that multiple use was 'not necessarily the combination of uses that will give the greatest dollar return or the greatest unit output'.

TABLE 19   Forest land use and ownership statistics, United States of America

Land ownership	(acres)	National forest use	
Total USA	2,216,487,000	154 national forests	182,854,000
private	1,344,224,000	20 national grasslands	4,942,000
public	872,263,000	4,497,220 acres of national forest area	
of which federal	770,952,000	comprises wilderness of primitive areas	
including:		7 million cattle, sheep and horses graze	
Bureau of land		on about 98,840,000 acres of the total	
management	464,548,000	national forest area	
national parks	27,181,000	Total forest area USA 758,597,000 acres	
national forests	187,796,000	in 4,500,000 ownerships	

About half of the area of national forests is capable of yielding commercial timber crops. Presently about 20 per cent of industrial timber in the USA is from national forests.
receipts £74,000,000 ($207,000,000) 1968
visitors 157,000,000 *visitor-days* 1968

Data: Frome, *The Forest Service*, 1971 and Douglass, *Forest Recreation*, 1969

Table 19 summarises the distribution and management of the federal (or public) lands. The Forest Service is part of the Department of Agriculture, and the dominant philosophy in its creation was that of 'the best output from the land', exemplified by the writings of Gifford Pinchot and speeches of President Theodore Roosevelt. In contrast the National Park Service, part of the Department of the Interior, also contained forests, some of which have been preserved almost too well (forests and parks are shown in Figure 24). So strict has been the parks'

adherence to the principles laid down by their founder John Muir and their purpose of conserving 'the scenery and the natural and historic objects and the wild life therein', providing for their enjoyment and leaving them 'unimpaired for future generations', that sometimes fire prevention has hindered forest regeneration, thereby forcing away the wildlife that depends on young trees and glades rather than a climax canopy. About 8 per cent of the national forests are 'wilderness' or 'primitive'

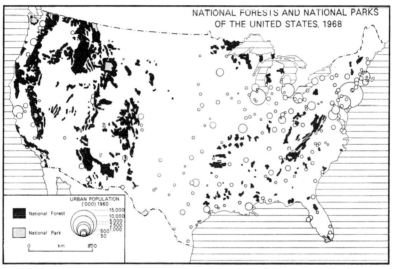

Fig 24   National forests and parks and population centres in the United States

areas 'where the earth and its community of life are untrammelled by man, where man himself is a visitor who does not remain . . .'[13]

Thus many forests in the United States are managed, and sometimes unmanaged, for purposes other than timber production. The Forest Service publications reflect the diversity of outlook, ranging from *Low-Cost Wood Homes for Rural America* (1969) to *Skiing the National Forests* (1970). Visits to the 200 winter sports areas in national forests increased from

1·5 million to 10 million in the period 1950–69. For summer visitors the Forest Service had created more than 50,000 camp sites by the mid-1960s.

Federal, interstate and regional co-operation in recreation planning in the United States has been promoted since 1962 by the Department of the Interior's Bureau of Outdoor Recreation. Further integration was planned, but President Nixon was unable to combine the Department of the Interior and Forest Service into a new Department of Natural Resources in 1971, one subdivision of which would have been entitled 'Land and recreation resources'. Meanwhile the Interior and Agriculture departments still 'compete': the 1,988 mile Appalachian Trail is supervised by the National Park Service, the 2,400 mile Pacific Crest Trail from Canada to Mexico by the Forest Service. Both services offer valuable experience for recreation managers, not least in their visitor interpretation services.

PATTERNS OF USE

In examining the capacity of forests for recreation, two kinds of data are required. First, something needs to be known about patterns of *use* of forests—the activities of people at particular locations and times. Such data will indicate the physical, ecological and psychological carrying capacities of different areas within a forest and can be collected by direct observation or even by air photography.[14] The second type of data reveals the profiles of *users* (or visitors) which are important in devising recreation strategies for regions or groups of forests.

The provision of recreation facilities varies considerably between countries. Ski resorts, snowmobiles and a whole armoury of North American 'off-road-recreation-vehicles' and sporting equipment are largely absent from British forests. Cooler summers and the proximity of the coast (never more than 110km distant) might help to account for the lack of swimming facilities in British forests. However, there are simi-

larities between all countries when patterns of visitor behaviour are observed.

Shafer, Hamilton and Schmidt have shown that North Americans prefer photographs of forested lakeside settings with an access road in view, to vistas of uninterrupted forest.[15] Dense, dark and deep forests are forbidding places to most people, who remember sombre fairy stories and warnings in nursery rhyme! Waterside and the edges of glades and clearings are the intensively-used focal points for public pressure. Heytze has observed this in the Netherlands and so has shown how people's desires for space on forest edges can be turned into planting schemes by the landscape designer who seeks to regulate visitor pressure.[16] Without knowing any of the jargon of social psychologists, who nowadays analyse people's comfort in different 'personal spaces', William Shenstone (1714–63) declared that 'A plain space near the eye gives it a kind of liberty it loves.'

Shafer and Burke have likewise seen policy implications in surveys of people's preferred locations and activities in forests.[17] State park visitors showed a penchant for open, grassy picnic areas, and for swimming areas surrounded by trees. (Hyde Park, London, has all these ingredients.) So in acquiring land for recreation near urban areas, open farmland, with scattered woods and lakes, or dammable streams, is ideal. Many of the evolving country parks of England and Wales offer combinations of grass, trees, water, views and good road access from urban centres.

SURVEYS OF USERS

Geographers have a particular interest in the problems of sampling spatially mobile populations in order to describe and explain patterns of spatial behaviour. Forest visitors are certainly a mobile target, and may stay at home in poor weather. But surveys on site are likely to be more rewarding than

telephone-administered surveys or household surveys, especially in Britain where less than 5 per cent of the population are thought to visit state forests and there are only 267 telephones per 1,000 people compared with 584 in the USA (1971 figures). It is easier and probably yields more accurate findings to interview forest visitors as a group in their car some time before they rush home. Interviews on site may be supplemented, or even replaced, by questionnaires issued for completion at home. Findings from four British surveys are summarised: Mutch 1963–4;[18] Colenutt and Sidaway 1968;[19] Countryside Commission 1969;[20] and the author 1969.[21] Most respondents were in motoring parties in forests where car access is allowed.

Methods

Interviews took place in the five forests chosen by Mutch, who interviewed visitors to the New Forest, Cannock, Loch Lomond, Allerston and Glen More Forests. Colenutt's interviewers questioned a stratified sample in the Forest of Dean and gave them a further postal questionnaire. Two scenic forest drives were opened to celebrate the overlapping royal investiture and Forestry Commission jubilee in North Wales in 1969; students interviewed and surveyed visitors and counted vehicles. The author used a simplified version of this method with a small team of voluntary national park wardens at both ends of the Dalby Forest Drive in the North York Moors (Figure 25).

Results

Most people visited the forests for a pleasant drive, picnic and short stroll, in that order. The two most common groups were an unaccompanied couple (aged over forty-five), or two adults (thirty to fifty years old) with two children. In the Forest of Dean visitors of social classes A, B and C1 outnumbered groups C2, D and E, even after allowing for higher rates of car-ownership among the richer groups. Mutch's sample travelled a mean distance of 25 miles to the forest on the day of interview.

Page 157 (*above*) New resort development on the Languedoc-Roussillon coast (*below*) new harbour and resort development, Port St Martin, Languedoc-Roussillon coast

Page 158 (*above*) holiday traffic, Ambleside, Lake District National Park (*below*) new resort development, Bay des Anges, Cote d'Azur

1 Shore road (C.D. 41)
2 Battery path.
3 Entrances.
4 5, 6, 7. Top storeys of the Amiral, Baronnet, Commodore and Ducal residences and their garden terraces.
8 Esplanade.
9 Gardens : 19 acres of greenery covering a 95,680 sq. yd concrete slab above a parking of 2,000 places and a private road network.
10 Quays and shopping centre.
11 Hotel of an international standing.
12 Swimming-pool.
13 Harbour-master's office, harbour administration, Customs, Weather Forecast Bureau.
14 Slipway. Ordnance and Supply stations.
15 Dry storage.
16 Quays and piers: 589 berths from 18 to 78 feet in length. Water, electricity, telephone, TV and connecting points.
17 Beach and beach shops.
18 Yacht club: bar, restaurant, showers, sailing-school, water-skiing, skin-diving, motor boating.

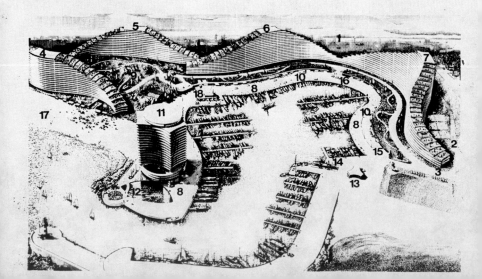

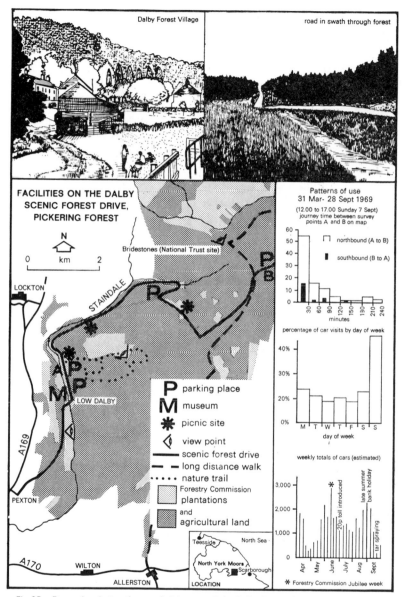

Dalby Forest Village

road in swath through forest

FACILITIES ON THE DALBY SCENIC FOREST DRIVE, PICKERING FOREST

N

0   km   2

Bridestones (National Trust site)

LOCKTON

STAINDALE

LOW DALBY

A169

PEXTON

A170   WILTON

ALLERSTON

P parking place
M museum
✳ picnic site
◊ view point
— scenic forest drive
– – long distance walk
• • • • nature trail
Forestry Commission plantations
and
agricultural land

LOCATION

Teesside   North Sea
North York Moors
Scarborough

Patterns of use
31 Mar- 28 Sept 1969

(12.00 to 17.00 Sunday 7 Sept)
journey time between survey
points A and B on map

□ northbound (A to B)
■ southbound (B to A)

minutes

percentage of car visits by day of week

40%
30%
20%
0%

M T W T F S S

day of week

weekly totals of cars (estimated)

3,000
2,000
1,000
0

Apr May June July Aug Sept

20p toll introduced
late summer bank holiday
tar spraying

✳ Forestry Commission Jubilee week

Fig 25   Recreational attractions and visitor use of the Dalby Forest Scenic Drive, Pickering, Yorkshire

10

Colenutt's visitor origin data showed a bell-shaped curve for Symond's Yat (a well-known beauty spot) with a maximum at 35–40 miles, and an expected distance-decay curve for the less well known Speech House site. Local groups—from within 5 miles—were important at both sites. The author identified holiday-makers from Scarborough, and day visitors from West Yorkshire and Humberside, as distinct groups within his sample. So each forest has a characteristic direction- and distance-related, and possibly socially defined, catchment.

Automobile Association road signs had attracted half the Dovey and Gwydyr respondents to those drives, and a similar proportion sought the North Yorkshire drive on the recommendation of friends; 44 per cent of respondents on this latter drive were there for the first time. Mutch had recruitment rates of 40–57 per cent for his Scottish sub-samples, and Colenutt's figures varied between 18 per cent for day visitors, to 55 per cent of tourists visiting the Dean Forest for the first time. Only one-third of North Yorkshire visitors thought the then novel 20p toll unreasonable: most were locals remembering when it was free. In North Wales 90 per cent expressed willingness to pay to use a forest drive.

Conclusions

These popular Forestry Commission forests were still poorly advertised, relatively unknown and badly signposted. Few people knew about the maps, leaflets and rather 'academic' guidebooks already available. Large display maps at forest entrances and simple plans given to all visitors—as in North Wales—might be considered. Sidaway hypothesised that *reducing* facilities at Symonds Yat in the Forest of Dean might increase turnover, and so alleviate overcrowding at peak periods. Even rough forest roads brought few objections.

All these forests would seem to offer scope for the further development of recreation functions without undue wear, tear and noise—especially at non-peak periods. However it is im-

portant to note that many of Mutch's respondents and those in North Yorkshire deprecated commercialisation.

RECREATION POTENTIAL

Britain's public forests would seem to possess two useful attributes for recreation development. The first is unified national ownership by an organisation which might be encouraged to develop recreation by its government masters. The second is the ability of forests to absorb cars, their occupants and noises, without excessive erosion or even fire risk.

Further examination is less encouraging. Sidaway and Oakes distributed a questionnaire to assess the recreation potential of 210 forests near cities and holiday areas.[22] To begin with, access to half the total was constrained by legal agreements. After analysing the population of car-owners within 30 miles of the remaining forests, only twenty-two could be shortlisted as having suitable terrain and a high potential demand for day recreation.

Forests, like recreation facilities of all kinds, are bedevilled by the problem of the peak loadings. Should picnic benches, toilets and car parks be installed sufficient for the demand on sunny Sunday afternoons in summer? And who would operate the facilities provided? Many foresters live in or near the forests where they work, and the weekend is for their leisure as well! Is a combination of retired foresters and voluntary forest wardens a possible answer, or should more foresters be trained to educate the visiting public about forest flora and fauna?

Foresters' attitudes

Whatever schemes are proposed for forest recreation, they will have to be implemented by foresters, most of whom entered the forest service to grow and harvest trees. Bultena and Hendee devised a questionnaire to gauge the attitude of foresters in the Pacific North West to timber management

and trail policy.[23] Their findings are summarised in Table 20.

TABLE 20   Foresters in the Pacific North West:
view of the expected response of interest groups to two policies

I TIMBER CUTTING POLICY

Their expected response

Interest group	*Increase allowable cuts*	*No clear position*	*Decrease allowable cuts*
Forest products industry	99	1	0
Superiors in Forest Service	94	4	1
Local town officials	76	20	2
Hikers, mountain climber clubs	2	13	84
Conservation organisations	4	7	89

II TRAILBIKE POLICY

	Open to trailbikes	*No clear position*	*Restrict forest to foot and horse*
Trailbike clubs	96	2	1
Hunter's organisations	63	21	11
Forest products industry	5	89	5
Superiors in Forest Service	23	42	22
Local town officials	9	83	7
Hikers, mountain clubs	6	3	90
Conservation organisations	3	8	86

Source: Bultena and Hendee, *Journal of Forestry*, 70 (1972), 337–42

So just as John Muir called sheep 'hoofed locusts' because of their ecological destructiveness, some foresters might see people as 'booted locusts' or conservationists see motor-bike riders as 'tyred locusts'. The 118 foresters interviewed happened to work in five of the most productive national forests in the USA. Furthermore, said the authors, foresters living in rural areas will have more contact (and therefore more sympathy?) with local commercial interests than with recreation-seeking townsfolk.

INTEGRATED MANAGEMENT PLANS

Recreation plans for forests will be drawn by foresters and,

especially in America, by private companies leasing or owning land within the forest curtilage. Douglass offers practical guidelines for site planning *within* the forest.[24] In the context of scale and urbanisation in Western Europe, three British and one Dutch recreation plan raise important principles.

The New Forest[25]

Over 100 miles of public highway traverses the forest—Crown Land managed by the Forestry Commission but also providing common rights which are preserved by the Verderers; 30,000 car-borne people might spill over the 1,200 access points from the roads on a hot Sunday. *Can the Forest Survive?* asked a pamphlet accompanying a consultative document, *Conservation of the New Forest*. User-groups, landowners and managers distilled their responses into a strategy for twenty-six car-free zones (shown in Figure 26a) and 166 locations for concentrating facilities.

The Chilterns Beechwoods[26]

Most of the beechwoods in the Chiltern Area of Outstanding Natural Beauty (AONB) are privately owned. A 'standing conference' of the four local counties, the Countryside Commission, Nature Conservancy and National Trust agreed that their main objective was 'to secure in the long term the rehabilitation of the Chiltern Beech and broad-leaved forest'. (Squirrels are more destructive than people.) They envisage considerable numbers of people in a very few places and argue that the bulk of the area 'should be left for those whose primary interest is natural beauty'.

East Hampshire AONB[27]

An inter-disciplinary team from central and local government, the Forestry Commission and Nature Conservancy considered what policies might be applied to agriculture, forestry, wildlife conservation, recreation and landscape in the area. A

study of likely trends and interactions between these various elements indicated the acceptability of different places for various activities, and so policies emerged for integrated land management.

Utrechtse Heuvelrug[28]

Close to the Royal Palace at Soestdijk in the Netherlands lies a thinly wooded area translated as the 'Utrecht hill-ridge'. Since 1959 an imaginative recreation plan, conceived by public authorities and private landowners, has brought the signpost Heuvelrugroute to the area, along which the motorist, moped and bicycle rider (four- and two-wheels are segregated) will find carefully designed and managed picnic and parking places. Interpretation services will satisfy those interested in the history and natural history of the region. The evolving recreation structure plan is shown in Figure 26b.

The methods incorporated in these plans are likely to be applied more widely in future. Management schemes for forests in the remoter uplands of Britain are likely to require much more thought about publicity, and may possibly involve the development of winter and summer *resort* centres in the forests.

Perspectives

Forest recreation needs to be viewed through several lenses. The first might be a geographical and topographical perspective. Development of recreation facilities in forests needs to be seen in the context of the existing and potential recreation assets of a touring region. The attractiveness of a particular forest for recreation will be a product of its accessibility and scenic resources.

From an administrative perspective, production foresters need to combine their appraisals of recreation potential with those of trained ecologists, user groups and adjacent landowners.

In a technical perspective, recreation management in forests calls for understanding of both visitor and forester behaviour,

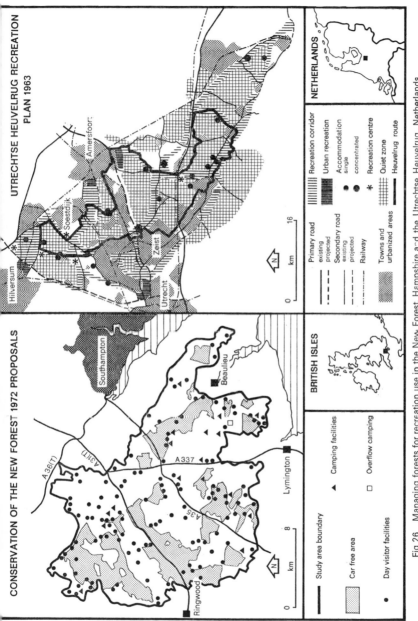

Fig 26 Managing forests for recreation use in the New Forest, Hampshire and the Utrechtse Heuvelrug, Netherlands

as well as the ecological responses of the resource system. Most foresters understand forest ecology and forest economics; a change in educational priorities is needed if social systems are to be better understood.

One further perspective has to be mentioned, that of politics, for forest management in both public and private sectors is subjected to government scrutiny. New priorities for state forestry may be recommended—perhaps to invigorate employment in otherwise decaying villages, perhaps to enhance the landscape, but more likely to give treasuries a better return on their capital. Recent reports have hinted at a cut-back in government support for forestry in Britain.[29] Even in the United States the proportion of the national budget allocated to natural resources (Forest and Park Services, Geological Survey and so on) fell from 1·5 per cent to a proposed 1·2 per cent in the period 1965–71.[30]

The geographer's training offers equipment, not only for examining patterns of spatial behaviour in the setting of man-made and natural forests, but also to understand the historical and legal patterns of forest clearance and present-day use which colour our *national* appraisals of this particular resource. Geographic perspectives offer valuable insights into the provision of forest recreation.

CHAPTER EIGHT

Resorts and Recreation

THERE are over 400 resorts* in Western Europe[1] with a total resident population in excess of 12 millions which is more than doubled during the holiday season. From the large brash seaside towns, such as Blackpool or Blankenberg, to the quiet inland resorts, such as Grasmere or Grasse, they all have one feature in common—a large part of their economy is bound up with catering for and entertaining visitors. This chapter sets out to identify and define the range of resort types in Western Europe, to discuss the history of resort development and to analyse the present-day distribution of holiday places in relation to population and recreation resources. The impact of recreation on the resort townscape and the diversity of resort hinterlands are also discussed. Finally the problems and prospects for the areas of new resort development are examined against the general backcloth of recreation resources in Western Europe.

In most cases national data on tourist* movements are used

* This term is defined in a glossary at the end of this chapter

and supplemented where possible with regional and sub-regional resort studies. The raw data on tourist movements origins and destinations are only available in aggregate form and neither the International Union of Tour Operators (IUOTO)[2] nor the national tourist boards make analyses of visitors by region or place of origin. Some bodies such as the British Tourist Authority (BTA)[3] carry out home holiday surveys but these represent a limited sector of the tourist market.* As most resorts and holiday areas in Western Europe attract visitors from a wide range of countries the absence of details concerning resort hinterlands is a major gap in tourist statistics. This problem is exacerbated by the variability and differing reliability of the extant data. Thus most countries collect data on foreign visitors by country of origin, but few have information on the travel patterns of their own residents taking holidays abroad. Moreover these gross figures give no breakdown according to purpose of visit. Such tourist data may come from several sources such as frontier records or hotel registrations, and in the latter case many visitors using camp sites or unofficial accommodation will be excluded. Double counting may occur where a tourist stops in a country en route to and from his main holiday destination. Methods of data collection and definition may vary through time. For example Peters[4] cites two sets of figures purporting to be UK visitors to France in 1963. The entry/departure estimate produced a figure of 1,630,000. Regional tourist estimates and a sample of the frontier crossing data gave 860,000. The former figure was probably inflated through including re-entry of visitors to France.

Moreover any discussion of the available aggregate data assumes that holiday-makers in general can be treated as a homogeneous whole, whereas there are many kinds with diverse demands and aspirations, and with different concepts of the sort of holiday they want. One can hypothesise that

* This term is defined in a glossary at the end of this chapter

several kinds of visitor hinterland exist simultaneously, which can be explained by the availability of recreation opportunities and an understanding of the behaviour patterns, motivations and socio-economic characteristics of the holiday visitors. In the absence of a detailed socio-economic analysis of the total holiday visitor population at resort or holiday region level, it is only possible to treat tourists as a general group, pointing out important variables where such data exist.

DEVELOPMENT OF HOLIDAY RESORTS IN WESTERN EUROPE

The European pilgrimage centres of the Middle Ages were the forerunners of resort towns and when this traffic declined, spas and health resorts gradually spread first on the Continent and later in Britain. Thus by the late sixteenth century there were twelve spas on the Continent[5] and two in Britain.[6]

The seventeenth and eighteenth centuries saw the growth of watering places and spa towns such as Bath, Buxton or Baden-Baden, which catered for a select and exclusive society. During the nineteenth century the Industrial Revolution in Western Europe encouraged a greater diffusion of wealth and with the advent of railway expansion this social and transport revolution produced a great number of new popular resorts. For example, once railways linked the expanding cities of Western Europe with the Mediterranean coast of France and Italy the select resorts of the upper classes were newly discovered by the growing middle classes anxious to emulate aristocratic fashions. In 1865 the railway arrived at Nice and two years later at Menton[7] leading, in the period from 1865 to 1914, to the appearance of a number of thriving resorts along the Riviera coast which transformed it into the premier holiday region of France. The early attraction of the Alpine resorts as part of the Grand Tour, and the growth of winter sports and mountaineering in the late-nineteenth century, led to the spread of winter sports

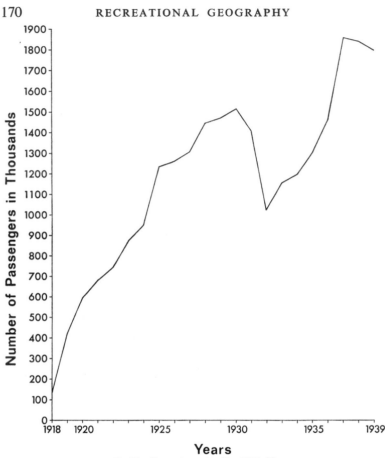

Fig 27   Cross-channel traffic, 1918–30

resorts in the Alpine districts of France, Italy, Switzerland and Austria.[8] More recently the Scandinavian countries have developed similar winter tourist centres.

The appearance of a large middle class with the Industrial Revolution in Britain provided a supply of potential tourists who were predominant in nineteenth-century Europe. Cross-channel traffic increased from 100,000 per annum in the 1830s to over 500,000 in the 1890s. By 1930 over 1,500,000 British travellers went to the Continent[9] (Figure 27). The major tourist

countries had an unprecedented boom in the 1920s when France, Switzerland and Italy each received well over a million foreign visitors.[10] In Britain, legislation enabling paid holidays was passed in 1937 (1936 in France), and the post-war impact of the motor car and charter travel led to the development of mass tourism with a dramatic impact on the major holiday regions of Western Europe. Spain, with its high annual sunshine totals and low cost advantages, developed resorts to cater for this new mass market: the annual average of 266,000 foreign tourists in the early 1930s rose to over 2 millions in the 1950s and over 12 millions in the 1960s. Four-fifths of these went to the coast, especially the Costa Brava.[11]

DISTRIBUTION OF HOLIDAY RESORTS IN WESTERN EUROPE

Tourist brochures produced by the national tourist authorities of Western Europe evoke the qualities of resorts through a wide range of nouns, including 'sun', 'sea', 'sand', 'beaches', 'mountains', 'historic'; and the association of resorts with these qualities can go some way towards explaining their distribution. As Figure 28 shows, resorts are in general peripheral; both nationally and in Western Europe most have a coastal location. The popularity of seaside holidays is borne out by the fact that 65 to 70 per cent of holiday-makers in Britain,[12] 29 per cent in France,[13] and 80 per cent in Spain[14] take all or part of their holiday at the coast.

Walter Christaller argued that the larger the agglomeration and the greater the population density, the greater the propensity to travel during holidays.[15] The French National Institute of Statistics and Economic Studies (INSEE) has established a close linear relationship between town size and the proportion of population taking a holiday, ranging from 75 per cent of the Paris agglomeration (1969) to 56 per cent for cities with populations over 100,000, and 19 per cent for rural communes of

less than 5,000 people.[16] Although a high correlation can be established between these two factors (R = + 0·89),[17] this almost certainly reflects the greater proportion of people with larger disposable incomes living in the major towns and cities.

Christaller also asserted that the landscape is the most im-

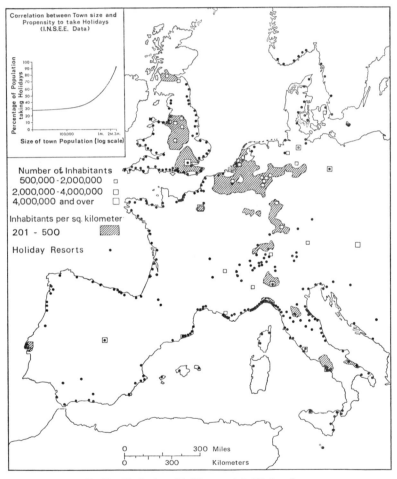

Fig 28   Distribution of holiday resorts in Western Europe

portant holiday destination.[18] This statement was echoed by
the work of Lewis in Wisconsin[19] where he identified major
landscape features of recreational attraction. These were water
surfaces (rivers, waterfalls, lakes, reservoirs, sea), scenic contrasts, vegetational contrasts, slopes and bluffs. Similarly in
France a survey of households by the INSEE found that

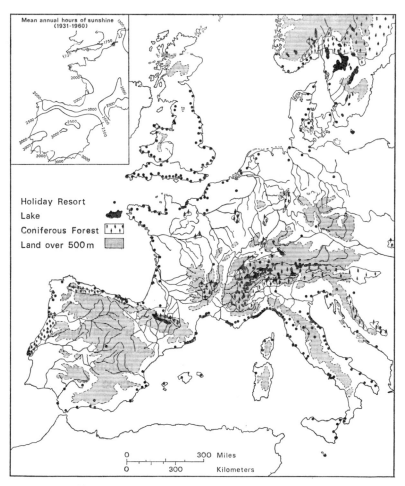

Fig 29   Landscape features of recreational attraction, Western Europe

respondents identified six types of holiday region.[20] These were: the sea, the mountains, the countryside, towns other than spas, the Paris region, spas and watering places.

Given the attempts by Christaller and Lewis to identify distinctive landscape features of recreational attraction, one could expect resorts to gravitate around such areas. To test this hypothesis, a map was prepared showing the distribution of resorts and recreationally attractive landscape features in Western Europe (Figure 29). Over 90 per cent of the resorts have a coastal location, although those on the Atlantic coast of Spain and the French and Italian Riviera have a backcloth of mountains and forests forming part of the general holiday region. Similarly Alpine resorts and many of the German resorts are associated with mountain areas.

Some of the landscape attributes such as the mountains, forests and lakes are inherently rural, and a distinction can be made between resort and non-resort holiday activities. Thus camping, caravanning, hiking, mountaineering and most water sports are non-resort based. These activities are widely scattered, often informal, and difficult to identify with a restricted locality; but they could be expected to be most prevalent in those areas with the greatest combination of recreationally attractive landscape features. With the exception of the Alpine massif, the resorts of Western Europe are peripheral to these attractive landscape complexes. While the resorts provide the whole range of more formal urban sports, together with visits to the beach, casino or theatre, they also serve as generators of sightseeing trips into the surrounding holiday regions. In promotional campaigns, these associated landscape features are commonly used as a setting for the resorts.

However, the distribution of landscape features only offers a partial explanation. Climate is an important factor, and the long sunshine hours of the southern European resorts help to explain the growth in their popularity. Areas in Western Europe with over 2,500 hours of sunshine (1931–65) (inset

Page 175 (*above*) water-based recreation, Lake Windermere, Lake District National Park (*below*) new marina, Languedoc coast

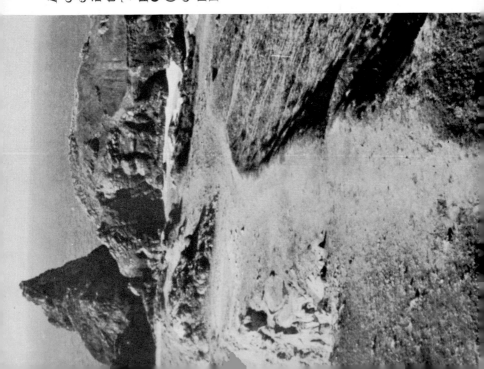

Page 176 (left) coastal path erosion resulting from visitor pressure, The Lizard peninsula, Cornwall (*right*) erosive effect of footpaths, the Pennine Way

Figure 29) emphasise the pre-eminent position of the Mediterranean resorts.

There is also a range of resorts with cultural, traditional and
historic associations whose location *per se* is not related to
recreationally attractive landscapes. Towns such as Haarlem
or Delft, York or Oxford are cases in point. A number of resorts
exist whose importance is due to their proximity to the major
population agglomerations. These are primarily but not exclusively day-trip resorts within one to two hours of the major
conurbations of Western Europe. The capital cities of Europe
function as a further category of resorts, with their long historical links with other countries, their identification with
national 'character' and their high standards of accommodation
and cultural amenities. Finally the distribution of spas and
health resorts is related to the geographical location of mineral
springs, associated with zones of faulting and rupture of the
rock strata.

IMPACT OF TOURISM ON RESORT TOWNSCAPES

While a varied range of towns function as tourist resorts in
Western Europe, the impact of the holiday industry on the
townscape shows a similar pattern in each case. The morphology of the resort towns reflects their holiday function and is
shown in their form, structure and land use. Buildings with a
tourist/holiday function and the associated resort infrastructure
are limited areally to a relatively narrow sector of the town,
with a gradation of declining tourist activity away from the
main foci of interest. As these towns evolved into holiday
resorts an accumulation of purpose-built and converted building types emerged. It has generally been a process of accretion
with the pattern of growth being influenced by typography.
Thus most of the seaside resorts have expanded parallel to the
sea front with relatively little development inland. The main
beach or promenade took over and aped the earlier spa

promenade, replacing the pump room as the focus of social life. The morphology of most resorts reflects their history of rapid development, with a great influx of capital investment in the form of hotels, entertainment features, promenades, piers and all the other facets of the resort townscape which are so familiar today.

The main periods of resort development have left a distinctive legacy of buildings and styles of architecture, well-represented by the large Victorian and Edwardian hotels in the select watering places and Riviera resorts of southern France. In Britain most resorts were well-established by the late nineteenth century and those towns which progressed from spas or watering places to holiday resorts have a townscape of Georgian and early Victorian origin. Having arrived by train, the resort was a self-contained provider of all the visitor's needs from accommodation to entertainment, for the visitor was not mobile and spent most of his holiday within the resort. This is reflected in the layout of the seaside resorts with the railway station, the main shopping and tourist streets leading to the front, the promenade and often the pier. Along this sea front area are grouped the hotels and boarding houses, shops and entertainment features.

A random examination of a variety of resorts in Western Europe shows a spatial association between tourist-oriented land and building uses which are separated very distinctly from the rest of the townscape. Figure 30, a schematic diagram of a 'typical' seaside resort, represents an amalgam of characteristic resort features. The tourist-oriented land and building uses are located in a zone between the railway station and the main beach or sea front area. Figure 31 emphasises this point which is most evident in the distinctive accommodation areas, where the prime frontal locations are occupied in almost unbroken succession by the larger hotels, with a gradation in land values and tourist-oriented land and building uses away from the sea front. In resorts which also function as gambling centres, such

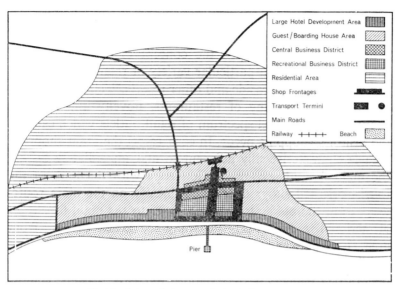

Fig 30 Schematic diagram of a 'typical' seaside resort

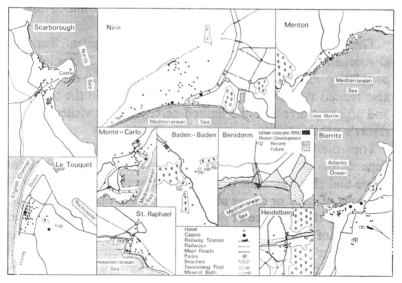

Fig 31 Characteristic morphology of selected resorts in Western Europe

as Monte Carlo, Biarritz or Menton, there are additional clusters of hotels around the casinos.

Stansfield has developed the concept of the Recreational Business District as a particular variety of retail district which can be observed in seaside and other resorts.[21] This is a seasonally oriented grouping of restaurants, novelty and souvenir shops and the general spectrum of retail outlets which cater to the visitor's shopping needs. In each resort the main shopping area is characteristically adjacent to and immediately behind the main frontal accommodation zone with the bulk of the tourist-oriented shops distributed linearly on the main routeways from the public transport termini to the main feature of attraction for the visitor—generally the beach or lake front area. This pattern is epitomised on the Belgian, Dutch and English coasts where those resorts which cater for large numbers of day trippers have developed intensive seasonal trading zones along the central sea front area. In all but the very large resorts most of these retail shops close during the off season, and seasonality is the keynote of the Recreational Business District (RBD).

The RBD is separated spatially from the Central Business District and has a quite different range of retail outlets, shopping population and shopping hinterland. The location of the RBD also reflects the concentration of visitor activity in the sea front and adjacent area and the limited perception by visitors of the resort's urban structure.

The role of the beach as a focus of recreational activity depends on several factors such as accessibility, the daily tidal range and the area which remains uncovered at high tide, the presence of cliffs or dunes separating it from the resort proper, its aspect, the presence of fine sands or rocks and pebbles, and the angle of slope of the beach.[22] Thus popular resorts such as Brighton or Zandvoort which possess long stretches of beach easily accessible at high tide commonly have peak season densities of over 1,200 persons per hectare.[23] The distribution of

visitors on the beach emphasises its close association with the Recreational Business District. Thus the greatest concentration of visitor numbers typically occurs on that part of the beach directly opposite the main route from the public transport termini and the centre of the RBD. The numbers and density of visitors on the beach take the form of a normal curve distributed around this most accessible point.

RESORT HINTERLANDS

A study of resort visitor hinterlands can show the areas contributing to present demand for holidays and recreation in Western Europe and the number of visitors that each resort draws upon. Unfortunately, published data at resort level on visitor numbers and origins are extremely scarce and the limited studies available are not directly comparable in time or methods. The national tourist bureaux have no detailed information about visitor source areas and no comprehensive survey has ever been made. Given the need for tourist advertising and publicity in actual and potential market areas, this is a glaring omission from official sources.

Some initial hypotheses may be put forward concerning resort visitor hinterlands:

1 The pattern of visitor hinterlands may be influenced by the social and economic characteristics of the major population concentrations.
2 The pattern of effective visitor demand may vary in direct proportion to the size of the town of origin.
3 With the day visitor population, distance may operate as a cost function, albeit a crude one. With staying visitors distance may act as a variable influencing the range of information available to holiday-makers.
4 The choice of holiday destination is a function of the type and amount of information available to the holiday-maker.

5   The spatial distribution of the demand for holidays may be affected by the range of intervening and competing opportunities.
6   The behaviour patterns of national and foreign tourists may differ.

Given these hypotheses, and the fact that no direct charge is made for the use of these resorts and associated holiday areas, the demand for their use as recreation places is a function of (i) their perceived attractiveness, facilities and so on, and (ii) the relative cost of reaching these places.

Day Visitor Hinterlands

Data are limited on day visitor movements and origins and only exist for a few resorts in Britain and North West Europe. Evidence collected from resorts in northern England and on the south coast suggests that most (over 80 per cent) day trippers are drawn from towns within a 60 mile radius of the resort.[24] This effectively represents up to two hours' driving time. On the Dutch coast the resorts within the Randstadt receive almost all their day visitors from places within 50 miles.[25] The only long-distance day-trip movements are to recreation sites in Zeeland and the central Netherlands close to the main routeways to the Ruhr.[26]

Resorts with an important day-tripper function are almost all concentrated on the shores of the English Channel North Sea coast, within easy reach of the major population clusters of North West Europe (Figure 29). There are three main groups of day-tripper resorts: along the Dutch coast from Egmond am Zee to Scheveningen; the Belgian and North West France coast from Knokke to Le Treport; and the coast of south eastern England from Felixstowe to Bognor Regis. Because these day-tripper resorts are clustered together, the Belgian coast, for example, consisting almost entirely of resort development, the potential visitor population is presented with a wide

range of intervening and competing recreation opportunities. Thus people in the Brussels region have a choice of five resorts within a 50-mile radius and much of the Dutch coast lies within one hour's drive from the cities of Randstadt, Holland. This variety of choice has effectively limited the day-visitor hinterlands of these resorts, and most of the visitor movements are on a sub-regional scale. Improved accessibility through the programmes of motorway development may marginally affect their catchment areas. The Rhine-Ruhr population agglomeration and the industrial towns of the Sambre-Meuse region lie just over 100 miles distant and, with a reduction in journey times, could provide further sources of day trippers in the 1980s. This raises the problem of over-use and peak-season congestion along these limited stretches of coastline. For example the Dutch coast has an estimated carrying capacity of 1 million at any one point in time.[27] Already 3 million people leave the Randstadt cities for outdoor recreation on summer Sundays, many of them heading for the coast.[28]

Evidence is available to suggest that distance does operate as a cost function and many day-trip movements involve relatively limited distances. Although the hinterlands are limited in extent, this is outweighed by the sheer volume of day trippers involved. For example the Kent coast resorts have a potential day-visitor population of over 10 millions. The Dutch and Belgian coasts will attract a similar total on a fine summer weekend.

Staying Visitor Hinterlands

The hinterlands of resident holiday visitors are much more complex in form and type, and discussion is restricted due to the limited studies available. Existing data suggest that most resorts have a regionally oriented market in terms of their nationals. Thus almost half the visitors to Welsh resorts in 1961 came from two adjacent regions, the North West and the Midlands.[29] Over half of the visitors to Scarborough and Whitby

came from the Northern Region, and at Keswick, Ambleside and Windermere over half the staying visitors lived in the North or North West.[30] Patmore, in his study of holiday movements in Britain, emphasised the pull of the South and West holiday regions over the past decade.[31] During the summer months the South West, South and Wales emerge as major net importers and the North/North East, Midlands and London as major exporters of population. He also identified largely regional holiday movements. Thus over one-third of those on holiday in Yorkshire in 1968 came from within the county. A similar pattern emerged for the South East and North West regions.

Studies at Le Touquet[32] and Biarritz[33] found that over one-

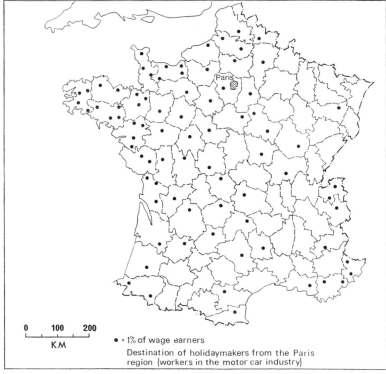

Fig 32a Staying visitor hinterland for selected parts of France

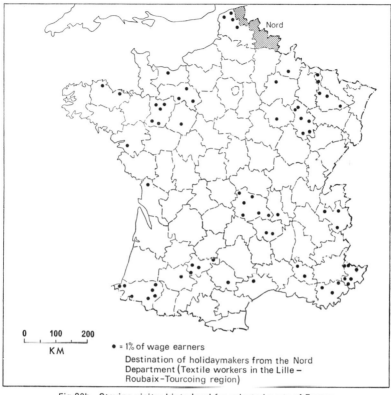

Fig 32b Staying visitor hinterland for selected parts of France

third of the staying visitors came from the two nearest departments and over half came from places within 120 miles of each
resort. The Biarritz survey was based on an analysis of non-
resident property-ownership (Figure 32), recognising an area
of second homes or property investment attraction. It was
argued that both types of ownership are closely linked to
holiday-making. Similarly a survey of holiday-makers at
Benidorm established that three-quarters of the Spanish visitors
came from the Madrid and Alcoya districts.[34]

Some limited additional information on choice of holiday
regions and propensity of populations to take holidays does

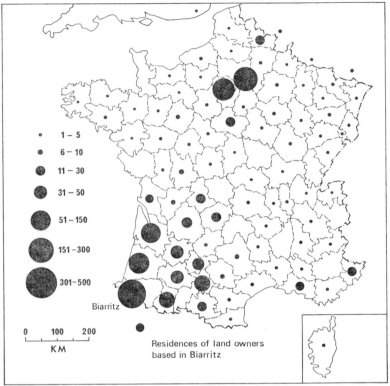

Fig 32c   Staying visitor hinterlands for selected parts of France

point to some general conclusions. INSEE studies of car workers in the Paris region and textile workers in the Lille-Roubaix-Tourcoing agglomeration emphasised a similar choice of holiday destinations.[35] Car workers preferred Brittany and the Massif Central; while the Vosges, French Alps and Provence were most popular among the textile workers (Figure 32). Both show preference for places with a seaside or mountain location which is typical of the overall pattern of European holiday movements, but it is not possible to say if *this* choice was influenced by occupation or place of residence.

The IUOTO *Survey of World Tourism* identified the twelve main tourist-generating countries and produced coefficients of

propensity to travel at national level (Table 21).[36] Unfortunately no regional or sub-regional breakdown was attempted within the countries of Western Europe.

TABLE 21   Main tourist generators (1965)

Country	Total tourist arrivals generated in world	Inter-regional arrivals generated	Intra-regional arrivals generated	Inter-regional arrivals as percentage of all arrivals
USA	21,689,920	9,763,321	11,926,599	45·0
UK	7,528,962	883,749	6,645,213	11·7
France	9,966,223	474,878	9,491,345	4·8
Germany	21,637,248	389,647	21,247,601	1·8
Canada	6,671,406	871,406	5,800,000	13·1
Belgium/ Luxembourg	3,787,409	50,011	3,737,398	1·3
Netherlands	4,075,100	98,456	3,976,644	2·4
Italy	3,139,669	153,822	2,985,847	4·9
Switzerland	2,194,407	95,284	2,099,123	4·3
Sweden	1,430,766	60,549	1,370,217	4·2
Denmark	1,366,350	30,130	1,336,220	2·2
Austria	2,079,350	41,180	2,038,170	2·0

Note: the smaller the percentage figure, the greater the propensity to travel abroad
Source: IUOTO Economic Review of World Tourism (Geneva, 1968)

In the absence of full regional or sub-regional analyses of visitor movements, it is clear that the factors influencing the visitor hinterlands of the resorts of Western Europe are complex and diverse. Size of agglomeration may act as one index although this could reflect higher incomes and greater mobility of people in the larger cities. The existing isolated studies are too limited to offer a unifying theory about visitor hinterlands, and little is known about the patterns of visitor movements below the national/international scale.

Data collected annually by the British Tourist Authority since 1951 give a broad picture of holiday movements within Britain.[37] Most holiday journeys involve limited distances and in almost every holiday area internal and adjacent regions supply the bulk of the visitors. As these nearby regions are

clearly the most familiar, this suggests that the choice of destination is related to the type and amount of information available to the holiday-maker. This bears out the findings of the author that resorts in the northern region had predominantly regional or sub-regional hinterlands.[38] Moreover there is a clear association between the socio-economic status of visitors and the type of holiday area used. In the Lake District and Wensleydale, where visual recreation and absence of commercialism are the keynotes, professional, managerial, and skilled workers form about half the visitors. At the gregarious, highly commercial seaside resorts of Scarborough and Whitby, less than one in ten of the visitors is of professional or managerial status:[39] 40 per cent are manual workers and a further 30 per cent office workers. Wall's analysis of holiday movements from one source area, Hull, shows that most (58·5 per cent) of the trips were to the coast and were concentrated on a few urban resorts.[40] (See also Chapter 4.)

TYPOLOGICAL CLASSIFICATION OF RESORTS

An attempt has been made to produce a typological classification of resorts based on their function and the extent of their visitor hinterland. Eight main categories of resort have been identified, making up a hierarchy of holiday places.

Resort type	*Characteristics*
1 Capital cities	High standard of accommodation, tourist facilities and entertainments. Concentration of national characteristics and identification with particular national 'character'. Long historical links with other countries.
2 Select resorts	Emphasis on large exclusive hotel accommodation with some development of guest/boarding/pension accommodation.

Resort type	*Characteristics*
	Located some distance from large population centres, usually in scenically attractive setting. Extensive visitor hinterland. Resorts in this category: Cannes, Menton, Biarritz, Deauville, San Remo.
3 Popular resorts	These attract large numbers of holiday visitors and offer a wide range of all types of holiday accommodation. Recent large-scale hotel and holiday apartment development is common. These resorts offer a wide range of entertainment and amusement features along the sea front region, and have a limited holiday season from Easter to October. Resorts in this category: Juan-les-Pins, Blackpool, Alicante, Scheveningen, Sorrento, Blankenberge.
4 Minor resorts	Small select resorts with limited clientele. Small towns in a rural inland or coastal setting. Absence of commercialism and organised holiday activity. Generally located in less popular, less accessible holiday areas. Resorts in this category: Granville, St Briac, Hendaye, Tenby, Le Trayas, Cap D'Ail.
5 Cultural/historic centres	These attract a high proportion of foreign tourists because of their cultural and historic associations, and characteristically they are the main centres for museums, art galleries and theatres. Resorts in this category: Stratford-upon-Avon, Canterbury, Florence, Avignon.

Resort type	*Characteristics*
6 Winter sports resorts	Generally in Alpine or Scandinavian location with whole resort infrastructure geared to skiing and associated winter sports. Resorts in this category: Chamonix, Davos, Grenoble, Klosters, Garmisch-Partenkirchen.
7 Spas/watering places	It is still fashionable on the Continent to 'take the waters' and a limited number of health resorts remain, particularly in Germany and France. Resorts in this category: Vichy, Aix-les-Bains, Baden-Baden, Evian.
8 Day-trip resorts	These towns are situated relatively close to the main concentrations of population and their visitor hinterlands are therefore very limited in extent. Day visitors predominate, and most of the resort amenities are designed/geared towards this type of visitor. Most resorts have a well-developed sea front trading area together with amusement parks and arcades. Great daily variations in visitor population due to changing weather conditions. Resorts in this category: Brighton, Southend, Margate, Ramsgate, Knokke, Scheveningen, Zandvoort, Katwijk, Ostia.

The distribution of these eight categories of resort was mapped at a European scale in an attempt to extend this typology (Figure 33). To some extent this classification is subjective and is used here descriptively. However, several clusters of similar resort types emerge.

The winter sports resorts of the Alpine region form the most distinct group. Predominantly day-trip resorts are also found in close association. The spas of Germany and the select resorts of the French and Italian Riviera form additional clusters of similar holiday places.

The landscape of each resort type is presented in schematic

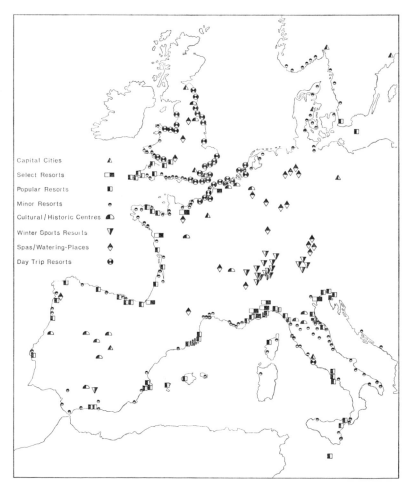

Capital Cities

Select Resorts

Popular Resorts

Minor Resorts

Cultural / Historic Centres

Winter Sports Resorts

Spas / Watering-Places

Day Trip Resorts

Fig 33   Distribution of resorts by type in Western Europe

form and, as Figure 34 shows, the main features are common to all; the distinction lies in their form and structure which relate to the resort function. In each case the tourist-oriented land and building uses are adjacent to the main focus of visitor attraction. The particular blend of resort activities and associated retail units gives a further measure of resort status and function.

Each category of resort has developed its building and land-use pattern in response to the particular demands of its pre-

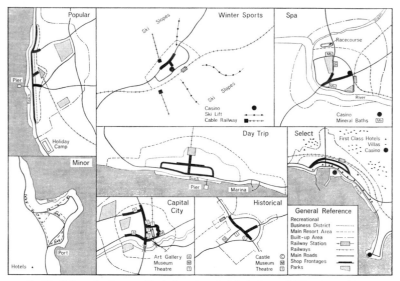

Fig 34   Schematic diagrams illustrating characteristic features of different resort types

dominant type of visitor. Thus the day-trip resorts attract a large proportion of working-class people from nearby conurbations and this is reflected by the resort sea front area with its amusement arcades and funfairs. Brighton, Southend and Zandvoort are typical examples. In complete contrast, those resorts whose main appeal lies in their historic or cultural associations attract higher income groups with very different tastes and requirements; there are many more museums, art galleries and similar cultural features.

The pattern of retail outlets also emphasises the distinction between resort types. Capital cities, select resorts, and to some extent the spas and cultural historic centres have more high-class retail outlets, bookshops, and expensive gift shops. The popular resorts and towns attracting large numbers of day trippers place more emphasis on cafes, restaurants, bars and brash novelty shops.

PROBLEMS AND PROSPECTS FOR FURTHER RESORT DEVELOPMENT

Although resort expansion is continuing apace along the Costa del Sol and Costa Brava, the most dramatic schemes for new resort developments are to be found in France where the government plans to spend well over £100 million up to the early 1980s.[41] A hundred miles of the Languedoc-Roussillon coast are being transformed from mud flats and marshes into a new Cote d'Azur. Six new resorts are being developed with a total capacity of 2 million visitors, and each has been zoned into areas for villas, apartments, hotels, holiday villages and camping sites.[42] Because of the harsh and arid coast a series of artificial harbours and lagoons have been created, with the emphasis on boating facilities. By the 1980s this massive development programme should provide 450,000 extra beds, moorings for 20,000 boats and 80,000 new jobs.[43] The high cost of developing the resorts' infrastructure (with land prices ranging from 50 to 2,000 francs per square metre)[44] has limited the availability of popular accommodation. In these low-density resorts a car is almost essential and this underlines their appeal to the middle-grade executive.

Resort development on a similar scale is planned for the Aquitaine coast. In 1970 the Aquitaine Coastal Development Commission began work on nine adjacent principal development units covering over 100 miles of coastline.[45] Over 22,000 new beds will be provided at sixteen selected points along the

12

coast,[46] with rapid new road and auto routes linking the resort complexes. New canals, marinas and lakeside developments are expected to attract thousands of pleasure craft to the region.

As part of the current five-year plan the French government is investing a further £23 million in the winter sports resorts of the French Alps.[47] Six resorts have been developed since 1946 and a further twelve are under construction, and by 1975 accommodation will be available for 100,000 extra people.

The vast scale of the French resort developments is reminiscent of the late Victorian/Edwardian era of resort growth when entrepreneurs had a great faith in the future of the holiday industry and poured in huge capital investments. Whether these new developments will relieve existing pressures on the popular holiday coasts as well as attract tourists otherwise destined for Spain or Portugal, is a question that must remain unanswered until the early 1980s.

The 1968 IUOTO *Survey of World Tourism* found that in ten European countries the growth of tourism had been hindered by lack of accommodation, and seven out of twelve countries felt that their planned increases in capacity would meet future demand.[48] The picture is bleak for Britain where the total of new and extended hotels has declined since 1970, and where a disproportionate share of the new building is concentrated on London.[49] The BTA estimated that 40,000 new beds would be needed by 1975 and it is probable that this shortage, if it continues, will inhibit the growth of tourism in Britain.

Camping grounds, caravan parks, holiday villages and holiday camps are increasing in number and competing with resorts for the present and potential tourist market. Because of their shorter season and much greater seasonal peak their overheads and general operating costs are much less and they are growing at a faster rate than the more traditional holiday accommodation.

Given these current problems there is a clear need for more market research on the part of resorts and their associated

regional tourist bodies. Any resort is interested in maintaining and increasing its share of the total tourist market and must seek ways and means of doing this. Until the market area or hinterland is known and a socio-economic profile of the visitors is obtained, publicity or promotional campaigns will not be fully effective. The potential tourist markets must be identified, together with their needs and preferences, if future resort development is to match potential demand. This research must be more than the mere collection and tabulation of facts as at present acquired by national tourist boards. The emphasis must be on the understanding of the basic relationships between the resorts or holiday regions and their existing tourist market. There needs to be an organised search for new knowledge so that rational policies and decisions can be arrived at in the holiday industry.

GLOSSARY

Resort Defined in the *Shorter Oxford English Dictionary* as: 'Place to which people go to for holiday-making, restoration of health, etc.'

Travel data Figures collected annually showing number of visitors by country of origin. The data are obtained either from frontier checks, hotel registrations, passport records or visa records.

Tourist In 1937 the League of Nations recommended the following definition of tourist: Any person travelling for a period of 24 hours or more in a country other than that in which he resides.
This would include:

(i) Persons travelling for pleasure, domestic reasons or health
(ii) Persons travelling to meetings
(iii) Persons travelling on business

(iv) Persons visiting as part of a sea cruise. Visitors travelling on holiday or for pleasure on day-trips to a country should be recorded separately.

Travel market For the purposes of this paper this term is taken to mean the country or geographic area that consumes the tourist-oriented goods and services at each resort.

CHAPTER NINE

The Planning and Management of Water Recreation Areas

WATER resources have long been a major element in the enjoyment of many forms of outdoor recreation, especially in maritime countries where a majority of holidays have traditionally been taken at the coast. More recently waterside areas, both coastal and inland, have become increasingly popular locations for second homes as well as the natural focus for recreation trips. The precise significance of water resources in the overall pattern of outdoor recreation is difficult to assess, but the available evidence suggests that it varies from area to area and in some may assume a dominant role. For example, in the United States the Outdoor Recreation Resources Review Commission estimated in 1962 that nationally about 25 per cent of all outdoor recreation was water-oriented,[1] while it has been suggested elsewhere that in the semi-arid western states the figure is charac-

teristically 60 per cent or more.[2] In smaller maritime countries with abundant water and a shortage of other recreation resources the figures may be even higher, most notably in the Netherlands where it has been estimated that 85 per cent of recreation activity days are spent at or in the water and another 5 per cent on the water.[3]

Such figures cover a wide variety of recreation experiences. Some activities, like swimming, fishing and boating, depend directly on the use of the water itself, while for other more passive pursuits the presence of water serves to enhance the recreation experience. Indeed it is in this role as a background and scenic asset that water is probably enjoyed by the majority of people in urbanised countries, for whom riverbanks and coast and lake shores are attractive locations for camping, picnicking and informal family recreation. Water resources are also often a vital element in wilderness areas, but it is not only in its natural state that water is a focus for recreation, for many of the dams and water projects of the western United States are themselves important tourist attractions. In many places the presence of water has been exploited by the development of recreation facilities with the effect of stimulating growth in the local economy.

The more active forms of water-based recreation may be conveniently divided into three categories: swimming and bathing, sport fishing and boating. Numerically most important in every country is swimming and bathing, which is typically enjoyed at some time by one-third or more of the total population. Relatively little organised swimming, however, takes place in outdoor waters and it is largely practised in an informal way as an adjunct to holidays and other recreation trips. As a result, swimming and bathing has shared in the rapid and continuous growth of outdoor recreation generally since the end of World War II. Associated with swimming are the more specialised activities of surfing and recreational diving which have also experienced considerable expansion in recent years.

Such activities, like swimming, are particularly associated with the coast, although swimming is also widely found on inland waters wherever it is not precluded by pollution or other considerations.

SPORT FISHING

Sport fishing has a long history in both Europe and North America, but it is in the United States that it is most highly developed. Here a high proportion of outdoor recreation opportunities are dependent on fishing and wildlife resources and fishing is often associated with other activities like camping, hunting, boating and the enjoyment of wilderness. It was estimated in 1970 that more than 24 million persons aged twelve and over regularly fished in fresh waters with another 8 million fishing at the coast.[4] If the under-twelves and those who fish occasionally are taken into account, there may be as many as 60 million anglers in the United States. Comparable figures for European countries tend to be very much lower, although everywhere sport fishing is by far the most important single water-based activity apart from swimming. In 1969, for example, England and Wales had nearly 3 million anglers[5] and the Netherlands more than 700,000.[6] Not only is the number of participants high but it appears to be growing rapidly, particularly in North America. The number of regular fishermen in the United States grew by one-third during the 1960s and is expected to double by 2000, while projections for Canada suggest that the demand for sport fishing may increase six times over the next thirty years.[7]

BOATING

Boating has always been a popular outdoor pursuit and in recent years it has experienced considerable diversification so that it now encompasses a varied range of activities, including

canoeing, rowing, sailing, power-boating, hydro-planing, water skiing and cruising. Again it is in the United States that boating has developed most rapidly and there are now well over 8 million recreational craft compared to 2·4 million in 1947.[8] This expansion has been made possible by the development of the outboard motor, the introduction of new construction techniques and the use of mass production methods which have meant that large numbers of small motor-powered boats have become available at relatively low cost. There is now one boat for every seven cars in the United States.

This wide extension of boat ownership may be attributed to a number of factors. In part it is simply a function of the prosperity of the American economy, for it has been shown that the ownership of boats and participation in boating tends to increase with age until the late forties, a trend which is presumably related to levels of disposable income.[9] Of equal importance is the fact that the abundance of inland waters in North America has provided relatively safe conditions for a massive expansion in the use of small motor boats. This has meant that recreational craft are often used primarily as a means of transport and most boating is done in combination with other activities, like picnicking, camping, sight-seeing, hunting and particularly fishing with which more than 80 per cent of all boating is associated. The possession of boats also enables people to explore lakes and rivers in otherwise inaccessible wilderness areas, often to seek out new fishing and hunting spots. Coupled with this is the desire for speed which is seen in the rapid development of water skiing and the use of powerful motor boats. The continuing increase in the size of motors in use has been one of the most significant trends within the general expansion of boating in the United States, where the overall horsepower of outboard motors sold rose from 4·7 in 1947 to 28·2 in 1965.[10]

Generally, boating appears to be at a much earlier stage of development in Europe, except possibly for Scandinavia where

relatively high levels of boat-ownership have been recorded.[11]
Here the long tradition of sea-faring together with extensive
inland lakes and a lengthy coastline in the relatively sheltered
waters of the Baltic have made boating one of the most popular
forms of outdoor recreation. Elsewhere the number of boats
remains small, although in all countries it is increasing rapidly.
In France, for example, the pleasure boat fleet increased five
times between 1950 and 1965 when it reached a total of 120,000
craft.[12] In such countries boating tends to be still the province
of a small minority of the population, a significant number
of whom belong to clubs dedicated to competition and other
organised activity. This is in marked contrast to the United
States where more than 40 million people enjoy boating as a
form of mass recreation in which clubs play only a minor role.
Such differences are also reflected in the relative importance of
outboard motor boats which make up about two-thirds of
America's recreational boats, whereas yachts and other more
specialised craft remain dominant in many European countries. The extent to which North American experience will be
repeated in Europe remains uncertain, but changes are already
taking place within the general expansion of boating. Traditional sailing craft have tended to decline in relative importance
as motor boats have grown in popularity, a trend which has
been particularly noted in Great Britain and the Netherlands.

THE GROWTH OF DEMAND

The factors underlying this expansion appear to be those
which have been identified with respect to the general growth
of participation in outdoor recreation. These include the shorter
working week, longer paid holidays, a higher proportion of the
population spending longer in full-time education, rising levels
of personal income and the increased mobility given by the
motor car. The motor car has been particularly important in
the water sports because of the need to move boats and other

bulky equipment and during the 1950s and 1960s the fastest growing item of boat sales in the United States was the trailer.[13] Greater mobility has had the effect both of spreading boating into new areas and of increasing the substitutability between different water resources. What such factors do not explain is why rates of growth in the water sports should have been faster than those in most other forms of outdoor recreation. To some extent, this is probably due to the recent introduction of many water-based activities, a factor which makes it difficult to predict future trends. Certainly there seems no reason why the water sports should not continue to be among the most popular outdoor activities and the projections which have been made suggest that participation in water-based recreation will increase dramatically during the last quarter of the twentieth century.

Until recent years the growth of water recreation was largely based on the use of natural resources and existing facilities. In maritime countries, for example, much activity was concentrated in sheltered coastal waters where ports and fishing harbours usually provided the necessary launching points, moorings and other facilities. Similarly the major rivers of both Europe and North America offered a wide range of recreation opportunities, while natural lakes accessible to the main centres of population were often intensively developed for recreation use. As recreation demands built up, these resources came under increasing pressure and growing attention has been paid to investment in purpose-built facilities and the use of man-made water resources usually created for some other purpose.

MARINAS

To some extent, the capacity of existing resources to support recreational use can be increased by the development of more permanent facilities. This applies particularly to coastal areas where the provision of moorings for recreational craft has

proved increasingly difficult. The problem is that such craft tend to be used infrequently for short periods and to spend most of the year in harbour where they require a permanent berth. The extent of such demand may be illustrated by an estimate made in West Germany that the space occupied by a single sport boat together with its associated car parking and other facilities may be equivalent to the site of a detached house.[14] In many areas the facilities available in existing ports and harbours proved inadequate, even where the original fishing function was completely superseded by a recreation function. The solution usually adopted is the creation of artificial yacht harbours or marinas, which have sometimes been used to stimulate growth in new areas rather than to make up existing shortages of facilities. Such specialised harbours were pioneered in the United States where they were typically developed by private enterprise, usually on a large scale and providing moorings for large numbers of pleasure craft together with extensive service facilities on which part of the profitability was based.

In Europe the marina has been a much more recent development and most have been built only since the early 1960s. The French government, in particular, has made extensive use of marina facilities in the development of tourist accommodation on the Mediterranean coast. Since 1965 the large-scale investment of both private and public capital on the French Riviera has led to a massive expansion of marinas so that facilities for 25,000 pleasure craft were available by November 1971.[15] Unlike the typical North American marina, these have been developed mainly as self-contained communities with residential accommodation and other facilities. Similarly the Languedoc-Roussillon project, which was approved in 1964, provides for the creation of twenty new harbours with facilities for 40,000 pleasure craft, again closely integrated with resort accommodation. Elsewhere marina development has tended to be more spasmodic and is mainly confined to the most popular sailing

areas. In Britain, for example, marinas are concentrated in the traditional sailing areas along the south coast of England and are generally smaller than their North American counterparts and lack the residential accommodation of those in France.[16]

INLAND WATERWAYS

Inland, some expansion of recreational use has been achieved by the creation of new access points to rivers and lakes and by the provision of marinas and other facilities, but more important has been the exploitation of man-made water resources. The first of these to have their recreational potential recognised were the canal and inland waterway systems of Europe and eastern North America. Some of these have long ceased to have any significant commercial function and are now mainly regarded as a recreational resource. This fact was formally recognised in Great Britain when the Transport Act 1968 committed the government to maintaining more than 1,100 miles of canal primarily for use by powered pleasure craft. Similarly the Department of Transport in Canada operates the canals of Ontario and Quebec which cater almost exclusively for tourist boating. Even where inland waterways are still heavily used by commercial traffic, some provision is often made for recreational craft. In West Germany, for example, the larger commercial locks on major waterways usually incorporate a small boat lock for recreational users, while the St Lawrence Seaway in North America similarly provides facilities designed to accommodate pleasure craft.

WET MINERAL WORKINGS

A rather different kind of resource is the wet pit created by abandoned mineral workings. Such resources appear to be of some importance in those parts of northern Europe where sand and gravel extraction has sometimes formed extensive

areas of water along the valley floors of major rivers. In many areas these gravel lagoons have long been used for fishing, but their exploitation for other forms of recreation has been more recent. In France, for example, the post-war period has seen the extensive development of sailing and other water sports on wet pits along the Seine around Paris where proposals have been put forward for the creation of water parks.[17] Ambitious plans have also been made for the recreational development of groups of gravel pits in several parts of Great Britain, most notably along the upper Thames where by 1980 some 3,000 acres of water within the Cotswold Water Park will provide facilities for a wide range of water sports as well as for passive recreation.[18] A rather different development is the National Water Recreation Centre at Holme Pierrepont on the River Trent, where a 2,000 metre rowing course together with facilities for water skiing and other sports has been created by the planned extraction of gravel.[19] Similar developments in North America have tended to be overshadowed by large federal multi-purpose projects, but they are sometimes important locally, as in Kansas where flooded strip pits left by open-cast coal mining have been opened up for fishing and other activities.[20]

MULTI-PURPOSE WATER PROJECTS

More important in the period since 1945 has been the growing recreational use of reservoirs. Such use has been most developed in the United States where the activities of three federal agencies have added significantly to the available recreational opportunities, although they were set up for other purposes. The dams of the Tennessee Valley Authority and the US Army Corps of Engineers were originally multi-purpose projects concerned with flood control, power generation, irrigation and the improvement of navigation, while those of the Bureau of Reclamation were primarily irrigation projects designed to

meet the water needs of the arid west. Some recreational development in association with these dams was carried out at an early stage by the National Parks Service and other agencies, but the acceptance of recreation as a valid purpose of such projects did not come until the 1940s. Since then many federal reservoirs have incorporated extensive facilities for camping, sight-seeing, fishing, boating and other water sports. As a result they have played a major role in meeting the rapidly increasing demands for water recreation facilities, particularly in the western states where they will become increasingly important because natural resources are so limited. Some indication of this growth is given by Lake Mead behind Hoover Dam, which attracted 3·6 million visitors in 1965 compared with less than 600,000 before World War II,[21] while it has been estimated that the recreational use of all federal reservoirs was increasing at the rate of 10 per cent a year during the mid-1960s.

Comparable projects have also been carried out in Canada, but the scale of reservoir construction in Europe tends to be very much smaller than in North America and they are more often designed for a single purpose, particularly domestic water supply. Probably the best-known multi-purpose water projects are those of the Ruhr Valley which have been mainly developed since 1945 and incorporated facilities for bankside recreation and for such active sports as swimming, water skiing and sailing right from the start.[22] A similar multi-purpose approach has been adopted in the Ijsselmeer project in the Netherlands, where the channels and peripheral lakes provide extensive shallow water areas well suited to the recreational use of small boats. Here facilities are being provided for both active and passive recreational use, including beaches with associated car parking and designated areas for fishing, speed boating and water skiing together with a range of boating facilities from sophisticated yacht harbours to simple slipways and landing stages.[23]

WATER SUPPLY RESERVOIRS

Some of the most important water resources which have not yet been fully developed for recreational purposes are water supply reservoirs. This applies particularly in Great Britain and the United States, where the introduction of limited recreational use has followed a remarkably similar pattern. In both countries municipal water utilities have traditionally sought to obtain their supplies from the cleanest possible source which they then protected from any possible contamination on the grounds that the prevention of pollution was better than unnecessary treatment. In the past this usually meant the exploitation of upland catchments from which the public was sometimes totally excluded. With the rapid growth of recreation demands such utilities have come under increasing pressure from sportsmen's organisations and other groups to open up their reservoirs for various kinds of water sports. This they have proved reluctant to do for a number of reasons, the most important of which was the increased risk of disease transmission that such a change of policy would involve. Other factors were that the introduction of recreational use might offend consumers, lead to increased treatment costs, require changes in reservoir operation or necessitate the acquisition of additional land and the improvement of access roads.

This does not mean that there was no recreational use of such reservoirs, for in both Great Britain and the United States public fishing was permitted at a few before World War I. Since then there has been a gradual extension so that by the early 1960s fishing was probably permitted at the majority of water supply reservoirs. The introduction of other activities has proved more difficult. The American Water Works Association issued its first policy statement on recreation in 1958, which was subsequently revised in 1965 and 1971.[24] This emphasised that the primary purpose of water supply reservoirs was to provide a safe and appealing product and that no uses should be

admitted which would lead to any deterioration in water quality. Any recreational use should be carefully controlled and unless there was full treatment body immersion activities such as swimming, boating and water skiing should not be permitted.

In Great Britain a similar set of recommendations was issued by the Institution of Water Engineers in 1963 and revised in 1972.[25] This suggested that no objection could normally be raised to fishing, providing that it was carefully regulated, and that sailing and rowing might also be allowed subject to a number of safeguards. Swimming, canoeing and water skiing were considered unsuitable and should be prohibited. These recommendations were followed in 1966 by a joint circular from the Department of Education and Science and the Ministry of Land and Natural Resources asking water utilities to consider whether they might be able to extend the recreational use of their reservoirs.[26] The result of this has been a significant relaxation of attitudes, although by 1969 sailing was permitted at only thirty-nine out of more than 300 reservoirs of 10 acres or more in England and Wales.[27] More important has been the fact that both sailing and fishing have been developed at all the major new reservoirs constructed since the early 1960s. In part, this is a reflection of the changing nature of the water supply industry which is depending increasingly on the use of regulating reservoirs where controls over water quality cannot be applied. A similar pattern has been followed in the United States as more water utilities are forced to make use of already polluted water.

MANAGEMENT PROBLEMS

The rapid expansion of water-based recreation has led to a number of management problems. One of the most serious is that most water resources are managed primarily for non-recreational purposes, including navigation, flood control, irrigation, water supply, power generation, nature conservation and the disposal of waste. In many cases these other functions

limit the nature and extent of the recreational use which can be permitted. The risk of pollution, for example, prevents the use of water supply reservoirs for certain activities, while the major changes in water level which are an integral part of flood control and irrigation projects sometimes makes the introduction of recreational boating difficult. Similarly, the needs of commercial traffic have led to growing demands for stringent controls over pleasure craft on the River Seine and some other European waterways. Even in the multi-purpose water projects of the United States recreation was traditionally permitted only so far as it did not interfere with the primary purposes of the project and the federal agencies involved have recently had to add recreation to other long-established management functions. In Great Britain the British Waterways Board has faced a similar problem since it was made responsible under the Transport Act 1968 for a waterway system the bulk of which would handle only pleasure craft.

A related problem concerns the financing of facilities. In both Great Britain and the United States a great deal of attention has been given to the assessment of benefits resulting from the recreational use of water resources, but methods of financing and of charging for such use remain unsatisfactory. One of the most common principles embodied in water resource policies is that the costs of management and investment should be borne by the beneficiaries so that development programmes should be self-supporting. Because recreation has traditionally been regarded as a residual use, this principle has normally been interpreted as meaning that recreational users should be charged only for those additional costs which they impose on the managing authority. In the United States charges for the recreational use of reservoirs vary considerably, but federal agencies have often received only token amounts for such use and the introduction of more realistic user fees has led to controversy.[28] Similarly those water utilities in Great Britain which have developed sailing and fishing on their reservoirs

usually set their charges at a level which is considered adequate to cover those additional administrative and other costs which can be directly attributed to recreational use.

The problem is that such charges are unlikely to produce sufficient revenue for further investment in facilities unless they are raised to unacceptable levels. In the United States federal agencies have tried to solve this problem by granting concessions at reservoir sites to private enterprise which then provides and manages the necessary facilities. The nature of these concessions varies widely, but generally admission to the reservoir itself remains free and the concessionaire makes his profit from the provision of camping sites, moorings, slipways, boat hire or other services and by the sale of food, drink and sporting equipment. It has been claimed that the availability of private investment has been a major factor in the rapid development of recreation facilities at reservoirs, although there has also been criticism of the standard of services provided and of the poor return to federal agencies. The development of marinas, in particular, has tended to follow this pattern in both Europe and North America, although even here an injection of public funds has sometimes been necessary, as has been recognised in the Canadian government's marina policy[29] and in the provision of boating facilities along France's Mediterranean coast.

A rather different approach has been adopted in some other countries, most notably in Great Britain and France, where water recreation facilities have largely been developed under the auspices of private sports clubs and organisations, sometimes with financial assistance from government sources. In Great Britain, for example, the use of water supply reservoirs for sailing has been granted exclusively to private clubs, usually under a lease giving them rights over the use of the water together with sufficient land to build a clubhouse and other facilities. The development of such facilities has sometimes been assisted by grants from the Sports Council or local authorities,

especially where provision is made for their use by school and youth groups. This approach has the important advantage to the water utility that responsibility for the day-to-day management of recreational use can be delegated to the club, generally subject to clearly defined conditions contained in the lease. Set against this is the fact that the granting of exclusive rights to a particular group of recreational users tends to create a situation in which it is difficult to respond to changes in the pattern of demand.

The provision and management of facilities for water-based recreation has also been hampered by the rather complex pattern of property and other rights associated with water resources in both Europe and North America. Such rights tend to vary from one country to another and between states in federal systems, and uncertainties about their precise nature are a common problem. Recreational users are particularly concerned with rights relating to fishing and navigation. Fishing rights to inland waters commonly belong to the owners of the adjacent land, so that in Europe most fishing is in private hands. Generally rights of public use for other activities are enjoyed on navigable rivers and waterways, although doubts sometimes exist about which waters are navigable, particularly in countries like France where the distinction is based on criteria which take no account of modern recreational uses. More important is the fact that the ownership of land adjacent to water tends to be widely dispersed and the recreational use of many resources is restricted because their banks are in private ownership. In North America land surrounding lakes and other water bodies has often been intensively developed, mainly for weekend cottages and other residential accommodation, and the resulting shortage of public access points has sometimes become a serious problem. Similar problems are found in France and other European countries where they are particularly associated with the recent development of second homes.

RECREATION AND WATER RESOURCE ADMINISTRATION

The major expansion of water-based recreation since the end of World War II has occurred at a time when industrial development and rapid urbanisation have also led to a massive increase in the demand for water. This, coupled with growing concern about the problem of pollution and water quality, has meant that the reform of systems of water administration and management has become an urgent need in many countries. Previously the development of water resources tended to be fragmentary and unco-ordinated and was carried out by a number of largely single-purpose authorities concerned with such matters as navigation, flood control, power production, irrigation and water supply. The value of a multi-purpose river basin approach was demonstrated during the 1930s by the Tennessee Valley Authority in North America and in Europe by the Compagnie Nationale du Rhône which has carried out an integrated programme of regional development in southern France, including power generation, agricultural improvement, irrigation, flood control and navigation.[30] As a result, reorganisation has generally taken the form of the gradual amalgamation of small authorities responsible for a single aspect of water management into larger units which could carry out more comprehensive planning.

This process is best seen in Great Britain where the progressive evolution of larger authorities responsible for water conservation and supply has been achieved through a series of reforms beginning in 1945 and culminating with the Water Act of 1973. This creates ten new multi-purpose regional water authorities in England and Wales which are responsible for most aspects of water management and which, for the first time, have been given the statutory duty of promoting the better use of their water space for sport, recreation and amenity. Elsewhere a number of countries have reorganised their water management

structures since the late 1950s, most notably West Germany in 1957, France in 1964 and the United States in 1965. In most cases the new structure has taken a similar form to that established in Great Britain since 1963, with a number of large river basin or regional authorities and a central advisory body. The objectives given to these authorities tend to be fairly general and concerned with such activities as water supply, the conservation of resources, regional development and the control of pollution. Recreation as such is not generally included and it is mainly in North America that this has been firmly established as a recognised purpose of water resource management.

CONCLUSIONS

It is clear that in the United States water-based recreation has reached a stage of development far in advance of that of most European countries. Favourable geographical conditions and a high standard of living have encouraged a rapid and continuous growth of participation in sport fishing and other activities which has been particularly associated with rising levels of boat-ownership. The various federal and state agencies have responded to these increased demands by providing extensive facilities, often of a high standard. This has been achieved by the evolution of a policy in which recreation is regarded as an important purpose of most water projects. The development of facilities at an early stage was made possible by the granting of concessions to private enterprise, especially for the construction of marinas which have provided increasingly sophisticated services, but the emphasis on commercial objectives which this involves has been counterbalanced by the wide availability of public waters. Federal funds have been of particular value here, both in the stocking and management of fisheries and in the provision of simple launching facilities for those who trail their boats to the water. In many areas public and commercial facilities co-exist without apparent conflict.

The extent to which American experience is relevant to the future development of water-based recreation in Europe is probably rather less than has sometimes been suggested. Certainly the various authorities concerned with the management of water resources will be faced with growing demands for the provision of recreational facilities, even where this is not explicitly included as one of their functions. At the same time, existing resources are more limited and their development is likely to follow a different pattern. There is little scope for the sort of large-scale multi-purpose project which has characterised federal involvement in recreational development in the United States. It also seems likely that the well-established club organisations in countries such as Great Britain and France will continue to play a significant role in the provision of facilities. Whether concessions to private enterprise will develop in the same way as they have in North America will depend very much on local conditions, although it is probable that they will become increasingly important.

Similarly the lack of suitable inland waters is likely to limit the popularity of the small outboard motor boat which has been so prominent in the United States. Even so, some of the most serious management problems will stem from the rapid growth of casual boating in which there is a high proportion of unskilled and inexperienced participants who take to the water only infrequently. This kind of demand will need to be accommodated largely on inland waters and in the most sheltered coastal areas where the introduction of intensive management techniques will probably be required to avoid congestion and prevent conflict. The growth of small craft with powerful outboard motors is a particular problem here, mainly because in inexperienced hands they can be a source of danger to other users. Generally the authorities responsible for the administration of these resources are inadequately equipped to deal with such problems and there is little experience of the use of the necessary management techniques in either Europe or North America.

CHAPTER TEN

The Economics of Outdoor Recreation

No single phrase or sentence is universally acceptable as an adequate definition of the subject matter of economics; however, one of its prime concerns is the choice between alternative uses of limited natural resources. Society is continually faced with choices; between schools and hospitals, beef and pork, new housing and subsidised railway lines. Economists attempt to help the decision-maker, who must choose, by comparing as objectively as possible the public's valuation of various goods and services. As the demand for outdoor recreation grows, more pressing questions will be asked about the relative merits of spending increasing amounts of money on recreation rather than on the many alternatives available. To answer these questions the benefits of recreation need to be measured in some way which will permit them to be compared directly both with the benefits of other goods and services and also with the costs of providing the recreation facilities. Economists, who

are accustomed to comparing benefits of different investments, over the last ten to fifteen years have shown increasing interest in the benefits of outdoor recreation.

The benefits of recreation can be expected to be related to the demand for the facilities.[1] It is thus necessary to measure present demand, predict future demands and then to associate with the demands a measure of recreation benefits. Prediction is a difficult and hazardous business, requiring considerable statistical expertise and often posing severe data problems; it is by no means a task only for the economist. Valuation of benefits of investments, however, is such an integral part of economic theory that the economist's most important contribution is probably his work on the measurement of recreation benefits. This chapter therefore concentrates on this issue.

THE MEASURABILITY OF RECREATION BENEFITS

If benefits of various goods and services are to be compared they must be measured in terms of some common denominator. The most usual such denominator is money, and little objection is raised to this in most cases; decisions as to how much of most commodities should be produced is left to private firms producing in response to the public's willingness to pay. The use of a monetary measure of benefits is especially helpful when benefits must be compared with costs.

Attempts to place monetary values on recreation benefits have aroused much opposition, basically on three counts. First, it is suggested that monetary valuation is inappropriate because of the subjective nature of the recreation experience. Secondly, recreation may give rise to substantial secondary benefits which the recreationist himself does not recognise in his willingness to pay for a facility. Thirdly, it is argued that recreation is a merit want, such as education, which should be provided free of charge to all citizens as a matter of social policy.

Two examples of the first argument are quoted by Hoch.[2] A California Public Outdoor Recreation Plan stated: 'The aesthetic values of fish and wildlife should be recognised in terms other than economic value.' A Forest Service pamphlet, discussing landscape stated that: 'Inspiration such as this cannot be measured in dollars and cents.' Trice and Wood[3] add to this argument the statement: 'Primary benefits from recreation are personal and varied and, therefore, not readily measurable in dollar terms.'

However, the benefits of *any* commodity depend on the consumer and are therefore also personal, varied, and subjective. The consumer himself, in fact, reduces his preferences and his subjective assessment of benefits to a monetary scale by his willingness to give up more of his limited income for some goods than for others. Price acts as a common denominator, giving some indication, free from planners' preferences, of the satisfaction derived by consumers from various commodities. Clawson and Knetsch[4] write:

For many significant purposes the personal values or intangibility of recreation are of little concern as such; they are reflected and gain importance by what people are willing to give up to obtain them.

The second argument against measuring recreation benefits is that secondary benefits (for example employment and health effects) are substantial, and that willingness to pay on the part of consumers themselves represents a small part of the total benefit. The existence of secondary benefits is not an argument for not measuring primary benefits; rather it is an argument for trying to measure both primary *and* secondary benefits.

The idea that recreation is a 'merit want' is put forward by Robinson;[5] he says that society intervenes where recreation is concerned because it does not like the allocation of resources resulting from a free market, so that 'the supplying of these services is therefore undertaken whether the consumer wants them or not'.

Mack and Myers[6] argue that recreation is a good to which superior merit is attached. Such arguments must be used with extreme caution; they imply that people ought to have something which they would not freely choose for themselves.[7] This may simply be an attempt to impose *planners'* preferences rather than working on the basis of *consumers'* preferences.

EARLY METHODS OF MEASURING RECREATION BENEFITS

Interest in monetary figures of recreation benefits developed in the late 1940s, chiefly among United States water-resource planners, and spread to Britain in the 1960s. The most popular approach has been based on 'informed judgement', as embodied in US Senate Document 97,[8] which suggested that the value of a general outdoor recreation day was within the range $0·5 to $1·5, while that of a specialised outdoor recreation day should be $2·0 to $6·0. Such values, though representing the consensus of experienced people and intended to reflect the public's willingness to pay, are essentially only planners' prices which may lead to a uniform but not to an economically correct treatment.

A method of evaluation based more firmly on consumer behaviour has been termed the 'gross expenditure method'. Primary recreation benefits are estimated as the aggregate of all expenses incurred by visitors, including costs of travel, food, hotel bills and other services. This procedure involves two principal errors. First, much of the expenditure relates not to the recreation itself but to ancillary services. Second, it implies that, in order to maximise benefits, recreation facilities should be so sited as to maximise the distance people actually travel; a recreation area within walking distance of one's home would give no benefit at all.

A further method, suggested in a report of the US National Park Service,[9] involves the assumption that benefits are always

twice the costs of any recreation development. Clearly this is of no help when choosing between alternatives, because all projects appear worthwhile and equally profitable. In the literature, reference can be found to a 'net value added' approach. The assumption implicit in this method is that the objective is to increase the prosperity of local residents, for benefits are measured as the increase in local incomes arising from recreation development. In some cases this method will be appropriate but, from the national point of view, much of the consumers' expenditure may represent no net benefit, because it is merely transferred from other areas.[10]

THE SURPLUS APPROACH TO MEASURING RECREATION BENEFITS

In this chapter it is assumed that recreation is being considered from the national point of view; interest must be focused on benefits to the consumers themselves rather than on increases in local incomes. In cost-benefit analysis, economists have made frequent use of the concept of 'consumers' surplus' as a measure of the benefits received from investments. This surplus is the difference between the maximum amount that consumers would be willing to pay and the amount they actually do pay. If a recreational site is of high quality, benefits are high, because people would be willing to pay a high price if

TABLE 22   *Hypothetical relationship of visit rates and costs for five distance zones*

Zone	Cost of visit (£)	No of visits per capita	Population	Total visits
A	0·20	0·05	1000	50
B	0·40	0·04	2000	80
C	0·60	0·03	3000	90
D	0·80	0·02	2000	40
E	1·00	0·01	1000	10

Total visits = 270

they had to. If the site is near to centres of population benefits are high because people do not actually pay much.

The correct procedure for measuring surplus will be illustrated by referring to the hypothetical data on visits and costs given in Table 22, which give the straight line relationship between visit rates and costs illustrated in Figure 35. In the case

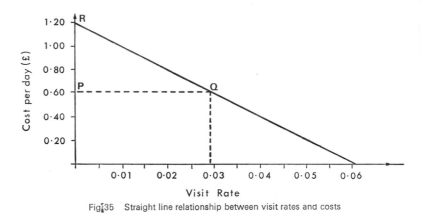

Fig 35   Straight line relationship between visit rates and costs

of zone C, the expenditure per capita is £(0·6 × 0·03) = £0·018, and total expenditure is £(0·018 × 3000) = £54. The benefit per capita, however, is the area PQR, which is equal to £0·009, so the total surplus will be £27. In a similar manner, the benefits to each zone can be calculated, and the results are given in Table 23.

TABLE 23   Recreation benefits (based on data in Table 22)

Zone	Benefits (£)	
A	25·00	
B	32·00	
C	27·00	Total benefits = £93
D	8·00	
E	1·00	

This method has been formalised somewhat by Clawson[11] who suggested a procedure for the derivation of a demand curve

for the recreation site itself, relating number of visits to levels of admission charges. The information in Table 22 gives us one point on this demand curve, namely 270 visits at the existing admission charge, assumed in this case to be zero. The effect of raising the admission charge to 20p will now be examined; the costs per visit from each zone will now be those shown in the second column of Table 24. To discover the likely visit rates at the new levels of cost it is necessary to look back at Table 22, where at a cost of £0·40 the visit rate was 0·04. If it is assumed that all the zones have homogeneous populations, the new visit rate from zone A at a cost of £0·40 will also be 0·04.[12] Similarly the new visit rate from zone C will be equal to the former rate from zone B and so on. Continuing this procedure it is possible to draw up the final demand schedule shown in Table 25.

TABLE 24   Visit rates and costs if admission charge is £0·20

Zone	Cost of visit (£)	Visit rate	Population	Visits
A	0·40	0·04	1000	40
B	0·60	0·03	2000	60
C	0·80	0·02	3000	60
D	1·00	0·01	2000	20
E	1·20	0·00	1000	0
			Total visits = 180	

TABLE 25   Final demand curve for recreation site

Admission Charge (£)	Visits
0·00	270
0·20	180
0·40	100
0·60	40
0·80	10
1·00	0

The demand curve for the site itself can be drawn from the information in Table 25, and the benefits of the recreation opportunity will be the area under the curve, the shaded area in Figure 36, which proved to be £93, the figure calculated in Table 23.

A serious shortcoming of the Clawson methodology is its

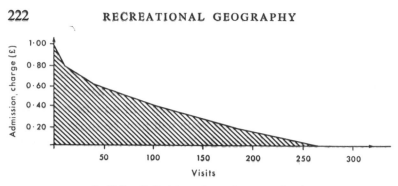

Fig 36 Hypothetical demand curve for a recreation site

failure to take account of benefits in the form of time savings; it only allows for savings in money costs. The visit rate from zone A at a money cost of £0·40 is likely to be higher than that from zone B at the same money cost, because the journey from B will take longer than that from A. The Clawson approach underestimates the number of visits from each zone for each simulated increase in admission charge and will therefore underestimate recreation benefits. This bias, which has not been overlooked in the literature, may be substantial, but at least it is consistent in direction and theoretically is not insuperable. A good deal of research effort is being devoted to the question of the value people place on the time they spend travelling, but until clearer results emerge the recreation analyst must remain content to employ sensitivity tests to see how benefits vary as the assumed value of time is altered. It is always possible to determine what the time value would have to be to make particular investments worthwhile.

From the point of view of economic theory the surplus methods of estimating recreation benefits are by far the most reliable. A further important consideration is how well the method works in practice.

THE CLAWSON APPROACH IN PRACTICE

The principle objective of the quantitative measurement of

recreation benefits is to be able to predict the benefits of any new facilities, so that a proper appraisal of investments in such facilities may be undertaken. Simple Clawson-type studies are useful, in that they establish the possibility of monetary valuations and also in that they provide experience of the possible magnitudes of such benefits when new facilities similar to existing ones are being contemplated. Such studies are not numerous. Clawson himself[13] and Knetsch[14] have illustrated the straightforward use of the method and work has continued in the United States, but empirical applications in the United Kingdom have been few. The method has been applied to sailing, angling and day visiting at Derwent Reservoir, Durham, by Lewis and Whitby,[15] and to day visiting in the Lake District by Mansfield;[16] and similar work on day visiting has been undertaken by Burton[17] and Colenutt.[18] However, the most detailed study of the Clawson methodology in Britain appears to be that undertaken by the author, in which the method was applied to trout fishing and sailing at Grafham Water in Huntingdonshire.

The most important requirement for a Clawson-type study is that data should be available on origins of visitors. As each angler has to sign his name and address in an anglers' register this provides a daily record of the number of anglers and of their geographical origin.

In the case of sailing, collection of the necessary data is not so easy. Access to a club membership list indicates where the members live, but is not sufficient to tell how many actual visits originate in each distance zone. In a postal questionnaire for Grafham (including questions on income, age and employment) a 62 per cent response rate was obtained.

A further problem in establishing sailing demand is the degree of institutional and educational use made of club facilities. Information on visits by university or college groups is likely to be difficult to obtain, while, for educational visits, the case for not trying to measure benefits is perhaps a reasonable one. In

taking children to sail one is offering them education, the *opportunity* to sample an activity to see if they like it. Sailing clubs often organise open meetings, and information on the geographical origins of such visitors may not be readily available.

Once each visit is allocated to a distance zone a problem common to both sailing and angling arises. A relationship between visit rates and costs must be estimated, and this requires

TABLE 26   Visit rates and costs, angling and sailing,
Grafham Water, 1968

| | ANGLING | | | SAILING | |
Zone	Visits per 100,000 population	Total cost per visit (including fishing charge of £1·00)	Zone	Visits per 100,000 population	Total cost per visit (£)
A	517	1·25	A	7,114	0·07
B	341	1·42	B	4,782	0·14
C	74	1·68	C	1,113	0·23
D	29	1·94	D	620	0·33
E	7	2·44	E	288	0·42
F	2·5	2·94	F	51	0·52
G	0·4	3·46	G	28	0·61
H	0·0	4·50	H	10·5	0·71
			J	1·2	0·80
			K	1·6	0·89
			L	0·5	1·04
			M	0·2	1·27

transforming distances into travel costs. The figure of money costs per mile used has a great impact on the estimates of the final demand curve. For example, in the case of angling in 1967, if a figure of 0·87 pence per mile is used it is predicted that, if a fishing charge increased from £1 to £1·60, the number of visits would be 5,739. If the cost per mile were 3·739p per mile, 12,722 visits would be predicted.[19] In view of the obvious importance of this issue the questionnaires distributed to anglers and sailing club members included a question designed to establish visitors' perceived costs of travel. Although the resulting estimates varied over a wide range, there was a marked cen-

tral tendency, giving an average (both mode and median) of about 1·25p per mile. This figure was then used in all subsequent calculations. To obtain accurate estimates of the cost per angler it was important to establish average car-occupancy and also the costs incurred by those persons who could not complete the return journey from home to Grafham in a single day.

As a result of the research described so far the data shown in Table 26 were obtained. The next step is to estimate the mathematical relationship between visit rates and costs. What form should the equation take? The usual approach is to estimate a number of different equations by the method of least squares regression and then choose the equation giving the best fit, measuring goodness of fit by the value of r^2. For both activities a number of equations gave values of r^2 in excess of 0·9, but they gave very different predictions of the impact of raising admission charges. Further research on angling showed that this sensitivity to the form of the equation could be virtually eliminated by increasing the number of distance zones from eight to twenty-seven; in the analysis of the 1968 data twenty-seven zones were used.

Before estimating the equation relating visit rates and costs, the figures of costs were increased to allow for the value of time spent in travelling. Various time values were used. Some resulting estimates of the final demand schedules are shown in Table 27. It can be seen that sailing appears much more sensitive to price than is trout angling, and this is evident also in Table 26. On this evidence it is more important that sailing facilities should be located nearer to centres of population than is the case with game fishing. This is not really surprising, because to obtain the full benefit of a sailing club subscription, members must visit the club regularly and this makes distance a most important factor.

The next task is the estimation, from these demand schedules, of recreation benefits. Strictly speaking the net benefit from recreation, the benefit over and above that from alternatives, is

14

TABLE 27 Final demand schedules for angling and sailing, Grafham Water, 1968

Fishing charge (£)	Angling visits if time value is:			Daily sailing charge	Sailing visits if time value is:		
	15p an hour	22½p an hour	30p an hour		15p an hour	22½p an hour	30p an hour
1·00	20,656	20,656	20,656	0·00	36,157	36,366	36,526
1·20	13,994	14,729	15,550	0·10	17,012	19,013	20,657
1·40	8,365	9,950	11,159	0·20	8,968	10,968	12,704
1·60	5,362	6,812	7,799	0·30	5,108	6,776	7,477
1·80	3,426	4,531	5,694	0·40	3,097	4,399	5,635
2·00	2,503	3,139	3,960	0·50	1,936	2,954	3,969
3·00	376	768	1,192	0·70	802	1,423	2,099
4·00	35	96	249	1·00	218	507	871
5·00	1	4	20	2·00	0	12	41
6·00	0	0	0	3·00	0	0	0

solely the consumers' surplus. In the case of sailing this will be the total area under the demand curve (cf Figure 36), while in the case of angling it will be the area under the curve but above a horizontal line drawn through the existing fishing charge of £1·00. However, if the economic return on recreation is to be compared with the rate of return on private investment, it appears necessary to include as a benefit the actual payments made by participants, ie fishing charges, sailing club membership fees and boat dues. Figures of benefits are given in Table 28.[20]

TABLE 28   Benefits from angling and sailing, Grafham Water, 1968

Time value	BENEFITS FROM ANGLING			BENEFITS FROM SAILING		
(per hour)	Surplus	Fees	Total	Surplus	Fees	Total
15 pence	9,697	20,656	30,353	5,624	12,500	18,124
22½ pence	11,640	20,656	32,296	6,800	12,500	19,300
30 pence	13,296	20,656	33,952	7,909	12,500	20,409

Clearly the benefits of sailing were substantially less than those of angling, despite the fact that there were 75 per cent more sailing than angling visits. This does not necessarily mean that there should be less sailing and more angling; it must be asked whether the marginal benefit of a unit of water provides a greater benefit to sailing or angling. It could well be that if there is spare angling capacity while the sailing club is fully subscribed the transfer of a unit area of water from angling would cause no loss, while permitting the benefit of an increase in sailing club membership.

A few further studies of trout fishing have been undertaken by Gibson,[21] with financial support from the Water Resources Board. His estimates of total benefits, for time values of 25p an hour, are:

(i) Tittesworth Reservoir (Staffs), 189 acres, £17,159
(ii) Derwent Reservoir (Durham), 845 acres, £15,667
(iii) Weirwood Reservoir (Sussex), 280 acres, £13,609

Day visiting has received less attention than angling, but the studies that have been undertaken illustrate that many more problems arise. For a start, expensive site surveys are necessary and it is not sufficient to interview on only one day; to obtain an estimate of annual benefits, it is necessary to establish the total number of visitors during a year and their geographical origin, and this requires surveys at regular intervals throughout the year. A requirement for the application of the evaluation methods outlined in this chapter is that there should be a clear figure of the cost of visiting the site being analysed. This requirement may not be met in the case of day visiting, where parties may visit a number of recreation areas in one afternoon and where the pleasure of merely driving around may be one of the objectives. Colenutt,[22] in his study of the Forest of Dean, noted that most journeys were not direct outward and return trips; in fact 70 per cent of visitors from major centres did not choose direct routes. He concluded that while distance travelled remains a strong predictor for both total and long-distance trips, it does not explain local trips. Mansfield,[23] however, did attempt to measure the benefits arising from trips to the Lake District; the problems encountered by Colenutt were to some extent by-passed by treating the Lake District as an entity rather than examining individual sites within the Lake District. This meant that trips originating within the national park had to be ignored. Mansfield's estimates of benefits were:

(i) Day visitors, £3,736 per average day
(ii) Half-day visitors, £1,140 per average day
(iii) Holiday trips, £27,700 per average week

Although the results described in this section give some guide to the benefits of new sites, in general more sophisticated analysis is needed if predictions are to be made. Account needs to be taken of many factors in addition to distance and population; particularly important is the location of alternative faci-

lities. This means that larger, regional models are necessary, including factors other than population and costs. Developments in this area are described in the next section.

MEASURING THE BENEFITS OF PROPOSED NEW SITES

Research results such as those described above could only be used to help predict the benefits of new facilities if considerable care were exercised. For example, the benefits of trout fishing at a new reservoir would be similar to the benefits from Grafham only if the new reservoir were identical to Grafham in respect of the quality of the fishing, the magnitude, distribution and socio-economic characteristics of the surrounding population, and the alternative recreation facilities available. This last point is particularly important and implies that the new facility must not noticeably improve the range of facilities available to the public. Clearly such conditions are unlikely to be met, and studies of the distances people are travelling serve only to value existing resources and are not a great deal of help in prediction.

One important study in Britain has been Mansfield's attempt to predict the recreation benefits likely to arise from any water resource development at Morecambe.[24] Unfortunately this study suffered from the problems outlined in the previous paragraph: the only data available were some statistics on day visits to the Lake District and Mansfield used these to great effect to arrive at some predictions. However, some sweeping assumptions were necessary; Mansfield has to assume that any Morecambe Bay complex would in effect be simply an extension of the Lake District. This gives benefits to people who, because a visit to the Lake District becomes cheaper, will visit the area whereas previously they did not, and it also gives benefits, in the form of cost savings, to people who would have visited the Lake District anyway but can now visit more

cheaply. Mansfield then had to make another assumption about the extent to which such savings would not accrue because some visitors would ignore the new facilities and continue to drive past Morecambe Bay to the older Lakes. Mansfield's work, though excellent in its use of the limited data, clearly illustrates the need for a deeper understanding of the impact on demand of other factors in addition to distances travelled if valid predictions are to be made for new sites.

A study by Merewitz[25] in the United States has attempted to explain visits from counties in Missouri to the Niangua Arm of the Lake of the Ozarks. The factors included were distance, population, density of population, urbanisation, availability of alternative sites, income of residents and mobility of residents. The most useful variables were the first three, while the lack of influence of the availability of alternatives could be accounted for by the fact that the indices tested took account only of the *number* of the alternatives and not of their quality.

A similar but larger-scale study, based on data for eight reservoirs, was that by Grubb and Goodwin,[26] whose explanatory variables were population and per capita income of the county of origin, round trip cost, a 'gravity' variable to reflect the competitive effect of other reservoirs and the size of the reservoir under specific consideration. Size was meant to reflect 'attraction', and was included also in the formulation of the gravity variable. All of the variables considered proved to have a significant influence on the level of visits. Studies of this type, taking account of the range of available alternatives and permitting the effect of new developments on the number of visits to existing facilities to be estimated, are required now in the United Kingdom. It appears that a start in this direction may be made in the recreation research being undertaken as part of the study of the feasibility of siting bunded reservoirs in the Wash estuary.

CHAPTER ELEVEN

Classification and Analysis of Recreational Resources

PLANNING for outdoor recreation requires information both on those resources which are currently used and on those which, on account of their inherent characteristics, would be suitable for recreational use at some future date. In this chapter, attention will be primarily focused on the latter, mainly by reference to investigations in central Scotland, although the approach adopted is thought to be of wide applicability.

RESOURCES CURRENTLY USED FOR OUTDOOR RECREATION

Identifying resources

In principle, establishing what resources are actually used for outdoor recreation should be a simple matter of survey, but in practice this is not the case. The principal difficulties are the very wide range of activities in time and space, difficulties which are aggravated by the fact that the most common form of

outdoor recreation, informal passive recreation, shows these characteristics to a marked degree; for by its very nature it is both unorganised and widespread. Furthermore, very little attempt has been made to record levels of recreational use, even for those activities which are clearly defined and occur within discrete areas. The only firm data relate to places for which there is a charge for admission or for the use of facilities, as in country houses open to the public, coastal car parks or golf courses, and even these data are normally confined to numbers participating, sometimes for each day (and ideally for periods within that day), but more commonly on a weekly, monthly or even annual basis. Rarely is there any other indication of intensity of use, such as length of stay; indeed, for most forms of outdoor recreation, it is not easy to obtain such information.

For the reasons already noted, passive recreation is the most difficult to record. Investigators have usually concentrated their attention at well-known sites which attract large numbers of visitors, but while these are clearly identifiable recreational resources, a much wider area of countryside can properly be regarded as a recreational resource; not only can small numbers of recreationists be found at many places within an area of attractive countryside, provided that it is reasonably accessible to major centres of population or to holiday resorts, but there is a growing body of evidence to show that the recreational journey through such countryside is in itself part of the recreational experience, and even an end in itself.[1] We do not know how important this widely diffused recreation is by comparison with that at well-known sites. Another major sector of outdoor recreation, embracing space-demanding activities such as field sports, hill walking and riding, though numerically much less important than car-based passive enjoyment of the countryside, is also poorly known, again because of the low intensity of use and the diffuse character of the activity, and because much of it takes place by private agreement on private land.

LEVELS OF USE

There is thus a need for techniques and procedures by which we can readily identify resources already used for outdoor recreation and, more important, levels of use of those resources. Remote sensing, whether by conventional vertical air photography, or, as has more commonly been the case in the United Kingdom, by observation and oblique photography from light aircraft,[2] offers one obvious possibility, though there are considerable practical problems, particularly the critical timing of flights and the difficulties of penetrating tree-cover, a matter of some importance in view of the well-known edge effect, the tendency for recreationists to concentrate at the boundaries between woodland and open space. A method known as the rural traverse was devised for the Scottish surveys to identify levels of recreational activity in areas of extensive recreational use: two observers patrolled an area by car at frequent intervals, recording and interviewing such recreationists as they encountered—an approach that ensured that this possibly important element of outdoor recreation was not overlooked.[3] Apart from these methods, aimed at acquiring the facts by direct observation, there remains a variety of data-dredging techniques which can be used to complement each other: consultation with the police, local authorities, motoring organisations, tourist and amenity bodies; surveys of households to identify those areas which respondents use; and surveys of clubs and associations, both local and national, concerned with or responsible for particular forms of outdoor recreation, eg angling associations, natural history clubs and such bodies as the Ramblers Association.

Yet identifying the areas used is only a first step, for it is probable that any reasonably comprehensive survey would show that most rural land is used for some form of outdoor recreation at some time and to some degree. What is needed is a measure of the level of use and, if outdoor recreation is to

be adequately planned, how nearly that level of use matches capacity. Though little progress has been made with either, assessing the level of use is essentially a matter of technique, whereas capacity is a concept which those researching in the field of outdoor recreation have not yet adequately defined.

Several approaches have been adopted to the measurement of levels of use, notably automatic counting devices, remote sensing and direct observation. Vehicle counters are a standard feature of traffic censuses and attempts have been made to count pedestrians by similar devices such as trample meters,[4] photo-electric cells linked to counters and the like,[5] though there are obvious problems of security of equipment against theft or vandalism. Air photographs have been used to enumerate numbers of visitors, and counts of those using the footpath to the summit of Arthur's Seat in Holyrood Park, Edinburgh, have been made from photographs taken at intervals with a hand-operated camera from a vantage point.[6] Experiments have also been undertaken using cameras suspended from balloons and controlled from the ground by means of a wire, and with cameras fixed to the struts of light aircraft and operated by clockwork motors.[7] A technique used to estimate caravan traffic,[8] employing a battery-operated ciné camera mounted at vantage points to take single shots at frequent intervals, has potential application at high-density sites, provided that security can be assured. Perhaps the most comprehensive attempt to record levels of use has been undertaken at two beaches in East Lothian—Yellowcraigs, to the west of North Berwick, and Whitesands, to the east of Dunbar—where teams of observers, located at vantage points, recorded at frequent intervals the numbers using each link of a network of footpaths and sections of beach.[9] Such an approach is expensive of labour, but provided that sufficient resources are available, there appear to be no insuperable difficulties in measuring levels of use.

CAPACITY

Although the term 'capacity' is widely used, there is little firm knowledge of the degree to which recreational areas differ in this respect. Furthermore, capacity can be conceived in a variety of ways (see Chapter 1). The most commonly used meaning is the capacity of the vegetative cover to support human use without deterioration;[10] but while it is not difficult to show that a site is being over-used to the extent that the vegetative cover has become discontinuous and accelerated soil erosion has begun, it is much more difficult to establish the point at which such deterioration begins. Many factors other than recreational pressure are involved and it is not easy to isolate those effects which are due to variations in weather or to biotic factors, such as changes in the rabbit population, from those which are due to recreational pressure; long-term programmes of research and careful monitoring will be necessary. Recreational use at much lower levels may affect populations of birds and animals, and red deer may be disturbed by a single walker a mile away; but there is great variation, and dotterel on the Cairngorm plateau seem to have adjusted very quickly to large numbers of visitors.[11] What is clear is that the measurement of capacity is difficult and that different environments and different communities of plants and animals vary greatly in their resistance to recreational pressure; dunes are particularly susceptible and mountain environments in the oceanic climates of the British Isles are much more vulnerable than similar areas in continental Europe.

POTENTIAL RESOURCES
FOR OUTDOOR RECREATION

This ignorance of capacity clearly presents a problem to those planning for future needs, who have no reliable indication of the extent to which additional resources will be needed as a

result of over-use of existing sites. Nevertheless, it will be generally agreed that additional recreational land will be required and that both planners and those who control rural resources will need some comparative measure of the suitability of the countryside to support sustained recreational use. Here, too, there are important gaps in information that need to be filled before recreational potential can be adequately assessed; they concern not only the capacity of different types of land and vegetation, but also a knowledge of what the recreationist seeks from different kinds of outdoor recreation, how far these desires are likely to change over time and even what constitutes suitability (in a technical sense) for different kinds of recreation. Recreational standards, both optimal and minimal, are rudimentary or non-existent; even in the much longer-established field of recreational planning in urban areas, one of the few firm standards used, that of 6 acres of playing fields and open space per 1,000 population, is both insecurely based and derived from circumstances which have changed (see Chapter 5). Current prescriptions of the resource requirements of different forms of outdoor recreation are at best based on the cumulative experience of practitioners and instructors, and at worst are little more than inspired guesses.

Just as virtually all rural land is in some sense recreational, so all forms of outdoor recreation require resources of some kind. Nevertheless, there is much virtue in the distinction between user-oriented and resource-based recreation. Many recreational activities are catholic in their requirements; provided that a sufficient area of land is available, its physical characteristics do not matter greatly so long as they are not extreme, eg steep and rocky or liable to flooding. Playing fields and golf courses can be established on most of the land surrounding towns, although some costs may be involved in using earth-moving equipment to mould the topography; many playing fields in industrial areas are on land formerly used for industrial purposes or worked for minerals. While, as with most

man-made structures, a fairly level, well-drained site is preferable, some investment can be justified if a site is to be used intensively, and ease of access to large numbers of people may be more important than physical attributes.

Resource-based outdoor recreation, on the other hand, is dependent on the availability of specific resources, and recreationists are often prepared to travel long distances to reach resources of high quality. Some activities, of which potholing is an obvious example, are possible only in the very few locations where a particular resource occurs; but more commonly, a range of sites can be used, differing chiefly in the quality of the recreational experience that they can provide. Skiing is possible at some time during the winter in quite a large number of places in Scotland; but there are only a few at which there is a sufficiently reliable prospect of sufficient snow each winter to warrant investment in ski lifts and other facilities. Even for these activities, any generally agreed and soundly based criteria for selection are lacking.

There is also a problem of scale. The criteria that would be relevant in a broad regional assessment, intended to provide information for strategic planning and to act as a screen for the identification of areas where further inquiries could be concentrated as the need for specific sites arose, are quite different from those appropriate to the selection and planning of a specific site. In the latter case, questions of ownership and availability of land will always be involved, major capital investment to alter accessibility may be justified and specific management techniques will be required. In the broad survey for strategic planning, most of these considerations can be disregarded. It is at this latter scale that most assessments of the suitability of natural resources for outdoor recreation have been attempted, most notably in the survey of Land Capability for Recreation of the Canada Land Inventory, which has involved the classification of nearly one million square miles of settled Canada.[12] Under such circumstances, it is the intrinsic qualities of land

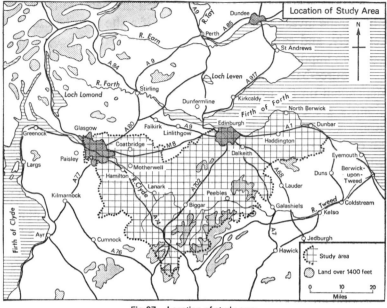

Fig 37   Location of study area

and water that must be assessed and any constraints on access or possibilities of major capital investments disregarded.

SURVEYS OF OUTDOOR RECREATION IN LANARKSHIRE AND GREATER EDINBURGH

The assessments undertaken as part of the recreation surveys of Lanarkshire and Greater Edinburgh were also of this kind and were further restricted in approach by the very limited resources available to the survey team to cover an area of 1,241,759 acres.[13] They are therefore primarily desk studies, amplified by fieldwork where this seemed necessary. The aim was to identify 'recreation environments', areas with a similar capacity to support various forms of outdoor recreation on a continuing basis. The results were intended to provide the sponsoring local authorities with a broad, comparative evalua-

tion of the study area and were not a plan for outdoor recreation, although, on the basis of this assessment and other surveys, recommendations were made and have, in the case of Lanarkshire, been accepted.

The method adopted was to make four separate, independent assessments of the components of land capability for outdoor recreation, and then to combine these into one single assessment. The four categories selected were: suitability for land-based recreation, suitability for water-based recreation, scenic quality and ecological significance. The basic spatial unit for all assessments was a 2km by 2km square of the national grid, dimensions that were partly conditioned by the size of the area and the degree of resolution that was thought desirable, and partly by the resources that were available for the project; a total of 607 squares covered the area. There were two additional reasons for choosing a square as the basic unit in preference to some more 'natural' unit, delimited, for example, by physical features that could be easily identified on the ground. First, the choice of a grid would emphasise the fact that the assessment was intended for use at the regional scale; and secondly, it would facilitate both comparison between data derived from a variety of sources, especially maps, and computation of relationships between the different sets of data. Additional advantages later proved to be the suitability of the grid square for mapping by computer and the increasing interest among local planning authorities in collecting data by grid cells.

In part, the reasoning behind this approach to assessment was that groups of recreational activities tend to have similar requirements, a view that was subsequently confirmed by analysis of data from household surveys, which showed that there were significant statistical correlations between some of the more popular activities. These relationships also had a practical application, by facilitating the identification of areas suitable for country parks; for these will more effectively fill their role as 'honeypots', relieving pressure on the countryside at large, if

they can provide resources for a wide range of outdoor recreation.

SUITABILITY FOR LAND-BASED RECREATION

Nine kinds of land-based recreation were considered in the first stage of this assessment, namely, camping, caravanning, picnicking, pony-trekking, walking, hiking, game shooting, rock climbing, and skiing. It was recognised that many forms of outdoor recreation are excluded from consideration, but these were either user-oriented, eg golf, or the concern of a very small minority of recreationists, eg scrambling, or had

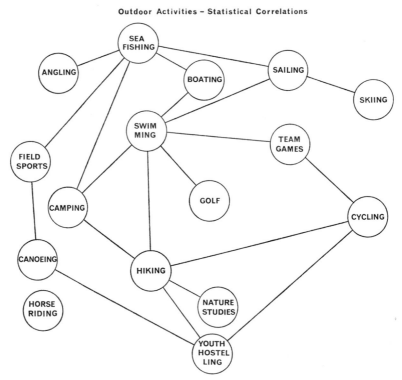

Outdoor Activities – Statistical Correlations

NOTE : lines linking activities denote a positive correlation significant at ·01 level of confidence

Fig 38   Outdoor activities: statistical relationships

characteristics similar to one of the nine chosen, eg orienteering. These activities were then grouped into six sets of activities with similar characteristics, and for each of these several criteria were identified indicating a minimum level of suitability; if these criteria were satisfied within a square, a point was scored for that square, so that a maximum of six points could be recorded if all criteria were satisfied.

The criteria used were:

(i) *Camping, caravanning and picnicking:* all countryside within 400m of a metalled road.

(ii) *Pony-trekking:* all upland areas above 300m in altitude and with rights of way or established footpaths and bridleways.

(iii) *Walking and hiking:* all upland areas above 450m, with rights of way or established footpaths and bridleways.

(iv) *Game shooting:* all areas assessed as shootings on valuation rolls.

(v) *Rock climbing:* all cliff faces over 30m in height.

(vi) *Skiing:* available relief of over 280m, with an average snow-holding period of more than three months.

These criteria are admittedly crude, but they were devised from what was known of the characteristics of the different activities and after consultation with experts in the different fields. Their range was restricted to enable scores to be established by inspection of maps and air photographs, supplemented where necessary by field observation. The least satisfactory is probably shooting, partly because only rateable shootings, ie mainly game shootings, were considered and because it is an assessment of present rather than potential use. Unfortunately, no method of estimating shooting potential was readily available, but it can be argued that the potential for expanding this kind of recreation lies in better management of areas already used in this way rather than in the identification of new areas.

15

Figure 39 shows the distribution of squares, shaded according to their scores. No square scored five or six points because none was adjudged suitable for skiing and only two contained cliffs suitable for rock climbing. Only 0·8 per cent of the squares scored four and 5·4 per cent three; on the other hand, only 4·1 per cent scored none. Most of the areas with above-average scores lies in the south and east of the study area, although the

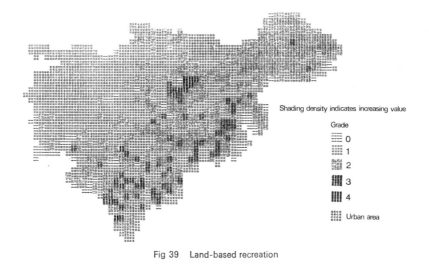

Fig 39   Land-based recreation

pattern is highly fragmented; these areas correspond with the main hill areas which mark the northern fringe of the Southern Uplands. The highest values, however, occur in the Pentland Hills immediately to the south of Edinburgh, an area that is already important for various kinds of outdoor recreation. In the lowlands, there is a contrast between those to the east of the Pentlands, which score two points, and those to the west, which score one. It is also clear that, with the notable exception of the Pentlands, the areas nearest the main centres of population have the lowest scores.

SUITABILITY FOR WATER-BASED RECREATION

Suitability for water-based recreation was assessed in a similar way, though separate criteria were also adopted for inland water and for sea coasts. Seven activities were identified —swimming and bathing, angling, canoeing, rowing, dinghy sailing and pleasure boating, motor boating and water skiing— and criteria were agreed, representing minimal suitability for each activity. Additionally, since water plays an important part in informal passive recreation, acting as the focus of many visits to the coast or countryside, ability to attract water-oriented informal recreation was also included. Since the demands of the various activities are often very similar in both nature and scale, they were also grouped according to the following criteria:

(i) *Angling on inland waters:* unpolluted rivers and streams and canals over 8m in width and enclosed water bodies over 5ha in area.

(ii) *Other active pursuits on inland water:* unpolluted waters with a minimum length of 1km and width of 200m, or an area of at least 20ha.

(iii) *Informal recreation oriented towards inland waters:* unpolluted waters within 400m of a metalled road.

(iv) *Active sea-based pursuits:* the presence of coastline.

(v) *Informal recreation oriented to the coast:* sandy or shingle beach within 400m of a metalled road.

These criteria were also devised after consultation with experts in the various fields and again represented minimal requirements. Information on pollution was obtained from the river purification boards and has since been published for the whole of Scotland by the Scottish Development Department.[14] As in the case of land-based recreation, suitability for informal recreation was judged in relation to present accessibility only and without regard for rights of access.

No square had scores in either of the two highest categories, chiefly because suitability for sea-based recreation and that based on inland waters were mutually exclusive in nearly all instances. The distribution of squares according to their suitability for water-based recreation is inevitably very different from that shown in Figure 39, for 73·9 per cent of the squares scored no points (Figure 40). The distribution of squares is essentially linear, picking out the main river systems and the

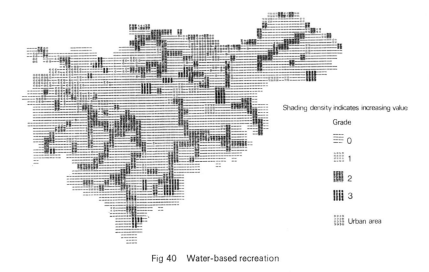

Shading density indicates increasing value

Grade

≡ 0

⦂⦂⦂ 1

▦ 2

|||| 3

⦂⦂⦂ Urban area

Fig 40   Water-based recreation

coast, although there are noticeable gaps in north Lanarkshire, reflecting the urbanised and industrial nature of that area. The highest values are in squares containing major bodies of inland water, all of which are reservoirs. This fact highlights the nature of this assessment, which is concerned solely with suitability; for these areas would generally rank low in respect of present use because it is the policy of the South East of Scotland Water Board to forbid water sports on direct supply reservoirs under its control.

SCENERY

Although the methods and criteria may, and indeed should, be criticised, it is unlikely that any critic would dispute the necessity of including assessments of land- and water-based recreation in any scheme for the identification of areas suitable for outdoor recreation. The inclusion of scenery, on the other hand, is more contentious, for the assumption is made that it is the principal resource in the countryside for informal outdoor recreation. What is not in doubt is that informal recreation, particularly the drive into the countryside or to the coast, is overwhelmingly the most important form of outdoor recreation, at least judged by the number of participants and the frequency with which they participate. All active forms of recreation are undertaken by small minorities, and although these proportions are likely to change with rising levels of education and affluence, the dominance of passive recreation, confirmed by all surveys undertaken in Great Britain, will persist for the foreseeable future.[15] There is therefore a strong case for giving particular weight to informal passive recreation in any assessment of suitability.

Some consideration has already been given to aspects of informal recreation by the inclusion of picnic sites and accessible coastline and water bodies in the assessments of land- and water-based recreation, and the prominence given to scenery accords with the Countryside Commission's decisions on its priorities; for it, too, has decided that its primary standpoint respecting the Scottish countryside generally and the use of land in particular is that of scenery or landscape.[16] In the Commission's view, the appearance and perception of landscape is the most important common denominator in the public enjoyment of countryside. This view receives some confirmation from the household surveys of recreational demand conducted in conjunction with this assessment, in that 'countryside' and 'coast' were the kinds of places that 80·9 per cent of respondents

liked to visit on a day out; but it is important to recognise that it is an assumption that has not been tested adequately. It is also perhaps significant that, when respondents were asked what facilities they desired for outdoor recreation, only 20 per cent mentioned any aspect of the countryside.

The assessment of scenic quality is in its infancy, though several approaches have been suggested and tested. These range from wholly subjective judgements, as in W. H. Murray's *Highland Landscape*,[17] through the matching of photographs of views against an international scale, to the prescription of sets of criteria, the approach employed here. The choice was again determined in part by the limited resources available, but the major reason was the success of D. L. Linton's classification of Scottish scenery.[18] His method has been adapted for this assessment, the main modifications being that, while Linton identified actual boundaries, used a system of scoring and drew on very extensive first-hand knowledge of Scottish scenery to moderate judgements where they appeared inappropriate, this assessment is based on a simple ranking of each grid square and has relied entirely on the prescribed criteria.

Linton identified two elements in the scenic resources of any area: 'One is the form of the ground, not as defined by the contour of the topographic surveyor, but rather by the landform categories of the geomorphologist. The other is the mantle of forests and moorlands, farms and factories, natural vegetation and human artifacts, by which the hard rock body of the landscape is clothed.' To these elements he gave the names 'landform' and 'land-use' landscapes.

Landform landscapes

Two criteria are used in the ranking of landform landscapes: absolute relief (the maximum height above sea level) and relative relief (the difference in altitude between the highest and lowest point in each square); and these have been combined to identify six classes of landform, which have been ranked

according to a subjective judgement of scenic attractiveness, particular weight being given to boldness and contrast of relief. In ascending order of importance, these are:

(i) *Lowlands:* below 500′ in height.
(ii) *Rolling countryside:* between 500′ and 1,500′ in height with an available relief of less than 400′.
(iii) *Upland plateau:* exceeding 1,500′ in height but with less than 400′ available relief.
(iv) *Hill country:* either between 500′ and 1,500′ in height and with available relief exceeding 400′, or between 500′ and 2,000′, with available relief between 400′ and 800′.
(v) *Bold hills:* either exceeding 2,000′ in height, with an available relief of between 400′ and 800′, or between 1,500′ and 2,000′, with available relief exceeding 600′.
(vi) *High hills:* exceeding 2,000′ in height and with more than 800′ of available relief.

These classes were given ranks from 0 (lowlands) to 5 (high hills). Linton included two further categories in his classification of Scottish scenery, but they are not represented in this area and have been omitted. High hills occur in only 4·9 per cent of the squares and, as would be expected, are located mainly in Peeblesshire; and upland plateau is barely represented (Figure 41). The other categories are fairly evenly represented among the remaining squares (lowland 18·6 per cent, rolling countryside 40 per cent, hill country 22·9 per cent and bold hills 12·9 per cent), and their distribution conforms with what would be expected from a consideration of the general relief of the area.

Land-use landscapes
Land-use landscapes are similarly divided into six categories, which are also ranked in ascending order of their contribution to scenic quality. This assessment is based on two untested but plausible assumptions, namely, that people prefer 'natural' or

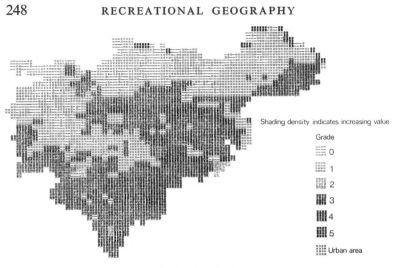

Shading density indicates increasing value

Grade

0

1

2

3

4

5

Urban area

Fig 41   Land-use landscapes

'semi-natural' landscapes to those where man's influence is more evident, and that diversity of use is more attractive than uniformity, judgements which, in Linton's view, are 'not so much personal as the judgements of our own society in a particular day and age'. Diversity was measured by comparing the actual percentages of each square under the different land uses with a theoretical distribution in which each land use occupies an equal share of the square[19] (ie 50 per cent for each of two components, 33·3 per cent for each of three components and so on). The theoretical distribution which the actual distribution most closely resembles indicates the number of significant land uses and hence the diversity of use; a land use may be present in a square, but may not be included in the estimate of diversity because it occupies too small an acreage. The merit of this approach is that the decision on diversity is made objectively. Those squares in which only one use is identified by this method are first ranked, and the squares in which two or three of the categories, improved farmland (crops and grass), moorland and woodland, are identified, ie diverse landscapes, are

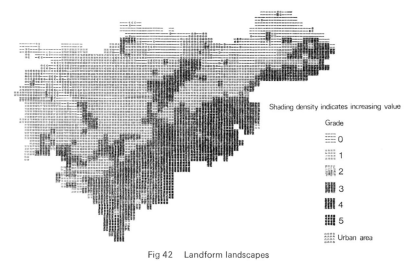

Shading density indicates increasing value

Grade

≡ 0

≡ 1

▓ 2

▐▌ 3

▐▌ 4

▐▌ 5

Urban area

Fig 42   Landform landscapes

ranked above them. The highest category is represented by those squares where there is a sufficient area of inland water for this to appear as a significant element.

The six categories in ascending order of importance are:

   (i) *Urban areas:* all built-up land and land within 1·5km of such land, ie the urban shadow zone.
  (ii) *Agricultural land:* crops and grass are the dominant use and no other use is significant.
 (iii) *Woodland:* woodland is the dominant use and no other use is significant.
 (iv) *Moorland:* moorland is the dominant use and no other use is significant.
  (v) *Diversified use:* at least two of crops and grass, woodland and moorland, make significant contributions.
 (vi) *Water:* squares where water makes a significant contribution.

As with landform landscapes, these ranks are equated with

scores from 0 (urban) to 5 (water). Both landscapes in which water is a significant element and those dominated by woodland occupy only a small proportion of the squares (2·3 per cent and 1 per cent respectively), although woodland is present in many of the squares classified as diversified. These latter, which account for 13·1 per cent of the squares, are located mainly along the boundary between the moorland and the improved agricultural land of the lowlands (Figure 42). Urban and urban shadow areas occupy 28·3 per cent of the squares, mainly in Edinburgh and north west Lanarkshire.

These two landscapes were then synthesised by adding the rank scores for landform and land-use landscapes, to achieve scores on a scale from 0 to 10, and then dividing these into five classes of scenery (in ascending order 0–2, 3–4, 5–6, 7–8, and 9–10). Over most of the study area, high values in the land-use assessment reinforce high values in the landform assessment, while most of the lowlands to the north rank low on both counts (Figure 43). Squares in the highest category occupy only 0·4 per cent of the area, while 40·6 per cent are in the lowest category; the remaining squares are fairly equally

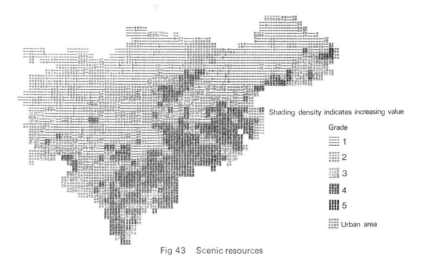

Shading density indicates increasing value

Grade

≣ 1

2

3

4

5

Urban area

Fig 43   Scenic resources

divided among the other categories. To the north of the Southern Uplands and their foothills, only the Pentlands stand out as an area of high quality scenery.

ECOLOGICAL SIGNIFICANCE

The fourth element in the assessment of recreational resources, ecological significance, is the most contentious and has been the subject of considerable debate among members of the research team. It was argued that areas of high ecological significance should be included as positive elements in the assessment, since they represent part of the attraction of the countryside, as is shown by the increasing numbers of visitors to nature reserves, such as that at Aberlady, and the growing interest in activities such as natural history. On the other side, it was argued that areas of high ecological significance should be protected against recreational development and so should have a negative score. It was decided to adopt the former course, but one merit of collecting the information on a grid basis and handling it by computer is that it is very simple to vary the weighting, and produce a new map. Thus, Figure 44 shows the effect on the

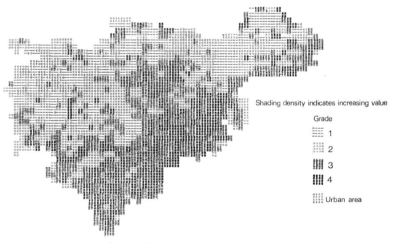

Shading density indicates increasing value

Grade

≡ 1

2

▓ 3

▓ 4

Urban area

Fig 44   Ecological evaluation of resources

final assessment of regarding high ecological significance as a factor making an area less suitable for outdoor recreation. The method adopted was derived from one devised by D. R. Helliwell, of the Nature Conservancy, for the rapid assessment of the conservation value of large areas.[20] No attempt was made by Helliwell to assess the quality of individual plant communities; instead, he relied on the diversity of habitats and ranked these in order of biological richness, his scoring reflecting 'the consensus of opinion among a number of conservation staff as to the relative weighting to be given to the different habitat types'. In the assessment used in this survey, the 2km by 2km squares were again used as the basic unit and the various types of habitat were simplified so that they could readily be identified from the available information. Six types were recognised, namely, water, broad-leaved woodland, marsh or bog, dunes, moorland, coniferous woodland and improved farmland. These were ranked according to the following rules. An exception was made in respect of any square that contained a nature reserve or Site of Special Scientific Interest (SSSI) for this was automatically placed in the highest class, a sensible decision in principle but one of doubtful relevance in this area where the great majority of such sites had been designated because of their geological or physiographic interest. Five grades of habitat were identified, in order of ascending ecological significance:

(i) *Grade 0:* urban areas, with no other habitat occupying 10 per cent of each square.

(ii) *Grade 1:* improved agricultural land accounting for at least 10 per cent of each square.

(iii) *Grade 2:* over 10 per cent of each square in either moorland or coniferous woodland.

(iv) *Grade 3:* over 10 per cent of each square in either broad-leaved woodland, or marsh or bog, or dunes, or water.

(v) *Grade 4:* over 10 per cent of each square in any two of broad-leaved woodland, marsh or bog, dunes, and water.

Clearly squares could be classified under a number of grades and each was given the highest possible score.

The resulting map provides a relative grading of ecological habitats (Figure 45). It is more fragmented than those of the previous three assessments, a feature which is partly due to the widespread scatter of SSSIs. There are very few squares in the lowest category (6·9 per cent), mainly round Edinburgh and Glasgow, but the next lowest occupies most of the lowlands and accounts for 27·8 per cent of the squares, although they are

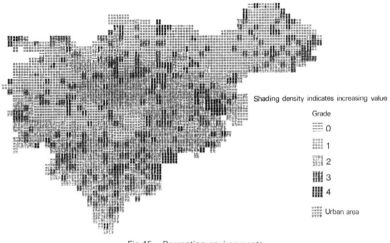

Shading density indicates increasing value

Grade

≡ 0

1

2

3

4

Urban area

Fig 45   Recreation environments

interspersed with numerous squares in higher categories. Most of the uplands are in Grade 2 (41 per cent of squares), while squares in the two highest ratings, which altogether account for 15·7 per cent and 8·6 per cent respectively, are widely distributed.

RECREATION ENVIRONMENTS

These four assessments were then synthesised to identify recreation environments. Each was given the same weight, 100 representing the highest score that could be (but rarely was)

achieved. There was thus a theoretical maximum of 400 points, though this was nowhere approached, and any score exceeding 250 represents an area with a high capacity to support outdoor recreation on a permanent basis. Areas with a score of less than 100 have only a very limited capacity for outdoor recreation as defined in this survey, though they might be suitable for user-oriented activities which were not very exacting in their physical requirements.

The scores were then divided into six grades, namely 0 (urban

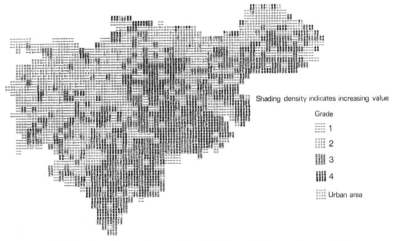

Shading density indicates increasing value

Grade

1

2

3

4

Urban area

Fig 46   Recreation environments (ecological evaluation scored negative)

areas), 1–99, 100–149, 150–199, 200–249, and 250 and over; their distribution is shown in Figure 46. The highest grade accounts for only 0·8 per cent of the squares and the next highest 6·7 per cent; urban areas account for a further 6·9 per cent. The lowlands generally fall into the second grade, while most of the uplands are in the higher ranking grades. As on all the maps, the Pentlands stand out as an anomalous feature in the lowlands and have considerable recreational significance both as a present and future recreational area, and as a barrier to recreational movements.

The effect of treating ecological significance as a negative factor, so that areas of high ecological value rank low as recreation environments, is shown in Figure 46; one inevitable effect is a general reduction in scores and a lessening of the contrast between uplands and lowlands. Since the criteria used to identify ecological significance are very similar to those on ranking land-use landscapes (apart from the inclusions of SSSIs), it might be more sensible to exclude this factor altogether, with the possible exception of SSSIs and nature reserves, which could be given a negative value.

CANADIAN CONTRASTS

It is instructive to compare the approach adopted in this investigation with that used in Canada, the only country where an attempt has been made to assess potential for outdoor recreation over the countryside at large[21] (or, more strictly, over that third which may be called settled Canada). Of course, it must be recognised that the context of such evaluations is quite different. Even in settled Canada there is more than 30 acres of land per head of population, while the allotment in this study area approximates to the British average of 1 acre. Perhaps even more important, the Canadian assessments are primarily concerned with vast tracts of little-disturbed vegetation in state ownership, which can properly be devoted primarily to outdoor recreation, and with a large and increasing acreage of farmland, on which production has ceased, whereas no part of this study area is unused and none is natural; thus, while in Canada there is abundant land which is both suitable and available for outdoor recreation, in Great Britain this has to be reconciled with the prior claims of existing land-users. One consequence is that the patterns of recreational use and recreational movement are rather different, a contrast accentuated by differences in personal mobility and in the availability of holiday cottages; for example, the scale and nature of

movement from Toronto on a summer weekend contrasts markedly with that from Glasgow, a conurbation of similar size.[22] Lastly, the much greater resources available for the Canadian assessments have enabled quite different methods to be used.

The scheme of assessment of suitability for outdoor recreation of the Canada Land Inventory, and likewise those of the provinces which adopted and implemented it, is primarily concerned with the identification of particular areas of ground by means of air photographs and extensive field checks. A wider range of recreational activities is covered, the holiday cottage is recognised as a specific factor and more attention is paid to water-based recreation and less to the drive into the countryside. Although both Canadian and Scottish methods attempt to provide an evaluation of suitability for outdoor recreation as a whole, the Canadian surveys do not include assessments to scenery as such, except as a factor in the guidelines provided for the classification of routeways and viewpoints, and the treatment of this topic is consequently less systematic than in Scotland. Similarly, although natural history interest is recognised as an attraction, no specific attention is paid to ecological significance. Again, while the methods of assessing suitability for recreational activities are quite similar, depending on empirically devised minimum standards, those applied in Canada are much more elaborate and are the product of extensive tests and checks carried out over a number of years, a reflection of the much greater resources available for this work. Perhaps the most striking difference, the contrast in the choice of the basic spatial unit for mapping, is revealed by the maps themselves; the Canadian maps, at a scale of 1: 125,000, show specific tracts of land with clearly demarcated boundaries, whereas the Scottish maps show information only by grid squares. The tracts on the Canadian maps vary considerably in size, so that it is difficult to compare the information they contain with that derived from other sources; and although the Canadian Geographic Information System has been specifically designed

to handle such maps, very much larger amounts of computing time are required for such comparisons than are needed for handling data by grid squares. Another disadvantage, at least in a British context, of using areas which can be clearly identified on the ground, is that they can immediately be related to the property of individual owners and occupiers who may object to their land being classified in this way. The importance of the kind of broad-brush treatment represented by the Scottish approach has been recognised in recent changes in town and country planning, for the new structure plans are to be essentially diagrammatic. In part, however, the decision about the basic mapping unit must be as much a matter of personal preference as of advantage.

CONCLUSIONS

This procedure for assessing recreational potential has inevitably been experimental, for it represents the first attempt to evaluate any large tract of Great Britain for this purpose in a comprehensive and systematic way. Many of its deficiencies, particularly those arising from the necessity of devising what was in essence a desk study, are due to the very limited resources with which the project was undertaken. Yet there are more fundamental difficulties. Research is urgently needed to identify much more precisely the space standards and other resource requirements of the different kinds of outdoor recreation, and to test the reactions of visitors to landscapes of different kinds and the extent to which the quality of scenery, however measured, is a major factor in their choice of areas for passive informal recreation. The values given to some of the elements and the choice of activities to be included in the assessments can, of course, be debated. In much the same way that SSSIs were singled out for attention in the evaluation of ecological significance, ancient monuments and other features which attract visitors to the countryside could have been

16

included as specific foci of attraction in the scenic assessment. It might also have been desirable to have incorporated all forms of outdoor recreation, including those that are user-oriented, but decisions were taken in good faith, with little other evidence to provide a guide. The decision to give equal weight to the four assessments and to their individual components could also be challenged (Figure 46), but it seems logical to adopt this procedure in the absence of any firm evidence to the contrary. Any subsequent evaluation can profit from this and other experience, and its organisers should seek in advance some more firmly-based indicators of the values that should be attached. What can justifiably be claimed is that, despite its acknowledged deficiencies, this approach offers a sounder basis for recreational planning than wholly subjective assessments; it has the added advantage that, since the steps are clearly identified and the original data retained, any evaluation can easily be modified as and when firm guidelines become available.

CHAPTER TWELVE

The Ecological Effects of Recreation

ALTHOUGH the increasing recreational use of rural land resources is evident, the accurate determination of recreationalists' attitudes towards alternative kinds of resource has proved elusive. Statements regarding the supply of land for recreational use, especially those concerning the availability of 'semi-natural' areas, are vague, reflecting the lack of a national inventory of semi-natural areas as well as the inability of interested parties to agree upon compatible management goals for their use. The existing acreage of semi-natural areas in recreational use could be increased to meet rising demand as some areas remain underdeveloped in private hands and others could be used more intensively. However, some areas currently in use are undergoing ecological change as a result of recreational activity and others are being lost to alternative land uses. Areas of high biological interest, once lost, are almost impossible to regenerate, and at present it is prohibitively expensive to attempt to do so.

Yet, in the long term, it could be argued that provided recreationalists are not too demanding in their view of the 'semi-natural', then the very increase in demand for outdoor recreation sites could create the necessary income from which to finance an expansion in the resource base. But recreationalists' criteria *are* demanding; therefore the market mechanism cannot place a meaningful value on unique, irreplaceable environmental resources.

The general lack of popular concern over ecological effects of recreation has led to planners placing a low priority on this issue. In Britain this is partly because the total acreage of land that has become degraded as a result of recreational activity is minimal. With the exception of a few well-publicised examples, such as the loss of vegetation near the Cairngorm ski-lifts[1] and a loss of stability in sand-dune ecosystems, for example at Gibraltar Point, Lincolnshire,[2] few areas appear to be under immediate threat. It may be, however, that the ability of many semi-natural ecosystems to resist extrinsically induced change results in a false picture of the real situation. Hidden stresses may be accumulating which, once they exceed the ecosystem's natural homeostatic controls, will result in rapid change leading to a new and perhaps less desirable equilibrium state. These are not easily reversed, and the lack of visual evidence of change in the environment of semi-natural areas should not lead to complacency. At present, knowledge about the rates and directions of change in ecosystems that result from the effects of recreational activity is limited, and detailed studies into the functioning of ecosystems known to be vulnerable to recreational activity, such as sand-dune ecosystems, and those known to be popular with recreationalists, such as chalk grassland, are therefore urgently required.

Reasoned discussion of the ecological effects of recreation has been limited by the lack of quantitative evidence and by the divergent interests of conservationists, planners and the general public. Most members of the public, for example, are totally

unaware of the potential effect on the environment that their presence may have, and are often largely unconcerned. Naturalists, on the other hand, may express considerable concern and demand the implementation of management programmes that ensure the survival of a rare association of plants or even a single species. On any given site the level of recreational pressure that is considered appropriate by each group may vary enormously. Moreover, the level of use deemed acceptable for the site in question will depend not only on its intrinsic qualities but also on its regional or national significance, which again may vary according to interest group. The lack of a national inventory of sites which describes their characteristics and assesses their significance for different interest groups may increase the naturalists' demands for the maintenance of the status quo, or even for a reduction in present levels of recreational use, and does little to help the planner formulate positive management policies other than those dictated by local needs. Mattyasovsky reports such an attempt to produce a regional inventory of recreation sites around Toronto, classified on the basis of their physical and biological characteristics, their 'naturalness' and intrinsic recreational interest.[3]

However it is not the intention in this chapter to examine the values of different interest groups nor to enter the controversies which surround policies aimed at protecting certain rare plant communities. Rather, it is concerned with the nature of semi-natural ecosystems, the known effects of recreational activity on such systems and management approaches designed to minimise change.

THE ECOSYSTEM

Ecosystems are dynamic, integrated systems consisting of numerous components which can be considered under the headings of plants, animals, soil and climate. The living components are dependent upon each other for energy which

originates from the sun and flows through the system, a proportion being fixed by plants, consumers and, ultimately, decomposers. Similarly, nutrients are cycled within the ecosystem, this cycling representing a further example of the functional inter-relationships of the components of the system, both living (biotic) and non-living (abiotic). Ecosystems are in a constant state of flux, with each of the major biotic components consisting of several, sometimes thousands, of species, and each species consisting of numerous individuals. Competition occurs between individuals and between species and, together with seasonally induced changes, year to year fluctuations and complications due to plant and animal behaviour, creates the inherently variable character of ecosystems as well as their constantly changing structures. Ecosystems should therefore be considered as highly complex systems because of their large number of component individuals and the various ways in which the components are interdependent. Whether or not they are integrated is a matter of debate.[4] However, it is universally accepted that they have the capacity to tolerate extrinsic change and are capable of continuous and infinite self-replenishment due to the reproductive power of their biotic components.

The degree of stability inherent in an ecosystem depends upon the time-scale over which it is viewed.[5] If the reference interval is only one day, a groundsel (*Senecio vulgaris*) population in an abandoned field would appear stable. Conversely, for a reference period of a few millennia the North European deciduous forest formation might appear relatively unstable. However, ecosystems in many areas show a directional change over a long period of time known as succession, a natural process which commences with the ecosystem in a relatively simple state and which progresses towards a more complex and better-ordered condition. It is a continuous process, the vegetation and associated fauna developing in terms of their species richness and structural complexity (degree of stratification in the vegetation and number of food-chain links) towards a relatively stable end-

point known as the climax. The level of productivity (energy fixed per unit area per unit time) increases through the earlier stages but may decline towards the latter stages whereas biomass (total carbon or dry matter content fixed per unit area per unit time) continues to increase regularly towards the climax at which time it stabilises.[6] Successions are often arrested at an intermediate (seral) stage by man's activities. For example, chalk grassland represents a seral stage maintained by grazing.

The significance of successional theory to the management of ecosystems and outdoor recreation lies in the fact that many ecosystems intensively used for recreation represent seral stages (for example, sand-dunes) and that larger management inputs are required to maintain a particular ecosystem at an earlier successional stage than at a later one. Also, the earlier the stage in the sequence the more easily its vegetation cover can be destroyed. This is because a simple system contains a smaller number of functional links than a more complex one and consequently has a reduced ability to absorb the effects of extrinsic change. Thus, in theory, forest is more stable than scrub, and scrub is more stable than grassland. However, this generalisation must be interpreted in association with other properties of the system. The most important of these is that plant growth forms vary in their resistance to recreational activity. Plants with apical buds at, near or below ground level are less likely to be damaged by trampling than plants with buds held aloft on delicate stems. Grasses in the vegetative state and herbs with a rosette of leaves are most resistant, and so grassland consisting primarily of these two growth forms is a particularly resilient vegetation type. The herb layer of a woodland is totally different, consisting largely of plants with their apical buds held well above ground level, and is very vulnerable to trampling.

The type of vegetation at a site may also be modified by local climatic, edaphic or biotic factors so that even climax vegetation may be vulnerable to recreational activities. Assessment of the

sensitivity of the vegetation cover of an ecosystem to recreational pressure has thus to take into consideration:

(i) its position in the successional sequence;
(ii) the proportion of ground covered by tolerant growth forms;
(iii) limiting environmental factors such as climate and wet, saline or nutrient deficient soils.

On the basis of these factors it is possible to generalise about the types of habitat or ecosystem which are most vulnerable. These include coastal systems, such as sand-dunes and salt-marshes, which represent early successional stages with unstable substrata, montane habitats where the capacity for growth and self-recovery is reduced by the climate, and systems with shallow soils (chalk grassland), nutrient deficient soils (lowland heaths) and excessively wet soils (fens).

THE EFFECTS OF RECREATIONAL ACTIVITY

Existing published research into the ecological effects of recreational activity has recently been reviewed by Speight who examined about fifty studies concerning effects on vegetative cover and twenty on animal life.[7] Most of these reflect research of rather a superficial nature and few describe designed experiments with a detailed analysis of the resultant data. The morphological evidence of recreational impact may be summarised as follows:

(i) Vegetation is bruised by trampling and most species are reduced in abundance or eliminated, although a few may increase in abundance. New species may be introduced. The height of the vegetation and its flowering frequency is reduced. Some species may adopt a more prostrate form.
(ii) The soil is compacted and its moisture content per unit volume of pore space is increased.

(iii) Animal life is disturbed and most species decline in number or move elsewhere.

There is considerable discussion at present about the effects of recreational activity on vegetational diversity and productivity. Much of the confusion surrounding the discussion on diversity has arisen from an inadequate definition of the term as it relates to a particular situation. It is important to distinguish between species diversity which can be equated with richness, that is the total number of species, and habitat diversity which concerns the variety of habitats in a defined area.[8] Recreational activity usually results in the disappearance of some species and the introduction of others. The species that disappear are usually the rare ones which, for that reason alone, are often considered to be the most important. For similar reasons, the introductions are considered undesirable because they are alien to that habitat. The net result is often the maintenance of, or a slight change in, species richness, although conservationists have often interpreted the change in species composition as a reduction in diversity. If habitat diversity is considered, a comparable difficulty is often encountered through the introduction of value judgements relating to environmental quality. Some areas have a high conservation value because they consist of extensive tracts of a single habitat, for example Pennine moorland, and if recreational activity creates new habitats, such as paths, then recreation may be considered undesirable. Generally, however, a wide variety of habitat types is considered to be of value, as there is a good chance that they will create greater biological and aesthetic interest than a single habitat. Finally, in the absence of scientific evidence, the effects of recreation on primary productivity will remain a subject of debate. The overall effect of trampling, for example, is probably to reduce the rate of biomass production but it is also likely that low intensities of trampling stimulate plant growth and marginally increase production. This effect

is comparable to the infrequent but repeated mowing of grass-land which produces a greater bulk of herbage than a single annual cut.

The primary objective of current ecological research is to monitor the changes taking place under increasingly intensive recreational activity in order to identify the stages at which different species disappear and, ultimately, at what intensity the vegetation cover is removed completely. The loss of certain species can act as indicators of general levels of wear and tear before the situation becomes too evident to the average recreationalist, and appropriate management decisions can then be taken. At present information is limited, although Huxley[9] lists seven resilient species (*Agrostis tenuis, Cynosurus cristatus, Festuca pratense, Lolium perenne, Poa annua, Poa pratensis* and *Trifolium repens*). Their presence is limited to lowland areas ($< 500m$) in Britain where in montane habitats the regular use of a footpath soon results in bare ground. Similarly, because the seven species are light-demanding, heavily used woodland trails are rapidly denuded of vegetation. In open lowland situations on neutral soils, however, the absence of one, two, three or more of these species is likely to be correlated with increasingly frequent trampling. Work in the Isles of Scilly has also revealed the resistance to trampling of *Plantago coronopus, Plantago lanceolata* and *Bellis perennis*.[10]

There are two particularly difficult sets of problems associated with this kind of research, neither of which has been satisfactorily resolved. First, there are those problems created by the need to measure in a single experiment changes in the state of the semi-natural ecosystem as well as in levels of recreational use. It is impossible to measure the presence, activities and spatial distribution of people to the same level of accuracy as is normally practicable in the mapping of vegetation, and indeed most investigators have been forced to resort to some surrogate measure of recreational activity.[11] Moreover, most recreational sites have different spatial boundaries from those of the existing

semi-natural ecosystems which adds to the difficulties of making an integrated functional approach to the problem. Secondly, many ecosystems react only slowly, at least in measurable terms, to recreational pressure, change sometimes only being observed long after the cessation of recreational activity. Both these sets of problems make it difficult to link specific recreational causes to particular ecological effects, especially as the ecosystem itself is in a constant state of flux.

MANAGEMENT APPROACHES

Two basic strategies, together with a combination of both, are open to the manager of a recreation site. These are either to manage the resource or to manage the visitor. The tendency is for resource management to be practised only when visitor management techniques are exhausted and the site still shows signs of wear. It is therefore more common in urban than rural situations. However, as recreational pressure has increased in rural areas, management of the resource itself has slowly become acceptable. As Beardsley and Wagar say, writing in the North American context:

> Until recently, cultural treatments such as watering, fertilizing, and seeding to increase the growth and durability of vegetation have not been applied to forest recreation sites. Such measures, normal in urban settings, may have been considered unnatural, uneconomical, or administratively awkward for use on 'wildland' areas. However, bare, compacted, and eroded recreation sites are as unnatural as those that are kept vegetated by cultural treatments, and they may be considerably less pleasant and attractive.[12]

Ecologists have contributed relatively little to management techniques so far, expertise being basically culled from knowledge gained in municipal parks, from agricultural practice and from the experience and intuition of site managers. Evidence is accumulating that single management techniques, such as draining, watering or fertilising, are unlikely to be successful

on their own, and that a comprehensive and on-going management programme is required.[13] This is particularly true where early seral stages (as on sand-dunes) or arrested successions (for example, lowland heath and chalk grassland) are used intensively. Chalk grassland requires a greater energy input, in the form of grazing or mowing, in order to maintain it, than does chalk scrub. Similarly, chalk scrub requires greater management effort than ashwood or yew-wood. The advantage, however, of dealing with an early successional stage is that the alternatives open to the manager are more numerous. A lowland heath can be allowed to develop into birch, gorse, oak or hawthorn scrub, grassland or bracken. The ecologist, however, still understands very little about the factors that control these developments, although it is well known that once scrub is established in a particular area it is very difficult to return the area to one of heather-dominated vegetation. The same argument applies to chalk grassland and other arrested successions.

The management of recreationists is much more widely employed, and the techniques instituted are numerous and variable and frequently designed to meet local conditions. These range from the use of physical barriers, such as fences and ditches, to more subtle approaches involving signposting, trails, alternative routes, the rotation of access points, and devices to attract people elsewhere. The latter vary from the provision of recreational facilities (car parks, refreshment huts, interpretation centres) to areas with a special designation such as country parks. Some sites are developed as part of an overall plan for a larger area, often as a means of relieving pressure on more sensitive sites. For example, Butser Hill near Petersfield, Hampshire, has been developed to attract people away from the coast as well as more sensitive chalk grassland nature reserves, and Northaw Great Wood, a country park in Hertfordshire, relieves pressure on the neighbouring Broxbourne Woods. Some areas are zoned with differing intensities of use in mind. The area near the car park at Old Winchester Hill National Nature Reserve,

Hampshire, is designed for more intensive use than the adjacent steep slopes which support the more interesting chalk flora and fauna. Flooded gravel pits are also often zoned, water activities being separated in both time and space. Small shallow pits, as at Cosgrove in Buckinghamshire, with graded banks and convoluted perimeters, may be set aside as nature reserves, and boating and angling may be prohibited.

CONCLUSIONS

Whilst there is general agreement that the number of visitors to the countryside engaging in unorganised recreational pursuits is increasing at over 10 per cent per annum, most people fail to appreciate that semi-natural areas are limited in extent and often sensitive to the effects of recreation. On sites where recreation management is practised the policies adopted are usually too concerned with managing the visitor and insufficiently concerned with monitoring changes in the resource. In many cases it is the properties of the ecosystem that effectively determine the capacity of an area to absorb additional recreational pressure and are therefore central to the development of a site plan. Unfortunately, there is little research being conducted into the relations between site management goals and ecological constraints and those studies that are being carried out are uncoordinated. In the long term, planners must be responsible for co-ordinating research in this field and implementing findings whilst ecologists and geographers have to accept responsibility for experimentation, analysis and interpretation. Moreover, it is essential that local authorities and private landowners are encouraged to implement or to permit management experiments within their recreation areas in order to provide the right kinds of opportunity for the collection of data. Only then will it be possible to establish a harmonious balance between the demands of the recreationalist and the resource characteristics of semi-natural areas.

CHAPTER THIRTEEN

Planning for Outdoor Recreation

THIS chapter examines the machinery for outdoor recreation planning in Britain with certain comparisons with the North American situation at national, regional and local levels. Specific reference is made to certain case studies. Planning for recreation must be considered as an integral part of the whole planning process with all the key procedures represented, from the determination of basic goals and objectives to the preparation of detailed designs, their implementation and continuous monitoring.

During the last six years there has been a rapid growth in planning and provision for recreation in Britain, brought about chiefly by the setting up of the Sports Council in 1966 and the passing of the Countryside (Scotland) Act 1967, the Countryside, Transport and Town and Country Planning Acts 1968, the Development of Tourism Act 1969 and the availability of more funds for recreation in the local and central government and

private sectors. As the *Countryside in 1970* study group on leisure aptly pointed out: 'A great deal of the machinery already exists; the task is to make it work effectively.'[1]

Efficient use of the recreational planning machinery is thus the key to effective outdoor recreational planning. A major problem in Britain and abroad is that the agencies for recreational planning have often developed for purposes far removed from recreation and great difficulties have ensued in adapting and co-ordinating them to meet present needs.

The history of development of the various agencies has been well-documented in publications by Cullingworth[2] and White[3] and this appraisal concentrates on the current situation with pointers to the future.

THE FUNCTIONS OF THE AGENCIES

National Planning

The Department of the Environment is the principal government department responsible for executive action concerning countryside recreation, as part of its control of and ultimate

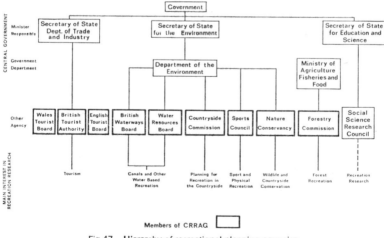

Fig 47   **Hierarchy** of recreational planning agencies

responsibility for the whole range of functions which affect people's living environment (Figure 47). Comparable central responsibility rests with the Secretary of State for Wales, the Secretary of State for Scotland and with the Minister of Development in Northern Ireland (when functioning) for their respective countries. However, even within this 'super' ministry, responsibility is somewhat fragmented; the Minister of Transport Industries looks after sport and recreation, and the Minister for Local Government and Development is responsible for water, the countryside and conservation. Regional offices of the Department have been set up to which considerable co-ordinating functions have been devolved.

The Countryside

Britain is unique in having set up a special body for the countryside (as opposed to recreation as a whole), with particular responsibilities for informal countryside recreation and conservation. This reflects strong popular feeling for the protection and enhancement of the countryside in a densely populated island.

The Countryside Commission was set up under the Countryside Act 1968 to administer powers for the 'conservation and enhancement of the natural beauty of the countryside, and to encourage the provision and improvement for persons resorting to the countryside of facilities for the enjoyment of the countryside and of open-air recreation in the countryside'. The Countryside Commission replaced the National Parks Commission, whose more limited powers under the 1949 Act[4] had become inadequate to deal with modern pressures on the countryside. A separate Countryside Commission for Scotland was set up in 1967. There is a separate Committee for Wales of the Countryside Commission, with a regional office at Newtown.

The total budget of the Commission compares unfavourably with that of other government bodies and with expenditure on urban recreation. In 1972–3 it was £1 million including grants

for national parks. The total national expenditure on country parks and picnic areas provided in England and Wales under the Countryside Act between 1968 and 1972 was only £2½ million, although there are indications that this is increasing. However, from a start in 1968 it is problematic whether the initial enthusiasm of local authorities to establish these areas will be maintained through local government reorganisation. So far the Countryside Commission has not made public any suggestions for the level of expenditure needed in this field. This is in marked contrast to the Sports Council's recommendation of £264 million to be spent on swimming baths, sports halls and golf courses by 1981.[5]

Between 1951 and 1957 ten national parks were created; an eleventh, the Cambrian Mountains National Park, was designated in 1972 and awaits confirmation. More than thirty areas of high landscape quality have been established as Areas of Outstanding Natural Beauty. Even in national parks access to open country may have to be negotiated, but a wide range of facilities can be provided. The creation of long-distance rights of way is grant-aided and over 800 miles of these have been approved, but there are no grants for the creation of links in routes at local or county level.

The Commission can recommend grant aid to local authorities providing access land, transit camping and caravan sites, country parks, picnic sites, tree planting and removal of eyesores. Assistance can also be given to private landowners tackling similar projects. Advice is given on landscape conservation and countryside recreation and the Commission carries out research, publishes a recreation news-sheet, prepares its own national countryside information material and supports information services operated in all the national parks.

Agriculture

Responsibilities of the government agricultural agencies in Britain and the United States towards recreation are essentially

indirect, although they play a very important part in shaping the appearance of the countryside in which much outdoor recreation takes place. Many of the conflicts and problems generated by these agencies through efforts to remove hedgerows or to conserve soil and water stem from the fact that the policies are carried through on private property with access controlled by the owner.[6] As the demand for outdoor recreation increases, however, the frequency and intensity of conflict will also increase. The nature and location of most such conflicts can be anticipated, plans can be formulated and programmes adopted to avert future crises.

It has been suggested[7] that there is no administrative machinery in Britain to deal with conflict at the level of the individual farm, where one carload of visitors comes into conflict with one farmer, and that new ways must be sought for bridging the gap between public and private interest in the countryside. Better management techniques are needed for landscape conservation and the design and running of recreation sites adjoining farmland. Information services on recreation provision and the need to conserve the countryside are vital for the farmer and general public. The Silsoe Conference paved the way by bringing together agriculturalists and conservationists.[8] Since this conference there has been a continuing dialogue resulting in a farm open day experiment involving the general public and proposals for additional landscape protection by the Countryside Commission. Greater assistance is needed for private landowners who wish to conserve wildlife, improve the landscape or provide recreation facilities. In the United States, on the other hand, such services are readily available through the Soil Conservation Service and Farmers Home Administration.

Forestry

Forest and woodland have a greater capacity than other types of land for absorbing people in the countryside without impairing the environment. It is thus particularly fortunate that govern-

ment agencies in both the United States and Britain are able to make available much of their forest for recreation, though the Forestry Commission's acreage of 3 million in Britain contrasts vividly with the 187 million acres managed by the US Forest Service. The *Countryside in 1970* report[9] commented that the Forestry Commission 'have become, if moving rather cautiously, a model for other landowners in providing informal picnic sites, laying out nature trails and interpreting forests for visitors by means of information centres, museums and guide books'. In 1970 the Commission had 15 million day visits,[10] although this is small beer indeed compared with the US Forest Service total which in 1968 reached 156 million.

Hitherto the facilities have been provided on a somewhat *ad hoc* basis, but it is now the Commission's policy[11] to prepare regional recreation plans. It is very important that these should be closely integrated with structure plans for the area concerned and that facilities are developed in those areas with the highest overall potential for informal recreation. Financing may be by either the Forestry Commission's own funds under the pro- visions of the Countryside Act or in partnership with local authorities for the development of country parks such as Afan Argoed, Glamorgan or Butser Hill/Queen Elizabeth Forest, Hampshire. The Commission have established forest parks over 600,000 acres of their holdings, chiefly in remote areas where recreational characteristics are noteworthy. While it is the Commission's policy to prohibit regular use of forest roads by motor vehicles, except where necessary for access to camping and picnic sites and car parks, where scenic drives for motorists have been established they have proved extremely popular (see Chapter 7). It is to be hoped that as a result of experiments such as Cwmcarn Scenic Forest Drive in Gwent, more such facilities can be created to take pressure off other roads. Thus a big change in emphasis has recently taken place in Forestry Commission policy, away from commercial forestry towards amenity and recreation provision.

National Parks

National parks occupy a special place in outdoor recreation in Britain: from 1949–68 they represented the only deliberate statutory attempt to provide areas for outdoor countryside recreation as well as for landscape preservation. They exist only in England and Wales, when it is arguable that by international standards it is in Scotland that large areas suitable for national parks are found. Because tens of thousands of people live, work and own land in British national parks, administration has been predominantly local, through county committees (see Chapter 6). Reorganisation of local government has not changed this essential feature, but has ensured that there is one executive board or committee for each park. Each park for the first time has to prepare a national park plan setting out its provisions for outdoor recreation and has to employ a national park officer to direct activities.

Other countries have used the term 'national park' more strictly and the most carefully thought-out structure is the National Park System of the United States, which is operated by the Department of the Interior through its National Park Service. This is responsible not only for the thirty-five national parks, but also for national monuments (such as Dinosaur National Monument, geological site), historic sites, national seashores and other sites of national importance. National ownership of most of the land and national planning and executive organisation have produced an impressive record in terms of conservation of landscape and provision of recreation opportunities, involving in national park status what is virtually a land use in its own right. To achieve a similar situation in Britain, the government would have to review the present boundaries of national parks and exclude areas, such as market towns, which cannot be managed or owned under national agency.

Water Recreation

There exists a strong and growing demand for the use of

rivers, lakes, canals and reservoirs for recreation (see Chapter 9). To satisfy this demand is only one of the many problems associated with the management and integration of water supply undertakings, bulk supply boards, river authorities, drainage and sewerage authorities which have encouraged the government to wave the magic wand of reorganisation and transform these bodies into regional water authorities which carry responsibility for water services as a whole. The new authorities which were set up on 1st April 1974 now have 'a duty to ensure the full development of rivers, canals and . . . reservoirs for amenity and recreation'.[12] A Water Space Amenity Commission has been set up to ensure the efficient performance by the regional water authorities of these functions outside Wales, which has its own Welsh National Water Development Authority.

Until now, the multiplicity of bodies involved have had to try to cope with water recreation demand in a classic situation where their primary role has been water supply, while the Countryside Commission, Sports Council and local authorities have all sought to guide and stimulate development of facilities. *Ad hoc* co-operation, as brought out in the admirable case studies by the Dartington Amenity Research Trust,[13] or as in the joint rehabilitation of the Monmouthshire and Brecon Canal by the British Waterways Board with Breconshire and Monmouthshire County Councils, supported by the Countryside Commission, has had some successes. The concern is that the new water authorities are now so large and all-embracing that provision for recreation may seem a minor item to them. Fortunately as far as canals are concerned, the British Waterways Board, which has been steadily improving its provision of healthy outdoor opportunities to users of the national canal system, has been exempted from the reorganisation.

Certainly, rational development of outdoor water recreation will not be ensured simply by the creation of the new regional authorities. It can only flow from full consultation by them

with planning authorities, the Department of the Environment, the Welsh Office, the Countryside Commission, the Sports Council and any others, such as the Central Electricity Generating Board, who may continue to control certain reservoirs.

Nature Conservancy Council

This government body, established through the National Parks and Access to the Countryside Act 1949, has two main functions: to conduct scientific research; and to conserve representative natural or semi-natural features of scientific interest through the creation of nature reserves and the identification of sites of special scientific interest. Particularly on its national nature reserves, the Conservancy has found itself involved in planning for or coping with outdoor recreation and has increasingly sought to cater for visitors to accessible reserves through nature trails and information centres as at Oxwich on the Gower Peninsula in South Wales, or at Ben Eighe in Scotland. It has also co-operated with planning authorities in the approach to county and sub-regional countryside plans to ensure that recreation proposals are compatible with ecological considerations.

National Trust

The National Trust (and, in Scotland, the National Trust for Scotland) is often thought of as a tweedy propper-up of mansions on hard times, but it should be regarded also as what it is: a charitable organisation empowered by Act of Parliament[14] to hold land and buildings in trust for the nation and to give access to them for recreation. It is not a government agency, but is run by its members and supported by public subscription and donation, yet it owns large parts of the Lake District, many other areas all over the country and operates selected places as picnic sites, caravan sites and country parks, usually in close co-operation with the recreation strategies of local planning authorities.

Private Developers

Grants or loans are available under the Countryside Act[15] from the national tourist boards in development areas and from the Council for Small Industries in Rural Areas for certain types of recreation development by private bodies. This has stimulated interest in projects such as country parks which might otherwise have been unable to attract initial capital. Several of the most popular day-trip targets in Britain, with a variety of attractions, are stately homes and their parklands. Many of these targets owe their origin to financial arrangements which have little to do with planning for outdoor recreation. As a break from the pattern of private development of existing resources, a recent experiment of particular interest has been the creation of the Landmark Centre in the Scottish Highlands,[16] offering in purpose-designed buildings a commercial package of information, interpretation of landscape and history through displays and films, craft shop, restaurant and plank-surfaced nature trail (for those who actually venture outdoors). Apart from the trail, the package could have been delivered equally well in the middle of Glasgow. Whether the Centre appeals because it helps visitors to relate to the countryside, or simply because it is a specific place to stop at, is hard to tell. Certainly it demonstrates that part of the demand for countryside recreation in terms of 'driving for pleasure' can be satisfied with comparatively little direct drain on countryside resources.

Tourism

Under the Development of Tourism Act 1969,[17] a British Tourist Authority was set up, with three national boards in England, Wales and Scotland carrying out executive functions. These include the administering of the Hotel Development Incentive Scheme and of subsequent government grants to new or expanding enterprises. A regional structure has been established, with, for example, in Wales, three regional tourism councils bringing together representatives of the tourist trade

and local authorities. A close liaison can be maintained between planning authorities and tourist boards. At a local level the structure provides for the affiliation of district and resort tourist associations. The range of activities covered is from advice of farmers on taking bed-and-breakfast guests to the arranging of national tourist promotions overseas, as well as the collection of data on holiday patterns and expenditure which should provide increasingly useful information for recreation planning on a regional scale.

Organised Sport

In Britain the Sports Council, a government-appointed body, deals with certain more organised recreation in the countryside, particularly water sports, golf, motor sports and other specialised activities. The great growth of these and the problem of resolving conflicts have been dealt with elsewhere (Chapters 1 and 9). Unlike the ministries of sport in some European countries, the Sports Council acts primarily in an advisory role, with the benefit of grants for facilities, coaching and development of sport, and information and research.

Great increases are evident in the levels of expenditure on sport as a whole, with special emphasis in the countryside on the provision of golf courses. A national assessment suggests that as many as 485 new eighteen hole courses will be required by 1981, costing over £43 million at current prices.[18] Further assessments are being made by the Sports Council in conjunction with the governing bodies of sport to determine specialist facilities needed by sport at regional and sub-regional level for high-level competition or advanced training purposes.

CO-ORDINATION OF GOVERNMENT DEPARTMENTS FOR RECREATION

It is useful to compare governmental machinery for co-ordinating outdoor recreation in Britain with that in the United

States. Both countries have effectively integrated research programmes through the two agencies: the Countryside Recreation Resources Advisory Group (CRRAG) in Britain and the Bureau of Outdoor Recreation in the Department of the Interior in the United States. CRRAG is an advisory body of all those government agencies which have powers to undertake research into aspects of countryside recreation in England, Wales and Scotland, but it has been instrumental in promoting joint research which is of benefit to recreational planning (Figure 47). Recent examples of such studies are the survey of mobile caravanning and camping[19] sponsored by eight of the member agencies and the water recreation case studies financed by the Countryside Commission and Sports Council. The Countryside in 1970 Conference[20] recommended that this co-operation should be extended to development projects. Both CRRAG and the Sports Council have published documents recommending further research needs.[21] Since only very large planning authorities are able to carry out original research on any scale, the link by continuous dialogue through these national agencies between planners and research workers is of vital importance in effectively disseminating research results.

The Bureau of Outdoor Recreation was set up in 1964 to deal with the problem of conflict and lack of any national policy for recreation.[22] The report found that 'Recreation has been an incidental, and almost an accidental by-product of the "primary purposes" of Federal agencies'. There are few activities, the report states, in which the relationships between federal, state and local government are so intertwined as in outdoor recreation. The study came to the important conclusion that the only satisfactory solution was the addition of a separate co-ordinating agency.

The recommendation was accepted. Public Law 88–29, *An Act to promote co-ordination and development of effective programs relating to outdoor recreation, and for other purposes*,[23] is a landmark in the history of recreational planning.

Its objectives are worth quoting at length:

(a) INVENTORY. Prepare and maintain a continuing inventory and evaluation of outdoor recreation needs and resources of the United States.

(b) CLASSIFICATION. Prepare a system for classification of outdoor recreation resources . . .

(c) NATIONWIDE PLAN. Formulate and maintain a comprehensive nationwide outdoor recreation plan . . .

(d) TECHNICAL ASSISTANCE. Provide technical assistance and advice to and co-operate with States, political sub-divisions and private interest . . . with respect to outdoor recreation.

(e) REGIONAL CO-OPERATION. Encourage inter-state and regional co-operation in the planning . . . of outdoor recreation resources.

(f) RESEARCH AND EDUCATION. (1) Sponsor, engage in, and assist in research relating to outdoor recreation . . . (2) co-operate with educational institutions . . . in order to assist in establishing educational programmes . . . to encourage public use and benefits from outdoor recreation.

(g) INTER-DEPARTMENTAL CO-OPERATION. (1) Co-operate with and provide technical assistance to Federal departments and agencies . . . (2) promote co-ordination of Federal plans . . .

In addition to the above functions, the Bureau of Outdoor Recreation administers the Land and Water Conservation Act programme[24] which makes 50 per cent grants to states and political sub-divisions for outdoor recreation planning, land acquisition and facility development, and makes funds available to certain federal agencies for acquiring land and water for outdoor recreation and preserving wildlife.

The scale of co-ordination needed for the federal outdoor recreation programmes is considerable. Eight cabinet-level departments and their fifty-five agencies, bureaux, services, administrations and offices, forty-one independent agencies, advisory boards, commissions and councils and 262 individual programmes were involved in February 1970. The Bureau conducts a continuing analysis of all phases of the federal outdoor recreation effort which provides a foundation for necessary adjustments and for identifying gaps and overlaps in existing programmes.

No similar co-ordinating body exists in Britain, although the chairmen of the bodies on CRRAG meet annually to discuss major policy issues of common interest.[25] There is a general requirement in the Countryside Act[26] that 'every Minister, government department and public body shall have regard to the desirability of conserving the natural beauty and amenity of the countryside'.

In both countries, outdoor recreation problems constantly cross administrative and spatial boundaries and call for solutions based on nationally co-ordinated policies.

RECREATIONAL PLANNING AT THE REGIONAL LEVEL

Regional planning in Britain today suffers from inadequate machinery for effectively co-ordinated action, although technical expertise and regional information are often available. In 1964–5 the government set up regional economic planning councils in England, with nominated members, and regional economic planning boards, a parallel administrative organisation. The latter now form the regional offices of the Department of the Environment. Similar arrangements apply in Wales, but in Scotland the Scottish Development Department has a slightly different function. In many regions local authorities have set up their own standing conferences on regional planning (not

necessarily covering the same regional areas as the government councils).

Regional sports councils were set up by the Sports Council in 1966–7 and in some cases took over earlier co-ordinating bodies. They advise on investment in sport and have carried out some noteworthy studies.[27] Local authority planning officers play a leading role on their technical panels and help to ensure that effectively co-ordinated proposals for sports development are put forward. Unfortunately, with the introduction of a new policy on grants,[28] the regional sports councils have lost the important function of vetting local authority projects for loan sanction. Hitherto they were able to make sure that there was joint planning and provision and the approval was not given to unduly extravagant facilities planned in isolation. However, enlightened authorities have been able to overcome these problems by agreement between county and district councils.[29] There are no parallel organisations of the Countryside Commission dealing with informal countryside recreation except for the Committee for Wales.

Joint governmental/local authority study teams have been created to make special regional planning studies the first of which to be completed is the Strategic Plan for the South East.[30] Sub-regional studies have been mounted by groups of local authorities and have contributed substantially to the techniques of regional planning. Such *ad hoc* groups and their studies are of an advisory nature and it is at government and local authority level that executive action is taken.

The complexity of administrative areas dealing with different aspects of outdoor recreation is illustrated in Figure 48 showing the current situation in Wales. A notable feature is the wide divergence in boundaries used by different bodies which can give rise to considerable delays, duplication of effort, wastage of resources, and which often frustrates the implementation of particular policies.

As Cullingworth and Senior have pointed out,[31] regional

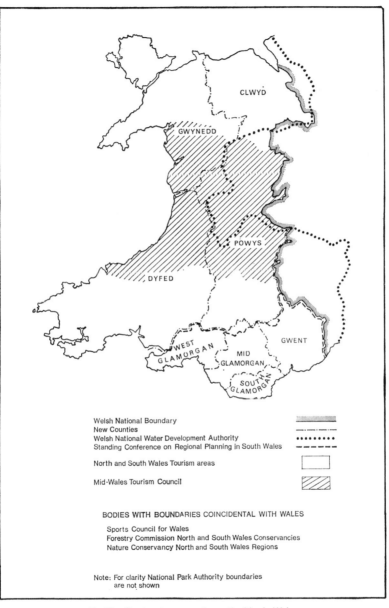

CLWYD

GWYNEDD

POWYS

DYFED

WEST GLAMORGAN

MID GLAMORGAN

SOUTH GLAMORGAN

GWENT

Welsh National Boundary	
New Counties	
Welsh National Water Development Authority	
Standing Conference on Regional Planning in South Wales	
North and South Wales Tourism areas	
Mid-Wales Tourism Council	

BODIES WITH BOUNDARIES COINCIDENTAL WITH WALES

Sports Council for Wales
Forestry Commission North and South Wales Conservancies
Nature Conservancy North and South Wales Regions

Note: For clarity National Park Authority boundaries
are not shown

Fig 48   Overlapping recreation authorities in Wales

planning means different things to central and local government. To the central government, regional planning is chiefly concerned with correcting the imbalance between one region and another; only with reluctance does it become involved in the making of investment decisions within regions on a territorial as well as a functional basis. Local government, on the other hand, sees regional planning as the expression of national policies primarily, in terms of a comprehensive long-term strategy for economic and physical development within each provincial region, in the context of which local planning authorities can work out meaningful structure plans.

Because of differences in their interpretation, regional plans for recreation will be likely to suffer from the same deficiencies in implementation as the rest of the regional studies, particularly where investment is involved. For instance, under the present system one local authority could decide to make a large investment in a country park which might not in fact be needed, while another authority might need to provide such a facility to meet regional needs, but have no inclination to do so.[32]

The context of some of the regional studies is examined later in this chapter. Even the new structure plan process provides only for voluntary joint structure plans[33] and the minister cannot force such action. Little progress can therefore be made on true regional recreation plans unless the government introduces an additional tier into the system of regional recreation planning.

Where ad hoc regional park authorities have been set up they have achieved notable success, provided their master plans are closely related to the needs of the communities they serve. To date there is only one such body in Britain, the Lee Valley Regional Park Authority, although further such bodies are under active consideration. An admirably illustrated description of its proposals is given in the Master Plan.[34] The authority comprises representatives of fifteen local authorities and has powers to raise finance by rate precepts from the Greater

London Council and the county councils of Essex and Hertford-shire. The general power and duty of the authority is 'to develop, improve, preserve and manage, or to procure or arrange for the development, improvement, preservation and management of the park [amounting to nearly 10,000 acres] as a place for the enjoyment of leisure, recreation, sport, games or amusements or any similar activity, for the provision of nature reserves and for the provision of entertainments of all kinds'. Thus the em-phasis is on intensive as well as informal countryside recreational use. Regrettably, special legislation is necessary every time such a separate body is set up.

Local Government and Recreation Planning

While local government in Britain has a statutory responsi-bility for provision for recreation in the limited spheres set out in the National Parks and Countryside Acts, interpretation and implementation of these powers varies very widely. The first conference (in 1965) of the *Countryside in 1970* recommended the setting up of special countryside committees of county councils, and with the passing of the Countryside Act these have made appreciable progress in many counties. A feature of these committees is the number of co-opted bodies representing the more important, voluntary countryside interests, water authorities and government departments. These committees are usually closely linked with the planning committees.

The Bains Report[35] on management of the reorganised local authorities in England and Wales from 1974 gives prominence, in suggested alternative committee structures, to special com-mittees for amenities and countryside. In the top tier non-metropolitan counties such committees are likely to include country parks, rights of way, commons, caravan sites, gipsy sites, recreation, tourism and entertainment. At the second tier new non-metropolitan districts are also likely to group together leisure and recreation functions, including recreation and tourism, entertainments, museums and commons.

There is much hidden expenditure on outdoor recreation at a local level. For instance, footpath signing and maintenance may be hidden in a wide variety of headings in highway authority budgets. Judging by results[36] this varies widely from authority to authority, but is often a low priority. Certain important activities such as horse-riding may receive no financial assistance at all. On the other hand a local authority may opt to spend all its resources under locally determined expenditure[37] on a grandiose swimming pool to the exclusion of far more cost-effective jointly planned recreation facilities in the urban and rural sector.

THE RECREATION PLAN PREPARATION PROCESS

National Plans

No national plan for countryside recreation is being prepared in Britain today, although this is being attempted in the United States. In Britain the emphasis is on policy guidelines to local planning authorities, and on the hierarchy of national parks (nationally determined), areas of outstanding natural beauty, country parks and picnic sites. Countryside Commission policy towards grant aid for picnic areas and country parks is set out in a description by Zetter. Since country parks have only been possible since 1968, the Commission acknowledge that 'there is a need for country parks almost anywhere in the country', but they have judged applications for grant in the light of known recreation facilities within a radius of about thirty miles and in relation to main traffic routes.[38] Also considered is the extent to which the park could be expected 'to attract people who would otherwise go to the coast, to a national park or to some other vulnerable area where over-use would cause erosion or other physical damage'. Zetter feels that in the short period since the Countryside Act came into force it would be unrealistic to expect a mature policy to have evolved, but firm guidelines have been set for a sound policy to be developed.[39] In practice

the tendency has been for some authorities to make a substantial contribution in providing country parks and picnic sites, while in areas of apparent need other authorities have done little.

It is to be expected, as the competition for funds between one scheme and another becomes greater and appraisals of need, by local and regional studies in conjunction with the Countryside Commission, are completed,[40] that a more sophisticated system of assessing grant aid could emerge which could form the basis of a national plan for country parks.

In Britain there is no comprehensive national or regional record of the resources available for outdoor recreation and it is important to ensure that the knowledge that voluntary bodies possess is fully utilised.[41] However, the Countryside Commission have carried out what is probably the world's most thorough study of a country's coastline[42] in conjunction with local authorities, and most regional sports councils have carried out studies of the recreational use of inland and coastal waters. However, these two types of area form only a small proportion of the total amount of land available for outdoor recreation. More than one-quarter of county planning authorities in England and Wales have also done comprehensive surveys of countryside recreation resources, but almost all of them have classified these resources differently. Attempts are being made by the Countryside Commission to advise on standardised mapping notations, but there continues to be wide divergence of content in county studies.[43]

When the Bureau of Outdoor Recreation was set up in 1964 in the USA, with one of its prime functions to prepare a national plan for outdoor recreation, it was in the knowledge that provision for countryside recreation by state, federal and other agencies was already very extensive, as documented in the ORRRC reports. Although the Nationwide Plan[44] will take into account information provided by the states and their political sub-divisions, it will not simply be an amalgamation of fifty state plans but will provide an overall view of outdoor recreation

18

in the US. This National Plan is intended to examine supply and demand factors for outdoor recreation, to identify present and future needs for areas, facilities and opportunities, and to make recommendations for meeting these needs projected to AD 1980, 2000 and 2020. It is intended as a framework and device for co-ordinating and developing federal, regional, state, local and private outdoor recreation programmes. Detailed inventories will range from small town parks to multi-million acre forest areas, and will cover most types of recreation activity.

Public participation through a series of forums has already featured significantly in the preparation of the Plan.[45] Work groups have been organised among the many federal agencies with an interest in outdoor recreation to deal with particular topics, to consider views expressed at the forums and make recommendations for alternative solutions to the problems. A Federal Task Force made up of policy-level representatives from the various departments is providing a steering group to the work group findings. This combination should enable the Bureau of Outdoor Recreation to produce a plan which is both practicable and sensitive to the needs of the people.

Structure Plans

Local planning authorities in Britain today are gradually moving over to a new planning process to prepare structure plans within their areas under the provisions of the 1971 Town and Country Planning Act. The recreation element in the structure plan[46] is now assuming a much more positive and important role than in the old-style development plan. It is seen to be closely related to transport, employment, and landscape and conservation and cannot be treated separately. The 1972 Town and Country Planning Act encourages the preparation of joint structure plans by neighbouring planning authorities which form cohesive sub-regions, such as South Hampshire and Norfolk and Norwich.

The underlying purposes of a structure plan[47] are that:

(i) it represents a local authority's broad intentions, not finite and definitive, but evolutionary in character;

(ii) these intentions are part of a broad process of reaching social and economic objectives, recognised in part through prediction of demand for a variety of facilities or resources;

(iii) it is a continuous planning process, where it is important to monitor consequences of decisions and actions;

(iv) it is not restricted to the arrangement of land uses, but is concerned with a comprehensive management of investment and land.

As Cherry has written:[48]

> The planner's task is therefore to facilitate the development of a wider range of leisure outlets which are both personal and purposive. This takes him away from traditionally conceived concepts of planning for recreation which were seen mainly in terms of land use. It extends his interest and concern beyond standards for playing fields or allotments or the provision of facilities such as tennis courts or swimming baths. Instead he is given the opportunity of developing a new co-ordinating role, with the requirement to provide a comprehensive range of provision from local to district and to regional scale. In short it is important to recognise the place which recreation planning occupies in the total planning process; it is integrating and central, not exclusive and peripheral.

The structure plan for recreation needs will have a 'broad brush' basis, highlighting the provision of major facilities in both town and country which have strategic or other implications from the point of view of investment or planning requirements. It is through the structure plan process and the public participation machinery that alternatives become identified and conflicts of interest, rather than consensus, identify priorities. The use of new planning techniques enables goals of structure plans to be broken down into objectives which can then be quantified and compared with one another.

Local plans and individual countryside projects will be

prepared within the framework of structure plans. Figure 49 illustrates the complex processes involved even at this level.

Planning Techniques

Rapid advances have taken place in the techniques of outdoor recreation planning in recent years on the supply side of the equation, though this has not been matched on the demand side. It is not proposed here to dwell in detail on demand prediction techniques, as these have been amply covered in Chapter 1. Suffice it to draw attention to the uncertainty of accurate predictive techniques at local planning authority levels, although CRRAG agencies have sponsored very useful studies on particular recreation activities.[49] The greatest promise for the future is in the mounting of regional studies on a collaborative basis along the lines of the admirable North West Leisure Activities Survey.[50]

Development of techniques on the supply of outdoor recreation resources has been chiefly in response to an appreciation of the complexity of conflicts to be resolved, the great growth in activity levels, and the availability of new data-processing methods at a time when planning methodology as a whole is undergoing fundamental change. Hitherto the new techniques have been developed at regional and sub-regional levels. While the systems approach to planning originated in the United States,[51] the practical application of new theories to planning problems has seen a great leap forward in Britain in recent years. Probably one of the most promising techniques for identifying potential informal recreation areas is the potential surface technique,[52] basically a technique for making a comparative evaluation of the areal distribution of resource potential, in accordance with the capability of land for meeting certain predefined objectives. Best results are obtained when it is used across the board for structure plan purposes as in the Coventry-Warwickshire-Solihull Sub-Regional Study (Figure 50).[53] The recreation component has been the subject of further

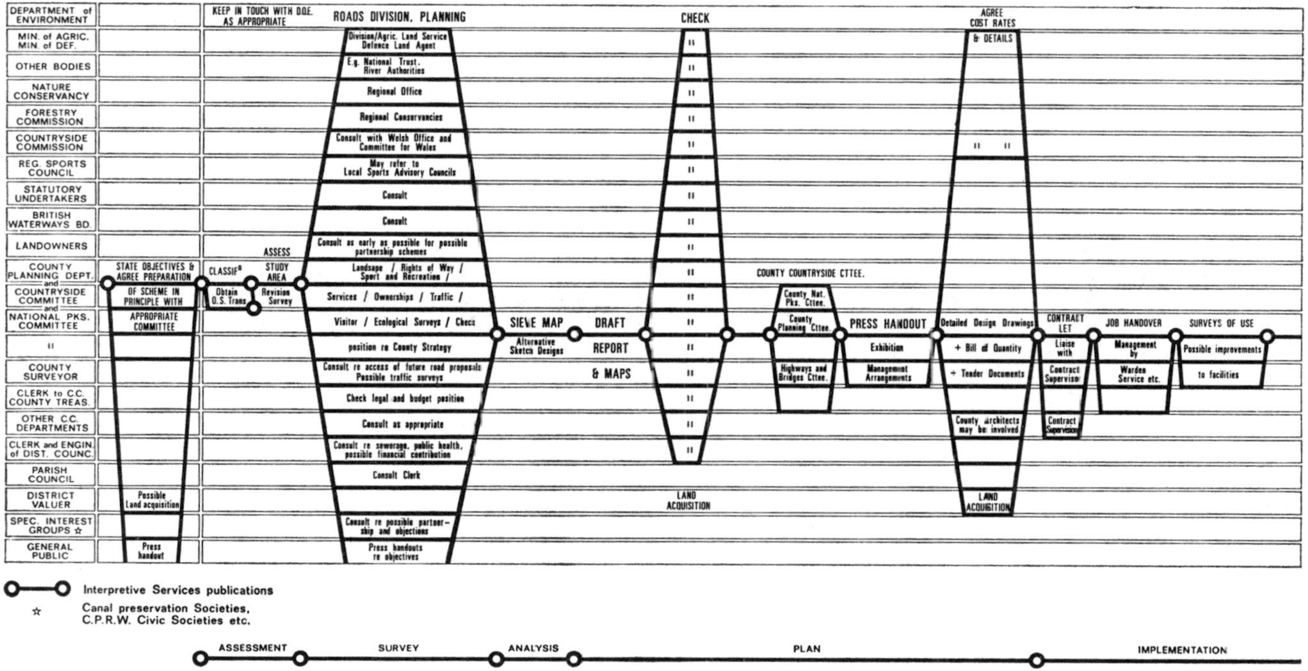
DEPARTMENT of ENVIRONMENT
MIN. of AGRIC. MIN. of DEF.
OTHER BODIES
NATURE CONSERVANCY
FORESTRY COMMISSION
COUNTRYSIDE COMMISSION
REG. SPORTS COUNCIL
STATUTORY UNDERTAKERS
BRITISH WATERWAYS BD.
LANDOWNERS
COUNTY PLANNING DEPT. and
COUNTRYSIDE COMMITTEE and
NATIONAL PKS. COMMITTEE
COUNTY SURVEYOR
CLERK to C.C. COUNTY TREAS.
OTHER C.C. DEPARTMENTS
CLERK and ENGIN. of DIST. COUNC.
PARISH COUNCIL
DISTRICT VALUER
SPEC. INTEREST GROUPS ☆
GENERAL PUBLIC
STATE OBJECTIVES & AGREE PREPARATION
OF SCHEME IN PRINCIPLE WITH
APPROPRIATE COMMITTEE
Possible Land acquisition
Press handout
KEEP IN TOUCH WITH D.O.E. AS APPROPRIATE
CLASSIF
ASSESS
STUDY AREA
Obtain O.S. Trans
Revision Survey
ROADS DIVISION, PLANNING
Division/Agric. Land Service Defence Land Agent
E.g. National Trust, River Authorities
Regional Office
Regional Conservancies
Consult with Welsh Office and Committee for Wales
May refer to Local Sports Advisory Councils
Consult
Consult
Consult as early as possible for possible partnership schemes
Landscape / Rights of Way / Sport and Recreation /
Services / Ownerships / Traffic /
Visitor / Ecological Surveys / Check
position re County Strategy
Consult re access of future road proposals Possible traffic surveys
Check legal and budget position
Consult as appropriate
Consult re sewerage, public health, possible financial contribution
Consult Clerk
Consult re possible partnership and objectives
Press handouts re objectives
SIEVE MAP
Alternative Sketch Designs
DRAFT
REPORT
& MAPS
CHECK
LAND ACQUISITION
COUNTY COUNTRYSIDE CTTEE.
County Nat. Pks. Cttee.
County Planning Cttee.
Highways and Bridges Cttee.
PRESS HANDOUT
Exhibition
Management Arrangements
AGREE COST RATES
& DETAILS
Detailed Design Drawings
+ Bill of Quantity
+ Tender Documents
County architects may be involved
LAND ACQUISITION
CONTRACT LET
Liaise with
Contract Supervisor
Contract Supervision
JOB HANDOVER
Management by
Warden Service etc.
SURVEYS OF USE
Possible improvements
to facilities
Interpretive Services publications
☆ Canal preservation Societies, C.P.R.W. Civic Societies etc.
ASSESSMENT
SURVEY
ANALYSIS
PLAN
IMPLEMENTATION

Fig 49 Complexity of recreational planning within the structure plan framework

detailed research in a South Wales regional exercise and further work is being undertaken by the South East planning agencies.[54] The technique ensures comparability between structure plans in neighbouring counties. The public participation process can

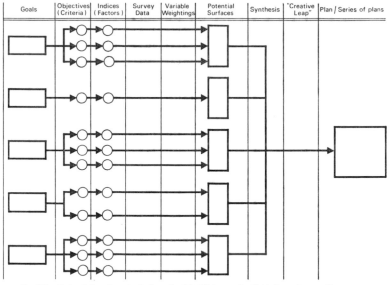

Fig 50 Potential surface technique for identifying potential informal recreation areas

be used in the weighting of the objectives and indices. Use of the computer can speed the technique so that alternative strategies may be generated and a large number of factors combined in a systematic way. Monitoring of the effectiveness of any plan is facilitated and, finally, short-term investment decisions for the siting of such major facilities as country parks can be on the basis of the preferred surface in advance of a structure plan.

Management Training

The planning and provision of facilities for outdoor recreation must be complemented by adequate management of those

facilities. Ideally, management should provide a feedback to the planning process so that continuous monitoring of performance is possible and future provision can be related to it. A problem arises in that many of the facilities are new to the authorities providing them, and management tends to be on an *ad hoc* basis. There are at present no recognised qualifications for national park or countryside wardens, or for supervisors or managers of country parks or countryside centres. A wide range of existing qualifications and/or experience will provide some sort of background for such staff, who will usually have to 'learn on the job' without formal training. With growing numbers involved and growing realisation of the benefits to be had from more organised training, the time is now ripe for the introduction of, for example, in-service courses for wardens. In the absence of a national lead, groups of authorities may have to pool their resources or support such suggestions as that made recently for a university-based course at Salford.[55] This is certainly a major gap in the British system at present. With so many agencies involved, the situation contrasts strongly with that in the US, where one of the key features of, for example, the National Park Service, is its management organisation.

CONCLUSIONS: THE FUTURE

In this brief review of planning agencies for outdoor recreation it is necessary to highlight certain basic issues and trends.

Co-ordination and co-operation of the many agencies involved is of paramount importance in Britain at a period of rapid change following reorganisation of local government and of water undertakings in 1974. This will be needed not only between authorities, but also within their own departments, particularly highways, planning and education, where integration is vital. At a national level the strengthening of co-ordinating bodies such as CRRAG to include development projects as well as research would be highly advantageous. The recreational use

of forests and water areas in particular is likely to grow and the agencies responsible should be appropriately strengthened, while care should be taken to avoid overlapping functions. Greater understanding of the linkages between urban and rural recreation needs and provision could lead to more effectively balanced investment programmes at national and local levels. We are likely to see greater precision in recreation planning techniques and an increasing awareness of the interaction of policies.

It is unlikely that a national plan for recreation will be prepared in Britain. More likely is the sum of regional and/or structure plans. However, greater central government guidance is needed on priorities for country parks. More effective regional planning is vital since many recreation planning problems require solution at regional level.

While legislation already available provides a good framework for the development of outdoor recreation facilities, there are three areas where, to assist planning agencies, change is required in Britain; first, for the streamlined setting up of regional park agencies without the need to promote separate parliamentary bills; secondly, for clearer indications of the use to which common land may be put for recreational purposes; thirdly, for the reform of the boundaries and functions of national parks.[56]

Research priorities have been well documented in the outdoor recreation field. Far greater knowledge of recreation traffic movements and their inclusion in land use transportation studies would be of great benefit to many planning agencies.

Britain has a great deal to learn from the United States in the field of professional management of recreation areas, particularly in interpretative services and warden (ranger) training. Co-ordination of information and publicity services is becoming increasingly important with the proliferation of bodies involved in countryside interpretation, education, tourism and recreation.

NOTES

No detailed bibliography is included in this volume, since the notes to each chapter given in the following pages contain much bibliographical material and a comprehensive review of the literature on the subject.

CHAPTER ONE

1 Countryside Recreation Research Advisory Group, *Countryside Recreation Glossary*, Countryside Commission (1970)
2 Countryside Commission, *The Demand for Outdoor Recreation in the Countryside* (Report of a seminar held in London on 15 January 1970)
3 Countryside Commission, 5
4 Knetsch, J. L., 'Assessing the Demand for Outdoor Recreation', *Journal of Leisure Research*, 1, No 2 (1969), 85–7
5 North Regional Planning Committee, *Outdoor Leisure Activities in the Northern Region* (1969)
6 Patmore, J. A. and Rodgers, H. B. (eds), *Leisure in the North West* (North West Sports Council, 1972)
7 Sillitoe, K. K., *Planning for Leisure* (Government Social Survey, HMSO, 1969), Table 8, 41
8 Central Statistical Office, *Social Trends*, No 3 (1972), Table 125
9 British Tourist Authority, *Digest of Tourist Statistics*, No 2 (1971)

10 For further details see: British Tourist Authority (formerly British Travel Association), *Home Holiday Surveys* (1951 onwards); Countryside Commission, *Digest of Countryside Recreation Statistics* (1969); *Britain 1972 An Official Handbook* (HMSO, 1972)

11 British Tourist Authority University of Keele, *Pilot National Recreation Survey*

12 North Regional Planning Committee, op cit

13 Patmore, J. A. and Rodgers, H. B., *Leisure in the North West*

14 House, J. W., 'Whitby as a Resort', *A Survey of Whitby*, ed. G. H. J. Daysh (Shakespeare Head Press, 1958)

15 Hutchins, H. Clifton and Trecker, E. W., *The State Park Visitor, A Report of the Wisconsin Park and Forest Travel Study*. Wisconsin Conservation Department (1961)

16 Lund, Richard E., *A Study of Wyoming's Out-of-State Highway Travellers* (University of Wyoming, 1961)

17 Copeland, Lewis C., *Travellers and Arkansas Business 1948–1956* (Arkansas Publicity and Parks Commission, Arkansas State Highway Commission, US Bureau of Public Roads and the University of Arkansas, 1951)

18 Countryside Commission, *Research Register No 5* (Autumn 1972)

19 Mansfield, N., 'Recreational Trip Generation', *Journal of Transport Economics and Public Policy*, 3, No 2 (1969), 152–64

20 Colenutt, R., *An Investigation into the Factors Affecting the Pattern of Trip Generation and Route of Choice of Day Visitors to the Countryside* (PhD thesis, University of Bristol, 1970, unpublished)

21 Colenutt, R. op cit

22 Outdoor Recreation Resources Review Commission, *Outdoor Recreation for America*, Summary Report and 27 Study Reports (US Government Printing Office, 1962)

23 Outdoor Recreation Resources Review Commission, *Prospective Demand for Outdoor Recreation*, Study Report No 26 (US Government Printing Office, 1962)

24 Outdoor Recreation Resources Review Commission, *National Recreation Survey*, Study Report No 19, Appendix A, 77–94 (US Government Printing Office, 1962)

25 Outdoor Recreation Resources Review Commission, *National Recreation Survey*

26 Burton, T. L. and Wibberley, G. P., *Outdoor Recreation in the British Countryside* (Wye College Department of Economics, 1965)

27 British Travel Association/University of Keele, *Pilot National Recreation Survey*, Report No 1 (1967); Report No 2 (1969)

28 Sillitoe, K. K., *Planning for Leisure*, Government Social Survey (HMSO, 1969)

29 North Regional Planning Committee, *Outdoor Leisure Activities in the Northern Region* (1969)

30 Patmore, J. A. and Rodgers, H. B. (eds), *Leisure in the North West* (North West Sports Council, 1972)

31 Ibid

32 North Regional Planning Committee, op cit, 3

33 Sillitoe, K. K., *Planning for Leisure*

34 Greater London Council Planning Department, *Surveys of the use of open space, Volume 1* (Greater London Council, 1968)

35 South Western Sports Council, *Initial Appraisal of Major Facilities* (August 1967)

36 Figures for participation rates were taken from Government Social Survey publication *Planning for Leisure* (1969)

37 The Sports Council's recommended standard is one eighteen-hole golf course for 20,000–30,000 persons

38 Willmott, P., 'Some Social Trends', *Urban Studies*, 6, No 3 (1969), 286–308

39 Rodgers, H. B., 'Leisure and Recreation', *Urban Studies*, 6, No 3 (1969), 368–84

40 Young, M. and Willmott, P., *Family and Kinship in East London* (Routledge, 1957)
Young, M. and Zweig, F., *The Worker in an Affluent Society* (Heinemann, 1961)

41 Rodgers, H. B., 'Leisure and Recreation', op cit

42 Willmott, P., 'Some Social Trends', op cit

43 Quoted by M. O'Rianain in a paper on Traffic Forecasting contained in European Travel Commission *Seminar on Forecasting Tourist Movement* (British Tourist Authority, 1971)

44 Outdoor Recreation Resources Review Commission, *Prospective Demand for Outdoor Recreation*

45 European Travel Commission, *Seminar on Forecasting Tourist Movement* (Report of Proceedings, British Tourist Authority, 1971)

46 Patmore, J. A. and Rodgers, H. B. (eds), *Leisure in the North West*

47 Dower, M. and McCarthy, P. E., 'Planning for Conservation and Development', *Journal of the Royal Town Planning Institute*, 53, No 1 (1967), 99–105

48 Furmidge, J., 'Planning for Recreation in the Countryside', *Journal of the Royal Town Planning Institute*, 55, No 2 (1969), 62–7

49 Houghton-Evans, W. and Miles, J. C., 'Environmental Capacity in Rural Recreation Areas', *Journal of the Royal Town Planning Institute*, 56, No 10 (1970), 423–7

50 Quoted by the Planning Correspondent: 'Over Use May be Destroying the New Forest', *The Guardian* (25 November 1970)

51 Cesario, F. J., 'Operations Research in Outdoor Recreation', *Journal of Leisure Research*, 1, No 1 (1969), 33–51

CHAPTER TWO

1 Burdge, R. J. and Field, D. R., 'Methodological Perspectives for the Study of Outdoor Recreation', *Journal of Leisure Research*, 4 (1972), 63

2 Craik, K. H., 'Environmental Psychology', *New Directions in Psychology*, 4 (1970), 1

3 Campbell, F. L., 'Participant Observation in Outdoor Recreation', *Journal of Leisure Research*, 2 (1970), 226; Burch, W. R., 'The Play-World of Camping: Research into the social meaning of outdoor recreation', *American Journal of Sociology*, 70 (1965), 604; Etzkorn, K. P., 'Leisure and Camping—The social meaning of a form of outdoor recreation', *Sociology and Social Research*, 49 (1964), 76

4 Clawson, M. and Knetsch, J. L., 'Outdoor Recreation Research, Some Concepts and Suggested Areas of Study', *Natural Researches Journal* (October 1963)

NOTES 301

5 Mercer, D., 'The Role of Perception in the Recreation Experience: Review and discussion', *Journal of Leisure Research*, 3 (1971), 261

6 La Page, W. F., 'The Outdoor Recreation Culture—Implications for commercial development', paper presented at 1972 Society for Range Management Meeting, Washington DC (mimeo), 8

7 Leigh, J., *Young People and Leisure* (Routledge, 1971)

8 Van Doren, C. S. and Lentnek, B., 'Activity Specialization among Ohio's Recreation Boaters', *Journal of Leisure Research*, 1 (1969), 312–13

9 Murphy, P. E., 'The Role of Attitude in the Choice Decisions of Recreational Boaters', *Journal of Leisure Research* (in press)

10 Hendee, J. C., 'Rural-urban Differences Reflected in Outdoor Recreation Participation', *Journal of Leisure Research*, 1 (1969), 338

11 Rogers, T. W., 'Migration Prediction on the Basis of Prior Migratory Behaviour', *International Migration*, 7 (1969), 13

12 Michelson, W., *Man and His Urban Environment: A sociological approach* (Addison-Wesley, 1970), 70

13 Rawley, K. and Peucker, T. K., 'Park-Awareness and Park-Use in Cities', *Western Geographical Series*, 1 (1970), 125

14 Hendee, J. C., Gale, R. P. and Catton, W. R., Jr, 'A Typology of Outdoor Recreation Activity Preferences', *The Journal of Environmental Education*, 3 (1971), 28

15 The concept of the mental map was initially outlined by P. Gould in *On Mental Maps* (1966), Michigan Inter-University Community of Mathematical Geographers, Discussion Paper No 9

16 Mercer, D., 'The Demand for Recreation at the Urban Fringe: The Example of Fern Tree Gully National Park', *Australian Geographer*, 11 (1971), 504

17 La Page, W., 'The Impulse Camper', *USDA Forest Service Research Note*, Northeastern Forest Experiment Station, USA (1972)

18 See, for example, Brown, L. A. and Moore, E. G., 'The Intra-Urban Migration Process: A perspective', *Geografiska Annaler*, Series B (1970), 1; Brown, L. A. and Holmes, J., 'Search Behavior in an Intra-Urban Migration Context', *Environment and Planning*, 3 (1971), 307

19 Golledge, R. G., 'Conceptualizing the Market Decision Process', *Journal of Regional Science*, 7 (1967), 239

20 Mercer, D., 'Beach Usage in the Melbourne Region', *Australian Geographer*, XII (1972), 123

21 Mercer, D., 'Discretionary Travel Behaviour and the Urban Mental Map', *Australian Geographical Studies*, IX (1971), 133

22 Barker, M. L., 'The Perception of Water Quality as a Factor in Consumer Attitudes and Space Preferences in Outdoor Recreation' (mimeo; paper presented at the annual meeting of the Association of American Geographers, Washington, DC, August 1968)

23 Cole, A., 'Spatial Behaviour of Camping Vacationists in the Grampian Ranges of Victoria' (mimeo; report submitted to the Recreation Branch, Forests Commission of Victoria, 1971). This was based on Lynch, K., *The Image of the City* (Harvard, 1960)

24 Murphy, P. E., 'The Potential and Problems of Experiments in Geography: A case study', *B.C. Geographical Series* (in press)

25 See, for example, Brown, P. J. and Hunt, J. D., 'The Influence of Information Signs on Visitor Distribution and Use', *Journal of Leisure Research*, 1 (1969), 79

26 Campbell, C. K., 'An Approach to Research in Recreational Geography', *BC Geographical Series*, 7 (1966), 85

27 Wolfe, R. I., 'The Inertia Model', *Journal of Leisure Research*, 4 (1972), 73

28 Lentnek, B., Van Doren, C. S. and Trail, J. R., 'Spatial Behavior in Recreational Boating', *Journal of Leisure Research*, 1 (1969), 103

29 Rostron, J., 'The Contribution of Attitude Studies to Outdoor Recreation Planning', *Western Geographical Series*, 3 (1970), 31

30 See, for example, Lime, D. W. and Stankey, G. M., 'Carrying Capacity: Maintaining outdoor recreation quality', *Recreation Symposium Proceedings*, Northeastern Forest Experiment Station USA (1971), 174

31 Sonnenfeld, J., 'Personality and Behavior in Environment', *Proceedings of the Association of American Geographers*, 1 (1969), 136

32 Knopp, T. B., 'Environmental Determinants of Recreation Behavior', *Journal of Leisure Research*, 4 (1972), 136

CHAPTER THREE

1 Allen, C. J., *Swiss Travel Wonderland* (Ian Allan, 1972)
2 Her journey was made on the uncompleted Liverpool & Manchester Railway, 25 August 1830. Her companion on the open footplate of the Northumbrian was George Stephenson himself. See Rolt, L. T. C., *George and Robert Stephenson: The railway revolution* (Longmans, 1960), 190–2
3 Granville, A. B., *The Spas of England and Principal Sea-Bathing Places* (I, Henry Colburn, 1841), xliii–iv
4 Simmons, J. (ed), *Journeys in England, an Anthology* (David & Charles, 1969), 34
5 Quoted in Gregory, L. F., 'View-Hunting with Genevieve', *Town and Country Planning*, 33 (1965), 151
6 Patmore, J. A., *Land and Leisure* (Penguin, 1972), 36
7 Yapp, W. B., *The Weekend Motorist in the Lake District* (HMSO, 1969), 22
8 Ibid, Table 12, 18
9 Hampshire County Council *et al*, *East Hampshire AONB, A study in countryside conservation* (Hampshire County Council, 1968), 21
10 Picozzi, N., *Breeding Performance and Shooting Bags of Red Grouse in Relation to Public Access in the Peak District National Park, England* (Unpublished report, Peak Park Planning Board, 1971), Table III
11 Ibid, 6, recording observations by N. Bayfield
12 Brathay Exploration Group, *The Gairloch Conservation Unit, Wester Ross: A technique for monitoring recreational use in upland areas* (Brathay Hall Trust, Field Studies Report No. 19, 1972), para 7.3. The survey period was 20–29 July 1972, in 'near perfect' weather conditions. It was estimated that about 90 per cent of people who entered the area of survey were recorded, some 1,239 people in all
13 Clawson, M., *Land and Water for Recreation: Opportunities, problems, and policies* (Rand McNally, 1963), 42
14 Ibid, 40, 42
15 Patmore, J. A. and Rodgers, H. B. (eds), *Leisure in the North West* (North West Sports Council, 1972); see especially chapters 5 and 6

16 Huron–Clinton Metropolitan Authority, *1965 Park Users Survey* (unpublished staff report, 1965)

17 Quoted in Gilbert, E. W., *Brighton, Old Ocean's Bauble* (Methuen, 1954), 118; the discussion of Brighton is derived largely from this source

18 Ibid, 152

19 Barrie, D. S. M., and Clinker, C. R., *The Somerset & Dorset Railway* (Oakwood Press, 1948), 27

20 Dorset County Council *et al*, *Land Use and Transportation Study of South East Dorset and South West Hampshire: Survey of holidaymakers, 1968* (Dorset County Council, 1971), Table 15

21 Ibid, Table 10

22 Jackson, R. T., 'Motorways and National Parks in Britain', *Area*, 4 (1970), 26–9

23 Wilson, H. and Womersley, L., *Traffic Management in the Lake District National Park* (The Friends of the Lake District, 1972), 6

24 Hennessy, B. and Mansfield, N. W., *Pleasure Traffic and Recreation in the Lake District: A research report based on a survey of weekend motorists* (Countryside Commission: British Tourist Authority, undated), Table 8

25 Colenutt, R. J., 'Modelling Travel Patterns of Day Visitors to the Countryside', *Area*, 2 (1969), 45–6; see also Colenutt, R. J. and Sidaway, R. M., *Forest of Dean Day Visitor Survey* (Forestry Commission Bulletin No 46, HMSO, 1973)

26 Rodgers, H. B., *Pilot National Recreation Survey, Report No 1* (British Travel Association/University of Keele, 1967), 69

27 Outdoor Recreation Resources Review Commission, *Outdoor Recreation for America* (US Government Printing Office, 1962), 34

28 Department of the Interior Bureau of Outdoor Recreation, *Outdoor Recreation Trends* (US Government Printing Office, 1967)

29 Cracknell, B., 'Accessibility to the Countryside as a Factor in Planning for Leisure', *Regional Studies* 1 (1967), 153

30 Forestry Commission, *Fifty-Second Annual Report and Accounts 1971–2* (HMSO, 1972), 16 and Table 13

31 Patterns of use of the Dalby Forest Drive are discussed in Mutch, W. E. S., *Public Recreation in National Forests: A factual survey* (HMSO, 1968), 37–52

32 *Fifth Report of the Countryside Commission for the Year Ended 30 September 1972* (HMSO, 1973), 9

33 Ministry of Housing and Local Government, Welsh Office, *Report of the Footpaths Committee* (HMSO, 1968), 3

34 Ibid, 3

35 Holroyd, M., 'Where Are the Footpaths?' *Rucksack*, 6 (1970), 6–7. The data quoted are based on returns by highway authorities to the Ministry of Transport, but their detailed accuracy cannot be guaranteed. 'Some of the mileages given are probably fairly rough estimates, but the majority are likely to be sufficiently accurate to indicate the main features of the distribution of paths.'

36 *Fifth Report of the Countryside Commission*, op cit, 20; a further seven schemes were under consideration at that time

37 Pritchard, T., *et al*, *Nature Trails* (Nature Conservancy, 1967), 4

38 *Nature Trails in Britain* (British Tourist Authority, 1972)

39 Forestry Commission, op cit, Table 13

40 The material in these paragraphs is derived from Alcock, J., *The Footpath Network in an Area of North Lancashire* (unpublished BA dissertation, University of Liverpool, 1971)

41 The 1949 National Parks and Access to the Countryside Act required local authorities, for the first time, to prepare definitive maps of rights of way. By December 1972, eleven counties had still to publish complete definitive maps. *Footpath Worker*, 8 (1972), 6

42 Bleasdale parish has 13·3 miles of public paths, 12·4 miles of private paths

43 See, for example, *Footpaths and Bridleways, A plea for their protection* (Ramblers' Association, 1967)

44 *Report of the Footpaths Committee*, op cit, 3

45 For a particularly valuable discussion of footpath management, see Huxley, T., *Footpaths in the Countryside* (Countryside Commission for Scotland, 1970)

46 *Evidence to National Parks Review Committee* (Peak Park Planning Board, 1971), 6

47 Miles, J. C., *The Goyt Valley Traffic Experiment 1970–1971* (Countryside Commission/Peak Park Planning Board, 1972)

48 *Routes for People: An environmental approach to rural highway*

planning (Derbyshire County Council/Peak Park Planning Board, 1972), 7

49 See, for example, *Report on Traffic in the Lake District National Park* (Lake District Planning Board, 1965); Wilson, H. and Womersley, L., op cit; Cosgrove, I. and Jackson, R. T., *The Geography of Recreation and Leisure* (Hutchinson, 1972), Fig. 5a

50 *A Road Policy for the Lake District* (Friends of the Lake District, 1939), 32–3

CHAPTER FOUR

1 Lickorish, L. J., in British Travel Association, *Conference on the Travel and Holiday Industry in Yorkshire* (Harrogate, 1963)

2 Calculated from US Bureau of the Census, *Statistical Abstract of the United States: 1970* (Washington, DC, 1970)

3 United Nations Statistical Office, *UN Statistical Year Book* (New York, various dates)

4 British Travel Association, *Patterns in British Holiday-making 1951–1968* (1969)

5 British Tourist Authority, *Digest of Tourist Statistics No 2* (1971), 72: 'The proportion of overnight visits to the Lake District varied from 18 per cent of all pleasure trips on Bank Holiday Sunday 1966, to 23 per cent on an August weekend and was as high as 45 per cent, or nearly half of all pleasure trips, on a September weekend. Whereas 42 per cent of holiday makers in the Lake District stayed in hotels and boarding houses, probably no more than 17 per cent of weekenders did so. On the other hand, while at least 56 per cent of weekend visitors used caravans or tents no more than 32 per cent of all holidaymakers did so.'

6 Wall, G., *Patterns of Recreation of Hull Car-Owners* (unpublished PhD thesis, University of Hull, 1970), 68

7 British Travel Association/University of Keele, *Pilot National Recreation Survey, Report No 1* (1967), 79

8 British Travel Association, *Patterns in British Holiday-making*, 18

9 Wall, *Patterns of Recreation of Hull Car-owners*, 93

10 Business Research Division, University of Colorado, *Travel Trends in the United States and Canada* (Boulder, 1969), 48

11 Countryside Commission and British Tourist Authority, *Pleasure Traffic and Recreation in the Lake District*, 3.2 (undated)

12 Jackson, R., 'Motorways and National Parks in Britain', *Area*, 2 (1970), 26–9

13 British Travel Association, *Patterns of British Holiday-making*, 35 and 63

14 Calculated from British Tourist Authority, *Digest of Tourist Statistics*, No 2

15 Lickorish, L. J. and Kershaw, A. G., *The Travel Trade* (1958), 191

16 British Travel Association, *Patterns of British Holiday-making*, 25

17 Wall, op cit, 104

18 British Travel Association, *Patterns of British Holiday-making*, 21

19 Wall, op cit, 104

20 Ibid

21 Boorstein, D. J., *The Image: A Guide to Pseudo-Events in America* (New York, 1961), 111–12

22 *1973 Motor Truck Facts* (Motor Vehicle Manufacturers Associations, 1973)

23 Barrett, J. A., *The Seaside Resort Towns of England and Wales* (unpublished PhD thesis, London University, 1958)

24 Cosgrove, I., and Jackson, R., *The Geography of Recreation and Leisure* (1972), 117

25 British Travel Association, *Patterns of British Holiday-making*, 35

26 Wall, G., 'Recreation and Cars', *International Journal of Environmental Studies*, 3 (1972), 259–64

27 Beazley, E., *Designed for Recreation* (1969), 35

28 Ontario Department of Tourism and Information, *Analysis of Ontario Cottage Survey, Travel Research Report No 55* (Toronto, 1971)

29 Maier, J., 'Development of Leisure-Time Homes', *International Geography*, papers submitted to the 22nd International Geographical Congress (Montreal, 1972), 692–4

30 County of Denbigh, *Second Homes in Denbighshire, Tourism and Recreation Research Report No 3* (Ruthin, 1972)

31 British Travel Association/University of Keele, 21

32 Davies, E. T., *Tourism and the Cornish Farmer* (University of Exeter, 1969)

33 Burton, T. L., *Outdoor Recreation Enterprises in Problem Rural*

Areas, Studies in Rural Land Use Report No 9 (Wye College, 1967)

34 Burton, T. L., 'Holiday Movements in Britain', *Town and Country Planning*, 33 (1965), 118–23

35 Wall, G., *Patterns of Recreation of Hull Car-Owners*, 88

36 Lavery, P., *Patterns of Holidaymaking in the Northern Region, Department of Geography Research Series No 9* (University of Newcastle-upon-Tyne, 1972)

37 Block, G., *Britons on Holiday* (1963), 14–16

CHAPTER FIVE

1 For a full discussion of the public open space movement, see Balmer, K. R., *Urban Open Space Planning in England and Wales* (unpublished PhD thesis, Department of Geography, University of Liverpool, 1972); Chadwick, G. F., *The Park and the Town* (Architectural Press, 1966); Olmstead, F. L., *Forty Years of Landscape Architecture* (G. P. Putnam's Sons, 1928)

2 9 Edw VII, c 44

3 The detailed requirements of the 1968 system are set out in *Development Plans: A manual on form and content* (MHLG, 1970), and in Circular 44/71 (Department of the Environment, 1971)

4 British Travel Association/University of Keele, *The Pilot National Recreation Survey* (1967); Sillitoe, K. K., *Planning for Leisure*, a Government Social Survey (HMSO, 1969); North West Sports Council, *Leisure in the North West* (1972); Greater London Council, Research Paper No 2, *Surveys of the Use of Open Spaces* (1968); Edinburgh Planning Department, *Open Space Plan for Edinburgh* (1969); Liverpool Planning Department, *Use of Open Space in Liverpool* (1972)

5 NPFA, *Review of NPFA Playing Space Target* (1971)

6 For a full discussion of this point, see Patmore, J. A., *Land and Leisure* (David & Charles, 1970), 84–5

7 See, for example, Sillitoe, op cit; BTA/University of Keele, op cit; GLC Research Paper No 2, op cit; Masser, I., 'The Use of Outdoor Recreation Facilities', *Town Planning Review*, 37, No 1 (1966–7), 41–53; Willis, M., 'Provision of Sports Pitches', *Town Planning Review*, 39 (1968); MHLG, *Provision of Playing Pitches in New Towns* (HMSO, 1967); The Sports Council, *Planning for Sport*

(Central Council of Physical Recreation, 1968); Winterbottom, D. M., 'How Much Urban Space Do We Need?', *Journal of the Town Planning Institute*, 53 (1967), 144–7

8 Gooch, R. B., 'Planning for Recreation', *Town and Country Planning*, 32 (1964), 480

9 GLC, op cit, 29, Table 20

10 Edinburgh Planning Department, op cit, 24, Table 6

11 Sillitoe, op cit, 20

12 Balmer, op cit, 130–40

13 The final sample included twenty-six county boroughs, sixteen non-county boroughs, and seven urban districts; response rate (usable) was 83 per cent

14 Gans, H., *Recreation Planning for Leisure Behaviour: A goal oriented approach* (unpublished PhD thesis, University of Michigan, 1957)

15 North West Sports Council, op cit, 60

16 Sillitoe, op cit, 38, Table 7; note: the figures in the text perhaps overestimate the percentage engaged in outdoor recreation as all those responding in the 'recreation' category were included

17 Clawson, M., 'Open (Uncovered) Space as a New Urban Resource', in Perloff, H. E. (ed), *The Quality of the Urban Environment* (Resources for the Future, 1969)

18 Lynch, K., *The Image of the City* (MIT Press, 1960)

19 See Darling, F. Fraser, *Future Environments of North America* (The Natural History Press, 1966); *Retrospect* xvi (April 16 1970); Dubos, René, 'Man Adapting: His limitations and potentialities', in Ewald, W. R. (ed), *Environment for Man* (Indiana University Press, 1968); Rapoport, A. and R. Hawkes, 'The Perception of Urban Complexity', *Journal of the American Institute of Planners*, 33, 210–21

20 Clawson, M., 'The Crisis in Outdoor Recreation', *American Forests* (March, 1959); Dower, H., *The Challenge of Leisure* (Civic Trust, 1965)

CHAPTER SIX

1 United Nations Organisation, *List of National Parks and Equivalent Reserves* (1971) (second edition), Brussels 1971

2 Phillips, A. A. C., *Conservation Planning in North America* (Countryside Commission, 1972)

3 National Academy of Sciences of the United States of America, *Biology and the Future of Man* (Oxford Univ. Press, 1970)

4 Shackleton, Lord, Speech at the 142nd Anniversary Dinner of the Royal Geographical Society (1972)

5 United Nations Organisation, op cit

6 Department of Education and Science, *Forestry, Agriculture and the Multiple Use of Rural Land*, a Report of the Land Use Study Group (HMSO, 1966)

7 Coleman, Alice, 'A Geographical Model for Land Use Analysis', *Geography*, 54, Pt 1 (January 1969)

8 Countryside Recreation Research Advisory Group, *Countryside Recreation Glossary* (Countryside Commission, 1970)

9 Countryside Recreation Research Advisory Group, op cit

10 Countryside Recreation Research Advisory Group

11 After Wager, J., 'The Carrying Capacity of Wild Lands for Recreation', Society of American Foresters, Forest Monograph 7 (1964)

12 Blacksell, M., 'Recreation and Land Use—A study in the Dartmoor National Park', *Exeter Essays in Geography in Honour of Arthur Davies*, Gregory, K. J. and Ravenhill, W. (eds) (Univ of Exeter Press, 1971)

13 Duffield, B. S. and Owen, M. L. (ed Coppock, J. T.), *Leisure + Countryside =* (Edinburgh, 1970)

14 Lewis, P. H., 'Quality Corridors for Wisconsin', *Landscape Architecture* (January 1964)

15 Linton, D. L., 'The Assessment of Scenery as a Natural Resource', *Scottish Geographical Magazine* (December 1968)

16 Forbes, Jean, 'A Map Analysis of Potentially Developable Land', *Regional Studies*, 3 (1969)

CHAPTER SEVEN

1 Payments and receipts of the Forest Fund are published in the *Annual Report and Accounts of the Forestry Commission*

2 The Forestry Act 1967, c 10, s 1 (3) repeats the fundamental orientation of the Commission

3 The seven forest parks are described in Edlin, H. L., *Forest Parks*, Forestry Commission Booklet No 6 (1969)

4 Countryside Commission, *Note on the Countryside Commission's views on the Consultative Document on Forestry Policy published 28 June 1972* (1972), 3–5; similar proposals were made in Ministry of Town and Country Planning, *Report of the National Parks Committee* (*England and Wales*), Cmd 7121 (1947), 77

5 The extended recreational use of state forests is encouraged in Amenity Lands Act (Northern Ireland) 1965, c 9, s 22; Countryside Act (Scotland) 1967, c 86, s 58; Countryside Act 1968, c 41, s 23

6 Richardson, S. D., 'The End of Forestry in Great Britain', *Advancement of Science*, 27, No 132 (1970), 153–63

7 Zehetmayr, J. W. L., 'The Future of Forestry in Great Britain', *Quarterly Journal of Forestry*, 66, No 1 (1972), 5–12

8 Appendix II, 40–41 of the Forestry Commission's *Fifty-First Annual Report and Accounts* (1971) comprised thirteen statements on recreation policy

9 Lord Taylor, quoted in Royal Society of Arts, *Proceedings of the Countryside in 1970 Third Conference* (1970), 40

10 Report of the Steering Group of the Study of the Long Term Problems of *Traffic in Towns* (1963), para 55

11 Fairbrother, Nan, *New Lives, New Landscapes* (1970; repr Harmondsworth, 1972) 285

12 Hall, John M., 'Leisure Motoring in Great Britain: Patterns and policies', *Geographia Polnica*, 24 (1972), 211–25

13 United States Wilderness Law, approved 3 September 1964

14 Direct observation is used by Atkinson, N. H. and Hetherington, J. L., 'Recreation Site Pressures and Their Variation with Site Location', *Forestry*, 45, No 2 (1972), 223–30

15 Shafer, E. L., Hamilton, J. R. and Schmidt, E. A., 'Natural Landscape Preferences: A predictive model', *Journal of Leisure Research*, 1, No 1 (1969), 1–19

16 Heytze, J. C., *Recreation in the Forest of Nunspect: A sociological approach to outdoor recreation in the Netherlands* (Utrecht, 1968)

17 Shafer, E. L. and Burke, H. D., 'Preferences for Outdoor Recreation Facilities in Four State Parks', *Journal of Forestry*, 63 (1965), 512–18

18 Dates in notes 19–22 refer to the year of survey, not the year of publication of reports
Mutch, W. E. S., *Public Recreation in National Forests: A Factual survey*, Forestry Commission Booklet No 21 (1968)

19 Colenutt, Robert J. and Sidaway, Roger M., *Forest of Dean Day Visitor Survey: An analysis of the demand for day visitor facilities*, Forestry Commission Bulletin No 46 (1973)

20 Countryside Commission, *Scenic Drive Survey: Dovey and Gwydyr Forests, July 1969* (1970)

21 Survey by author of use of Dalby and Newtondale Scenic Forest Drives, September 1969; findings not published elsewhere

22 Forestry Commission, *Report on Forest Research* (1971), 102–3, note on recreation research by R. M. Sidaway and R. Q. Oakes

23 Bultena, G. L. and Hendee, J. C., 'Foresters' View of Interest Group Position on Forest Policy', *Journal of Forestry*, 70, No 6 (1972), 337–42

24 Douglass, Robert W., *Forest Recreation* (1969), Pt II

25 New Forest Joint Steering Committee, *Conservation of the New Forest: Final recommendations* (1971)

26 Chilterns Standing Conference, *A Plan for the Chilterns* (1971)

27 Hampshire County Council *et al*, *East Hampshire Area of Outstanding Natural Beauty: A study in countryside conservation* (1968)

28 Vereniging De Utrechtse Heuvelrug, *1959–1969 Tien jaar De Utrechtse Heuvelrug* (Utrecht, 1970)

29 Forest Ministers of Great Britain, *Forestry Policy* (1972); Her Majesty's Treasury, *Forestry in Great Britain: An interdepartmental cost/benefit study* (1972)

30 Frome, Michael, *The Forest Service* (New York, 1971), 156

CHAPTER EIGHT

1 Western Europe is defined as France, West Germany, the Benelux countries, Switzerland, Austria and the Scandinavian countries, Spain, Portugal and Italy

2 International Union of Official Travel Organisations, *Economic Review of World Tourism* (Geneva, 1968)

3 British Tourist Authority, *Home Holiday Surveys* (1951 onwards). *Digest of Tourist Statistics No 1* (1969); *Digest of Tourist Statistics No 2* (1971)

4 Peters, M., *International Tourism* (1969)

5 Leonard, R., *Englishmen at Rest and Play* (1931)

6 Pimlott, J. A. R., *The Englishman's Holiday* (1947)

7 Burnet, L., *Villégiature et Tourisme sur les Côtes de France* (Paris 1963), 69

8 Defert, P. P., 'Quelques Repères Historique du Tourisme Moderne', *The Tourist Review* (January/March 1958)

9 *Board of Trade Journals*, passenger movements from Great Britain to the Continent

10 Lickorish, L. J. and Kershaw, A. G., *The Travel Trade* (1958), 42

11 Naylon, J., 'Tourism—Spain's Most Important Industry', *Geography* (1967)

12 British Tourist Authority (1951)

13 French Embassy Press and Information Service, *The French Tourist Industry* (1967)

14 Naylon, J., op cit

15 Christaller, W. 'Some Considerations of Tourism Location in Europe: The peripheral regions—underdeveloped countries—recreation areas', *Regional Science Association Papers XII Land Congress* (1963)

16 Institut National de la Statistique et des Etudes Economiques, *Les Vacances de Français* (annually)

17 The product-movement correlation coefficient was calculated for nine categories of settlement graded by size of population; because of the limited number of observations these results must be treated with caution

18 Christaller, W., op cit

19 Lewis, P. H., 'Quality Corridors in Wisconsin', *Landscape Architecture* (January 1964)

20 INSEE, *Les Vacances de Français*

21 Stansfield, C. A. and Rickert, J. E., 'The Recreational Business District', *Journal of Leisure Research*, 2, No 4 (1970), 213–25

22 For a thorough discussion of this theme, see Burnet, L., *Villégiature et Tourisme sur les Côtes de France*, Part 1, Chapter 2; also

Charlier, R. H., 'The Recreational Role of the Beach', *Tijdschrift voor Econ. en Soc. Geografie* (1960), 274

23 Sample counts taken by the author, summer 1971

24 For work on this theme, see Lavery, P., *Patterns of Holiday-making in the Northern Region* (Department of Geography, University of Newcastle-upon-Tyne, Research Series No 9, 1971); Henessey, B. W. and Mansfield, N., *Pleasure Traffic and Recreation in the Lake District*, Countryside Commission/BTA (1970); Duffield, B. S. and Owen, M. C., *Leisure + Countryside* = (Department of Geography, University of Edinburgh, 1970); Wager, J., *Public Use of Ashbridge* (unpublished paper, 1964); *Peak District National Park Survey* (British Tourist Authority, 1963, unpublished); British Tourist Authority Survey of *Whitsun Holiday Travel* (1963)

25 Roderkerk, E. C. M., *Experience in the National Park de Kemermerduinen* Haarlem (1970); also Provinciale Planalogische Dienst Suid-Holland, *Recreatieonderzoek Brielse Maas* (The Hague, 1968)

26 Poppens, B., 'Recreatie in het Lauwerzee', *Culturijp* (June 1970)

27 Hall, P., *World Cities* (Randstadt, Holland, 1966), 109

28 Ibid

29 The Council for Wales and Monmouthshire, *Report on the Welsh Holiday Industry* (Cmnd 1950, 1963)

30 Lavery, P., *Patterns of Holidaymaking in the Northern Region*

31 Patmore, J. A., *Land and Leisure* (1970), 155–61

32 Cribier, F., 'Les Estivans au Touquet', *Annales de Geographie*, 74 (1965)

33 Laborde, P., 'Propriété Foraine et Séjour Touristique à Biarritz', *Annales de Géographie*, 77 (1969)

34 Formica, C., 'La Costa Blanca et il suo svilluppo Touristico', *Revista Géographica Italiana*, 72 (1965), 42–65

35 Mentioned in Boyer, M., 'La Géographie des Vacances des Français', *Rev Geog Alpine*, 50 (1962)

36 International Union of Official Travel Organisations, *Economic Review of World Tourism*

37 BTA, *Home Holiday Surveys* (1951 onwards)

38 Lavery, P., op cit

39 Ibid

40 Wall, G., 'Socio-Economic Variations in Pleasure-Trip Patterns: The case of Hull car-owners', *Trans Institute of British Geographers*, 57 (1972)

41 Dower, M., 'The Fourth Wave', *The Architects Journal* (1965), 182

42 Special article, *The Economist* (18 July 1970), 72

43 Special Issue on France, *The Times* (11 October 1971)

44 *The Economist* (1970), 72

45 'Aménagement de la Côte Aquitaine', *Urbanisme*, 130 (1972)

46 *Urbanisme* (1972)

47 Mentioned in *The French Tourist Industry* (1967)

48 IOUTO, *Economic Review of World Tourism*

49 British Tourist Authority, *Digest of Tourist Statistics* (1972)

CHAPTER NINE

1 Outdoor Recreation Resources Review Commission, *Water Recreation—Values and Opportunities*, Study Report No 12 (US Government Printing Office, Washington, DC, 1962)

2 Price, R. C., 'The Increasing Impact of Recreation on Water Resource Planning, *Proceedings of the Second Annual American Water Resource Conference 1966* (1966), 187–92

3 Duin, R. H. A. and Loos, P., 'Water-en oeverrecreatie in het Ijsselmeergebid', *Stedebouw en Volkshuisvesting*, 50, No 4 (April 1968), 150–71

4 US Department of the Interior, *River of Life-Water: The environmental challenge* (Washington, DC, 1970)

5 National Opinion Polls, *National Angling Survey, 1969–70*, conducted by the Steering Committee of the National Survey of Angling (Natural Environment Research Council, 1971)

6 Duin, R. H. A. and Loos, P., op cit

7 Macniel, J. W., *Environmental Management*, Constitutional Study prepared for the Government of Canada (Ottawa, 1971)

8 'Cahiers de L'Institut D'Aménagement de la Region Parisienne', 12–13, *Loisirs Nautique* (December 1968)

9 Little, A. D., Inc, *Tourism and Recreation*, State-of-the-Art study prepared for the Office of Regional Economic Development (United States Department of Commerce, Washington, DC, 1966)

10 Little, A. D., Inc, op cit
11 Donaldson and Sons, *European Leisure, Recreation and Tourism: A brief report* (1971)
12 Cahiers de L'Institut D'Aménagement de la Region Parisienne, op cit
13 Little, A. D., Inc, op cit
14 Internationaler Arbeitskreis Sportstattan, *Yacht Harbours—Bases for planning* (Deutsche Bauzeitschrift, 1972)
15 Ambassade de France à Londres, *Bulletin Mensuel D'Information*, Ser 13, No 19 (November 1971)
16 Countryside Commission, *Coastal Recreation and Holidays*
17 Cahiers de L'Institut D'Aménagement de la Region Parisienne, op cit
18 Tanner, M. F., *Water Resources and Recreation* (The Sports Council, 1973)
19 Nottinghamshire County Council, *Holme Pierrepont: A national water sports centre* (1969)
20 Little, A. D., Inc, op cit
21 Cahiers de L'Institut D'Aménagement de la Region Parisienne, op cit
22 Economic Commission for Europe, *River Basin Management* (United Nations, New York, 1971)
23 'Rijkdienst voor de Ijsselmeerpolders', *Flevoland: Facts and figures* (Zwolle, 1972)
24 American Water Works Association, 'Policy Statement on Recreational Use of Domestic Water Supply Reservoirs', *Aqua*, 4 (1971), 15–17
25 Institution of Water Engineers, *Recreation on Rivers and Reservoirs* (1972)
26 Ministry of Land and Natural Resources, Circular No 3/66, *Use of Reservoirs and Gathering Grounds for Recreation* (1966)
27 British Waterworks Association, *Amenity Use of Reservoirs: Analysis of returns* (1969)
28 US Water Resources Council, *The Nation's Water Resources* (Washington, DC, 1968)
29 Canadian Council of Resource Ministers
30 Jones, I. E., 'The Development of the Rhone', *Geography*, 54 (November 1969), 446–51

CHAPTER TEN

Note: Much of the author's work on recreation was undertaken while he was a member of the Department of Industrial Economics and Business Studies at the University of Birmingham. His research there was financed by the Water Resources Board. The views expressed in this paper are those of the author and not necessarily those of the Water Resources Board.

1 This is not to say that mass recreation necessarily provides the greatest benefit; interest needs to be focused not only on *how many* people use a facility but also on the *strength* of the individuals' demands

2 Hoch, Irving J., *Economic Analysis of Wilderness Areas*, Ch 6 of Outdoor Recreation Resources Review Commission Study Report No 3, *Wilderness and Recreation—A report on resources, values and problems* (Washington, DC, 1962)

3 Trice, Andrew H. and Wood, Samuel E., 'Measurement of Recreation Benefits', *Land Economics* (August 1958)

4 Clawson, M. and Knetsch, J. L., 'Outdoor Recreation Research: Some concepts and suggested areas of study', *Natural Resources Journal* (October 1963)

5 Robinson, Warren C., 'The Simple Economics of Public Outdoor Recreation', *Land Economics*, No 1 (1967)

6 Mack, Ruth P. and Myers, Sumner, *Outdoor Recreation* in Dorfman (ed), *Measuring Benefits of Government Investments* (The Brookings Institute, Washington, DC, 1965)

7 Arguments based on the premise that consumers are making incorrect choices must be carefully distinguished from arguments concerning the distribution of benefits

8 US Senate, *Evaluation Standards for Primary Outdoor Recreation Benefits* (Washington, 1964); supplement to US Senate Document No 97, 87th Congress, 2nd Session (Washington, 1962)

9 US Department of the Interior, National Park Service, *A Method of Evaluating Recreational Benefits for Water-Control Projects* (1950)

10 An interesting study, using this method, is that by N. Wollman in New Mexico: Appendix D of *The Value of Water in*

Alternative Uses (University of New Mexico, Albuquerque, 1967)

11 Clawson, M., *Methods of Measuring the Demand for and Value of Outdoor Recreation*, Resources for the Future, Reprint No 10 (Washington, DC, 1959)

12 This assumption of homogeneity is quite reasonable if each zone is large, including a large population, and many different types of area and population; the concentric zones suggested by Clawson will tend to ensure that these conditions are satisfied

13 Clawson, M., op cit

14 Knetsch, J. L., 'Economics of Including Recreation as a Purpose of Eastern Water Projects', *Journal of Farm Economics* (December 1964)

15 Lewis, R. C. and Whitby, M. C., *Recreation Benefits from a Reservoir*, Research Monograph No 2, Agricultural Adjustment Unit (University of Newcastle upon Tyne, 1972)

16 Mansfield, N. W., 'The Estimation of Benefits from Recreation Sites and the Provision of a New Recreation Facility', *Regional Studies*, 5, No 2, 55–69 (1971)

17 Burton, T. L., *Windsor Great Park: A recreation study*, Study in Rural Land Use No 8, Department of Economics, Wye College (University of London, 1967)

18 Colenutt, R. J., *An Investigation into the Factors Affecting the Pattern of Trip Generation and Route Choice of Day Visitors to the Countryside*, (PhD thesis (unpublished), University of Bristol, 1970)

19 0·87p = cost of petrol only, 3·739p = total cost, including depreciation; both figures are 1967 prices

20 In the case of sailing fees exclude boat dues, figures of which were unavailable. Benefits of sailing exclude benefits from block memberships, and open meetings. Figures for angling exclude benefits to the small number of season ticket holders

21 John G. Gibson's present address is the Department of Transportation, University of Birmingham

22 Colenutt, R. J., op cit

23 Mansfield, N. W., op cit

24 Mansfield, N. W., op cit

25 Merewitz, L., 'Recreational Benefits of Water Resource Development', *Water Resources Research*, 2, No 4 (1966)

26 Grubb, Herbert W. and Goodwin, James T., *Economic Evaluation of Water-Oriented Recreation in the Preliminary Texas Water Plan*, Texas Water Development Board, Austin, Texas, Report 84 (September 1968)

CHAPTER ELEVEN

1 For further details see: Colenutt, R. J., *An Investigation into the Factors Affecting the Patterns of Trip Generation and Route Choice of Day Visitors to the Countryside*, (PhD thesis (unpublished), University of Bristol, 1970); Duffield, B. S., *The Nature of Recreational Travel Space*, paper given at Recreational Economics Symposium, Department of the Environment, London (1972)

2 Sidaway, R., *Assessing Day Visitors and Camping Use in the New Forest*, paper given at Recreational Economics Symposium, Department of the Environment, London (1972); Symmonds, A. E., *Monitoring Changes in Camping and Caravanning*, paper given at Recreational Economics Symposium, Department of the Environment, London (1972)

3 Duffield, B. S. and Owen, M. L. (ed J. T. Coppock), *Leisure + Countryside =* (Edinburgh, 1971)

4 Coker, A. M. and Coker, P. D., 'Some Practical Details of the Use of Pressure Sensitive Counters', *Recreation News Supplement*, No 7 (August 1972)

5 Bayfield, N. G. and Picknell, B. G., 'The Construction and Use of a Photoflex People Counter', *Recreation News Supplement*, No 5 (November 1971)

6 Huxley, T. and Pratt, J., *Preliminary Survey of Holyrood Park*, (Nature Conservancy, Edinburgh, 1966)

7 Duffield, B. S. and Forsyth, J. F., *Assessing the Impact of Recreation Use on Coastal Sites in East Lothian*, paper given at Conference on the Use of Aerial Photography in Countryside Research, Countryside Recreation Research Advisory Group, London (1972)

8 Duffield, B. S. and Owen, M. L. (ed J. T. Coppock), *The Touring Caravan in Scotland* (Edinburgh, 1971)

9 Duffield, B. S. and Forsyth, J. F., op cit

10 For full definition of 'capacity' see Chapter 1; also Countryside Recreation Research Advisory Group, *Countryside Recreation Glossary* (Countryside Commission, 1970)

11 Quoted in *Cairngorm Area*, Report of the Cairngorm Technical Group on the Cairngorm Area of the Eastern Highlands of Scotland, Scottish Development Department, Edinburgh (HMSO, 1967)

12 Canada Land Inventory, *Land Capability Classification for Outdoor Recreation* (Department of Regional Economic Expansion, 1969)

13 Duffield, B. S. and Owen, M. L. (ed J. T. Coppock), *Leisure + Countryside* = (Lanark, 1970; Edinburgh, 1971)

14 Scottish Development Department, *Towards Cleaner Water* (HMSO, 1972)

15 For more on this theme, see British Tourist Authority/University of Keele, *Pilot National Recreation Survey*, No 1 (1967)

16 Select Committee on Scottish Affairs, *Land Use Resources in Scotland*, III, Paper 511 iii (Countryside Commission for Scotland, 1972)

17 Murray, W. H., *Highland Landscape* (National Trust for Scotland, 1962)

18 Linton, D. L., 'The Assessment of Scenery as a Natural Resource', *Scottish Geographical Magazine*, 84, No 3 (December, 1968)

19 For a discussion on the use of this technique, see Weaver, J. C., 'Crop Combination Regions in the Middle West', *Geographical Review*, 44 (1954)

20 Helliwell, D. R., *Survey of Severnside—A method of evaluating the conservation value of large areas*, internal Leaflet produced by the Land Use Section, Nature Conservancy, Shrewsbury (1969)

21 Canada Land Inventory (1969)

22 Watson, A., Bayfield, N. and Mayes, N., 'Research on Human Pressures on Scottish Mountain Tundra, Soils and Animals', Proceedings of the Conference on Productivity Conservation in Northern Circum-Polar Lands at Edmonton, 1969 (International Union for the Conservation of Nature, 1970)

CHAPTER TWELVE

1 Watson, A., 'Public pressures on Soils, Plants and Animals near Ski-Lifts in the Cairngorms', in Duffey, E. (ed), *The Biotic Effects of Public Pressures on the Environment*, Monks Wood Symposium, No 3, The Nature Conservancy, Monks Wood, Huntingdon, (1967), 38–46

2 Lloyd, R. J., *Countryside Recreation: The ecological implications*, Lindsey County Council, Lincoln (1970); Schofield, J. M., 'Human Impact on the Fauna, Flora and Natural Features of Gibraltar Point', in Duffey, E. (ed), *The Biotic Effects of Public Pressures on the Environment* (1967)

3 Mattyasovsky, E., 'Recreation Area Planning: Some physical and ecological requirements', *Plan*, 8, No 3 (1967), 91–109

4 Raup, H. M., 'Some Problems in Ecological Theory and their Relation to Conservation', *Journal of Ecology*, 52 (suppl, 1964), 19–28

5 For a discussion on this point, see Harrison, C. M. and Warren, A., 'Conservation, Stability and Management', *Area*, 2 (1970), 26–32

6 For discussion, see Odum, E. P., 'The Strategy of Ecosystem Development', *Science*, 164 (1970), 262–70; Regier, H. A. and Cowell, E. B., 'Applications of Ecosystem Theory, Succession, Diversity, Stability, Stress and Conservation', *Biol Cons*, 4 (1972), 83 8

7 Speight, M. C. D., *Ecological Change and Outdoor Recreation*, Discussion Paper in Conservation, 4 (University College, London, 1973)

8 Williams, C. B., *Patterns in the Balance of Nature and Related Problems in Quantitative Ecology* (Academic Press, London and New York, 1964)

9 Huxley, T., *Footpaths in the Countryside*, Countryside Commission for Scotland (Perth, 1970)

10 Goldsmith, F. B., Munton, R. J. C. and Warren, A. W., 'The Impact of Recreation on the Ecology and Amenity of Semi-Natural Areas: Methods of investigation used in the Isles of Scilly', *Biological Journal of the Linnean Society*, 2 (1970), 287–306; for further results, see:
20

La Page, W. F., *Some Observations on Campground Trampling and Ground Cover Response*, US Forest Service Research Paper, NE 68 (1967); Burden, R. E. and Randerson, P. F., 'Quantitative Studies of the Effects of Human Trampling on Vegetation as an Aid to the Management of Semi-Natural Areas', *Journal of Applied Ecology*, 9 (1972), 439–57

11 La Page, W. F. (1967)

12 Beardsley, W. G. and Wagar, J. A., 'Vegetation Management on a Forested Recreation Site', *J Forestry*, 69 (1971), 728–31

13 Beardsley, W. G. and Wagar, J. A. (1971); see also Cordell, H. K. and James, G. A., 'Supplementing Vegetation on Southern Appalachian Recreation Sites with Small Shrubs and Trees', *J Soil and Water Cons*, 26 (1971), 235–8

CHAPTER THIRTEEN

1 Ad Hoc Group on Leisure, *Countryside in 1970*, Report 13 (1970)

2 Cullingworth, J. B., *Town and Country Planning in Britain* (4th ed, Allen & Unwin, 1972)

3 White, B., *A Sourcebook of Planning Information* (Clive Bingley, 1971), Ch 3

4 National Parks and Access to the Countryside Act 1949 (HMSO)

5 Sports Council, *Provision for Sport: Indoor swimming pools, indoor sports centres, golf courses* (HMSO, 1972)

6 Outdoor Recreation Resources Review Commission (ORRRC), *Federal Agencies and Outdoor Recreation*, Report 13 (US Government Printing Office, Washington, DC, 1962), 16–20; Bureau of Outdoor Recreation, *Federal Outdoor Recreation Programs and Recreation—Related environment programs* (Department of the Interior, Washington, DC, 1970)

7 Keenleyside, C. B., *Farming, Landscape and Recreation* (Countryside Commission, 1971)

8 *Farming and Wildlife—A study in compromise*, Silsoe Conference Proceedings (Royal Society for the Protection of Birds, 1970); *Farming and Wildlife in Dorset*, Report of a Study Conference (Dorset Naturalists' Trust, 1970)

9 *Countryside in 1970*

10 Forestry Commission, *Recreation Policy* (1971)

11 *Forestry Policy* (HMSO, 1972)

12 Central Advisory Water Committee, *The Future Management of Water in England and Wales* (HMSO, 1971); Department of the Environment and the Welsh Office, *A Background to Water Reorganisation in England and Wales* (HMSO, 1973)

13 Water Recreation Case Studies prepared by Dartington Amenity Research Trust, published 1973 onwards; this very thorough set of studies in depth comprises coasts, natural lake, upland and lowland rivers, reservoirs, canals and estuaries

14 National Trust Act 1907 (HMSO); also subsequent National Trust Acts of 1937, 1939 and 1953

15 Countryside Act 1968 (HMSO), s 5; Department of the Environment, *Memorandum on Grants*, National Parks and Access to the Countryside Act 1949 and the Countryside Act 1968 (HMSO, 1971)

16 Patterson, John L., 'Landmark Visitor Centre', *Official Architecture and Planning*, 33, No 10 (October 1970)

17 Development of Tourism Act 1969 (HMSO)

18 Sports Council, *Provision for Sport*

19 British Tourist Authority and Countryside Commission, *Survey of Mobile Caravanning and Camping* (1971)

20 *Countryside in 1970*

21 Sports Council, *Research Priorities for Sports Provision*, Second Report of the Sociological Surveys Study Group (1971); Countryside Recreation Research Advisory Group, *Research Priorities* (Countryside Commission, 1971)

22 ORRRC, Report 13

23 US Congress, *An Act to Promote Co-ordination and Development of Effective Programs Relating to Outdoor Recreation, and for Other Purposes*, Public Law, 88–29, 88th Congress S.29, 29 (May 1963)

24 BOR, *Federal Outdoor Recreation Programs*

25 Countryside Recreation Research Advisory Group Annual Report, *Recreation News Supplement* (Countryside Commission, 1971), 16–19

26 Countryside Act 1968, Section 11 (HMSO)

27 For example, North West Sports Council, *Leisure in the North West* (Salford, 1972)

South Western Sports Council, *Major Recreation Survey by County* (1966 onwards)

28 Department of the Environment, Circular 2/70

29 Munn J., 'Planning for Recreation—A fully integrated local authority approach', paper to *National Playing Fields Association Annual Conference* (1972)

30 South East Joint Planning Team, *A Strategic Plan for the South East* (HMSO, 1970)

31 Cullingworth, *Town and Country Planning*

32 Town and Country Planning Acts 1968 and 1972 (HMSO)

33 Thorburn, A., 'Towards an Effective Regional Framework', *Built Environment*, 1, No 1 (April 1972)

34 Lee Valley Regional Park Authority, *Report on the Development of the Regional Park with Plan of Proposals* (1969)

35 Bains Report, *The New Local Authorities—Management and structure* (HMSO, 1972)

36 Ramblers' Association, *Footpath Worker*, a quarterly bulletin for the information of all engaged in the care and protection of public paths

37 Department of the Environment, Circular 2/70

38 Countryside Commission, *Policy on Country Parks and Picnic Sites* (Countryside Commission, 1969)

39 Zetter, J. A., *The Evolution of Country Park Policy* (Countryside Commission, 1971); Waterhouse, *Country Parks and the West Midlands*, University of Birmingham, Centre for Urban and Regional Studies (1972)

40 Two such studies in the South East and South Wales Regions should help considerably in this respect: Standing Conference on Regional Planning in South Wales and Monmouthshire, *Recreation in South Wales* (1973); Davidson, J. M. and Sienkiewicz, J., *Study of Informal Recreation in South East England* (SIRSEE Project), paper given to Recreation Economics Symposium, London Business School (1972)

41 *Countryside in 1970*

42 *Coastal Preservation and Development: A study of the coastline of England and Wales*, reports of the nine Coastal Conferences (National Parks Commission, HMSO, 1967/68)
Coastal Recreation and Holidays, Special Study Report, Volume 1,

(containing reports by The Sports Council and The British Tourist Authority), Countryside Commission (HMSO, 1969); *Nature Conservation at the Coast, Special Study Report, Volume 2* (containing the report of The Nature Conservancy), Countryside Commission (HMSO, 1969); *The Planning of the Coastline: A report on a study of coastal preservation and development in England and Wales,* Countryside Commission (HMSO, 1970); *The Coastal Heritage; A conservation policy for coasts of high quality scenery,* Countryside Commission (HMSO, 1970); the Countryside Commission proposal to establish special heritage coast agencies for their management has not been adopted by the British government, but many of the other recommendations of these important reports are being implemented

43 Countryside Commission, *Recreation Resources Mapping Notation* (1970)

44 Bureau of Outdoor Recreation, *Planning Surveys Series Nationwide Plan—Bureau of outdoor recreation manual,* Department of the Interior (Washington, DC, 1964)

45 Correspondence with William E. Rennebohn, Chief Division of Planning and Research, Bureau of Outdoor Recreation (Washington, Sept. 1972)

46 Ministry of Housing and Local Government, *Development Plans —A manual on form and content* (HMSO, 1970); Appendix A contains a list of factors which should be considered in the preparation of the recreation component of a structure plan

47 Standing Conference on Regional Planning in South Wales and Monmouthshire, *Recreation in South Wales* (1973); Ch 1 contains a full discussion of the recreation element of the Structure Plan including a full list of goals being adopted

48 Cherry, G. E., *Town Planning in the Social Context* (Leonard Hill Books, 1970)

49 See Sports Council and CRRAG, *Research Priority* documents (note 21)

50 North West Sports Council, *Leisure in the North West* (Salford, 1972)

51 McLoughlin, J. B., *Urban and Regional Planning—A Systems Approach* (Faber, 1969)

52 Countryside Commission, *Planning for Informal Recreation at the*

Sub-Regional Scale, South Wales Standing Conference Area, January 1974

53 *Coventry–Warwickshire–Solihull Sub Regional Study*, Final Report on the Sub Regional Study and Supplementary Reports 3, 4 and 5 (Warwick, 1970)

54 Davidson, J. M. and Sienkiewicz, J., *Study of Informal Recreation in South East England* (SIRSEE Project)

55 Countryside Commission, *Countryside Recreation Staff*, 1974

56 Department of the Environment, *Report of the National Park Policies Review Committee* (Sandford Report) H.M.S.O. 1974

Acknowledgements

THIS book is the culmination of many months' work by a number of people, particularly the contributors, without whose efforts it would still be an idea and not a reality. My particular thanks go to Miss J. Holland and Miss J. Ford for their patience and care in typing the finished manuscript. Their help and ability have been invaluable in the lengthy process of editing and blending together the various chapters.

Many of the illustrations were produced by the staff of the Drawing Office of the Department of Geography, Birkbeck College, Mr G. Davenport, Mr G. Reeve and Mr W. Johnson, and I am grateful for the hours they have spent on my behalf. The following persons and organisations supplied plates and I would like to thank them for permission to reproduce this material: Dr J. F. Davis, Dr J. Gittins, Dr B. Goldsmith, Mr J. Hall, the Belgian Tourist Office, the French Tourist Board, Aerofilms, and the Peak Park Planning Board.

We should also like to record the valuable help given in preparing Chapter 7, by T. Johnstone, G. Simpson and H. Strickland (Forestry Commission, Pickering), R. Bell (North York Moors National Park Warden), ten voluntary wardens and R. Woolmore (Countryside Commission), when he surveyed motorists in Pickering Forest. R. M. Sidaway kindly

reported on recreation research in progress at the Forestry Commission headquarters, Alice Holt Lodge, where the library staff were most helpful. The maps in Chapter 7 were redrawn by Pauline Tillett, Don Shewan and Steve Pratt in the Department of Geography, Queen Mary College, with the kind permission of the copyright holders: Figure 23, Her Majesty's Stationery Office and Ordnance Survey; Figure 24, United States Department of the Interior, Geological Survey; Figure 25, Forestry Commission and Ordnance Survey: Figure 26a, New Forest Joint Steering Committee and Ordnance Survey; Figure 26b, Vereneging de Utrechtse Heuvelrug.

I am grateful for the comments and advice from Allan Patmore and to the series editor, Professor R. Lawton, for his patient and meticulous reading of the text. Keeping the good wine until the last, I must give special thanks to my wife Alma for her encouragement and tolerance over the past eighteen months.

PATRICK LAVERY

Index